The Woman Who Dared to Vote

LANDMARK LAW CASES

&

AMERICAN SOCIETY

Peter Charles Hoffer
N. E. H. Hull
Series Editors

For a complete list of titles in the series go to www.kansaspress.ku.edu

N. E. H. HULL

The Woman Who Dared to Vote

The Trial of

Susan B. Anthony

UNIVERSITY PRESS OF KANSAS

Published by the University Press of Kansas (Lawrence, Kansas 66045), which was
organized by the Kansas Board of Regents and is operated and funded by
Emporia State University, Fort Hays State University, Kansas State University,
Pittsburg State University, the University of Kansas, and Wichita State University

Library of Congress Cataloging-in-Publication Data

Hull, N. E. H., 1949–

The woman who dared to vote : the trial of Susan B. Anthony / N. E. H. Hull.

p. cm.

Includes bibliographical references and index.

ISBN 978-0-7006-1848-4 (cloth : alk. paper) —

ISBN 978-0-7006-1849-1 (pbk. : alk. paper)

1. Anthony, Susan B. (Susan Brownell), 1820–1906—Trials, litigation, etc.

2. Women—Suffrage—United States. 3. Election law—United States.

I. Title.

KF223.A58H85   2012

342.73'072—dc23

2012004015

British Library Cataloguing-in-Publication Data is available.

Printed in the United States of America

10 9 8 7 6 5 4 3 2 1

The paper used in this publication is recycled and contains 30 percent postconsumer
waste. It is acid free and meets the minimum requirements of the American National
Standard for Permanence of Paper for Printed Library Materials Z39.48-1984.

TO ALL THE WOMEN, AND MEN, WHO DEDICATED
THEMSELVES TO THE WOMEN'S MOVEMENT, WHOSE
SACRIFICES WE MAY HAVE FORGOTTEN AND WHOSE
ACHIEVEMENTS WE TOO OFTEN TAKE FOR GRANTED

CONTENTS

The Woman Who Dared to Vote is the first single volume to document fully the trial of woman's rights advocate Susan B. Anthony for daring to vote in a federal election. It seems an obvious topic for an inexpensive and easily accessible book, bringing together as it does important topics in post–Civil War Republican politics, the first feminist movement, and the Fourteenth Amendment's impact on constitutional law. The cast of characters—Anthony, Elizabeth Cady Stanton, Lucy Stone, Victoria Woodhull, U.S. Supreme Court Justice Ward Hunt, and Charles Sumner, to name but a few of the remarkable women and men who grace the following pages—in itself merits a recounting of the trial. It catapulted Anthony into the very front rank of the movement, and renewed the promise of full citizenship for women.

There is no shortage of primary sources to tell this story. Ann D. Gordon and the other editors of the multivolume *Selected Papers of Susan B. Anthony and Elizabeth Cady Stanton* spent over thirty years bringing together and annotating much of the primary sources. Anthony was a diarist and, like many in the movement for woman suffrage, a busy speaker and correspondent. Newspapers covered her travels and her trial extensively. She even arranged for publication of the transcript of the trial. Over the course of the late fall of 1872 and through 1873 the pretrial and trial proceedings were front page news.

Hull brings to the task of telling this story a noteworthy combination of teaching and scholarly credentials. She is a law teacher and historian who taught women's studies courses, legal history courses, and hard law courses during a long career as a classroom instructor, scholar, and practicing attorney. Her special training allows her to see in the records the tactics of counsel, the irregularities of the pretrial and trial process, and the political motives of all the parties to the trial, and thereby make a uniquely dramatic story an equally instructional one. For those in power that the woman's movement thought were friends turned out to be quite the opposite.

It is this complexity—legal, political, personal—that has made the trial of Susan B. Anthony a landmark case. Hull roots her unraveling of that complexity in the personalities and careers of the registrars, commissioners, prosecutors, and defense counsel. She has recreated the heady days before Anthony went to the polls and the worrisome weeks that followed. She has untangled every legal thread.

A concluding chapter relates the Anthony trial, from which there was no appeal, to the Supreme Court case of *Minor v. Happersett* (1875). Then the issues that Anthony tried to raise were resolved for a time. Women had no federal constitutional right to vote. State laws alone conferred that right. A postscript continues the story to the Twenty-first Amendment, suitably named the Susan B. Anthony Amendment.

This is a deeply moving story, told with great sympathy and verve. It is a story of courage and despair, of sisterhood and rivalry, of high purpose and low politics. It is a story we need to know.

ACKNOWLEDGMENTS

More than thirty years ago Michal Belknap asked me to write a chapter on the Susan B. Anthony trial for a book he was editing on *American Political Trials*. The subject intrigued me, but I was much too busy revising my Ph.D. dissertation, coauthoring a book on infanticide with my husband, and raising my first-born son to undertake the chapter for Mike's book. This book is the culmination, therefore, of decades of thought, and I thank Mike for planting the seed.

Though his childcare was one of the reasons I had to delay working on this project, Williamjames Hull Hoffer grew up to become my valuable "study buddy" on this project. For three summers (an imbecilic time to leave New Jersey for Georgia), as he toiled on his own book about the *Plessy v. Ferguson* case in the upstairs office of our townhouse in Athens, I worked downstairs on my mini-laptop. We met for breakfast, coffee breaks, and lunch and reinforced each other's work through our meaningful discussions. He was my go-to guy for help with the Civil War and Reconstruction eras of U.S. history.

My legal history seminar in the eventful political spring of 2008 focused on "Woman Suffrage." Thanks to all the women in the class who inspired me with their enthusiasm: Nicole Curio, Mojisola Dabney, Lynda Hinkle, Jamie Hutchinson, Hope Jamison, Katie Kepner, Erica Roby, and Mary-Elizabeth Sampsel. Most of all, to Lynda Yamamoto, whose paper on Alice Paul's Quaker feminism, enlightened me about the tenets of the Quakers and how those might translate to the story of Susan B. Anthony's own Quaker-inspired commitment to the cause of woman suffrage, I'm grateful.

Nancy Martin, the John M. and Barbara Keil University archivist and Rochester Collections librarian, Department of Rare Books and Special Collections, Rush Rhees Library, University of Rochester, was extremely helpful in getting me photocopies of Susan B. Anthony's scrapbooks. Dean Rayman Solomon generously supported my writing of this book with time off from teaching duties and arranging my teaching schedule to give me an additional semester off after my sabbatical. My colleague Rand Rosenblatt arranged for me to present the book at a Rutgers Law School Faculty Workshop and, as usual, the Camden law school community, in particular Donald Joseph, came through with extremely helpful corrections, comments, and criticisms. I would like to thank Ann Delasandro, head librarian at the law school (and a dear friend), who has permitted me to deposit a version of this book with footnotes for the benefit of interested scholars, and the UGA Library for its marvelous collections and its extremely helpful interlibrary loan department.

I am grateful to Ann Gordon and the other editors of the multivolume edition of the *Selected Papers of Elizabeth Cady Stanton and Susan B. Anthony*. Its carefully selected and annotated primary sources proved invaluable and provided an easily accessible print alternative to the microfilm of the originals. Confirming that such edited collections are often the backbone of scholarly works, I made copious use of the documents and here acknowledge that debt with gratitude.

Thanks also to the wonderful team at Kansas, including director Fred Woodward and associate director Susan Schott, and especially editor in chief Mike Briggs, who have been so encouraging and patient.

And, as always, my debt is profound to my editor Peter Charles Hoffer. Not only did he edit the manuscript in his capacity as coeditor of this book series, he also acted as a sounding board at every stage of its development, pushed me every day to get my work done, and sometimes even acted as a research assistant.

Why the Trial of
Susan B. Anthony Matters

Susan B. Anthony is generally accounted the foremost, and most effective, advocate for woman suffrage in nineteenth-century America. Or so she appears in public prints, history textbooks, and mass media. Certainly there is much truth in that description, but even these encomia obscure the importance of the trial. For, until her trial for violating a federal election law designed to prevent ex-Confederates from voting illegally, Anthony, despite her vigorous nationwide campaign for a woman's right to vote, always stood in the shadow of Elizabeth Cady Stanton. The trial brought Anthony the attention she wanted and deserved.

Stanton was one of the founding mothers of woman's rights in the United States. She and Lucretia Mott had called the first woman's rights convention at Seneca Falls in 1848, and there Stanton had added a plank for woman suffrage to the Declaration the convention approved. Stanton was far better educated and more articulate than Anthony, and until the trial Stanton was more respected in the movement. Whenever Stanton and Anthony appeared on a platform together, everyone in the audience—supporters and press alike—paid more attention to the older and more matronly Stanton. After one particularly galling episode for Anthony, when the two women appeared before an audience together in San Francisco at which Stanton garnered cheers and Anthony jeers, Anthony wrote to her mother: "whoever goes into a parlor or before an audience with that woman [Stanton] does it at the cost of a fearful overshadowing, a price which I have paid for the last ten years."

As 1872 opened, Anthony had gathered a loyal coterie of supporters of her own, but she was far from the icon or face of woman suffrage. What was more, the movement itself had split into two separate and antagonistic suffrage associations. Attempts to unify them in which Anthony had taken a prominent role had failed; the movement for a woman suffrage constitutional amendment Anthony had endorsed had stalled; and the charismatic and controversial Victoria Woodhull had captured the attention of Congress and the public as the new voice for woman suffrage. Anthony at first allied and then dramatically divorced herself from Woodhull, causing a strain on Anthony's relationship with Stanton and many other allies. By the time the election of 1872 rolled around, Anthony was on the verge of relative irrelevance, and the woman suffrage movement she had devoted nearly twenty-five years of her life to was almost at dead stop.

When Anthony voted in the 1872 election she did so along with many other women; indeed, she was not the first woman to claim to successfully cast a ballot in an election. In the early post-Revolutionary era the state of New Jersey had allowed and then disallowed women the vote. In 1869 the ladies of Vineland, New Jersey, had the honor of successfully casting their ballots despite the law that restricted the franchise to men, followed by Nannette B. Gardner in Detroit, who in March 1871 succeeded in registering to vote under the claim that she derived the right under the Fourteenth Amendment. But Susan B. Anthony was the only woman to be tried in a federal court for the crime of voting. The uproar generated by the trial captured the attention of the press and the general public. Disheartened women in the suffrage movement used it as a rallying cry.

If federal authorities had intended her trial to suppress the woman suffrage movement, it backfired. But if their goal was to avert a massive civil disobedience movement of women appearing at the polls to vote, which for a time the leaders of the woman suffrage organization led by Anthony and Stanton had advocated, the Anthony trial and the subsequent U.S. Supreme Court decision in the *Minor v. Happersett* case forced the woman suffrage movement to rethink its strategy. After the intense reaction to the trial quieted, the battle for woman suffrage inched forward, through state-by-state legislative changes and the slow build-up toward passage of a federal constitutional amendment.

Henceforth, there was no question who stood as the champion of the woman suffrage movement. The case, and media coverage of the case, had anointed Anthony as the avatar of the movement,

{ *Introduction* }

more than Stanton or Lucy Stone or even the venerable Lucretia Mott. Without the trial the Nineteenth Amendment would not have been called the Susan B. Anthony Amendment. What was more, the case revived Anthony's energy and ensured that the cause she made her life's work survived its post–Civil War tribulations. The trial of Susan B. Anthony was a turning point in the story of the woman suffrage movement, American legal history, and women's history.

The following book is not a history of woman suffrage. My focus is the trial of Susan B. Anthony. The constraints of the series format and limits on word length meant I had to create a coherent narrative that captured the sense of what took place but could not be comprehensive. Many events and incidents that took place in the years I covered were, of necessity, only touched upon or omitted altogether. In the prologue I introduce Susan B. Anthony and explore how she and her close circle of associates came to the woman's rights and suffrage movement. The first two chapters of the book provide the reader with background on the woman suffrage movement in the critical post–Civil War era, its betrayal by former allies in the abolitionist movement, and how it had devolved into dissension before the Anthony trial. The third chapter tells the story of Anthony's vote, arrest, and the preliminary hearings. Chapter 4 relates the legal and public relations maneuvering in the six-month run-up to the trial. The following two chapters narrate the story of the two-day trial, with all the drama created by Anthony, her attorneys, the politically ambitious prosecutor, and the recently appointed Supreme Court Justice Ward Hunt, who presided over the trial. Chapter 7 discusses the aftermath of the Anthony trial as well as the civil suit challenging the state of Missouri's law limiting suffrage to men instituted by Anthony's ally, Virginia Minor, and husband, Francis, a suit that reached the U.S. Supreme Court. The postscript follows the major players in the case through the passage of the Nineteenth Amendment, the happy culmination of Anthony and millions of women's dreams dating back to 1848.

"Is Not This a Wonderful Time— [An] Era Long to Be Remembered"

According to later histories and autobiographies (no documentation contemporary to the event exists), Susan B. Anthony met her future collaborator and dear friend Elizabeth Cady Stanton on a street corner in Seneca Falls, New York, in May 1851. Stanton, thirty-five years old at the time, lived in Seneca Falls with her lawyer husband and four small sons, the youngest born only three months earlier. Though a small village in the middle of the nineteenth century, Seneca Falls was at the center of a "burned over region" of reform movements, most notably the abolition of slavery, women's rights, and temperance. It was probably Anthony and Stanton's temperance activities rather than women's rights issues that prompted their introduction by Amelia Bloomer, the editor of the *Lily*, a temperance journal to which both Stanton and Anthony contributed articles. Stanton, in her memoirs published thirty years later, claimed to clearly remember the event. She described "Miss Anthony on the corner of the street, waiting to greet us."

According to Stanton, Anthony had come to Seneca Falls to hear the fiery British abolitionist George Thompson, touring the States at the time. Anthony may very well have stopped in town while on her circuit of upstate cities and villages stumping for temperance. Stanton continued her recollection: "There she stood, with her good, earnest face and genial smile, dressed in gray delaine, hat and all the same color, relieved with pale blue ribbons, the perfection of neatness and sobriety." Thirty years after the fact Stanton recalled, I "liked her thoroughly."

In 1851 Anthony was thirty-one years old, the second oldest of seven children. She remained close to her remarkably long-lived siblings (she lived eighty-six years herself). Her parents were members of the Society of Friends, and she remained a Quaker in many ways throughout her life. Much of her oratory was in the nature of Quaker witness, speaking without fear of reprisal, moved by her inner light. She testified, just as the first Quakers did in England and Ireland, though the wrath of the established church and the Crown's courts fell on their covered heads.

A precocious child, her formal education was interrupted by her father's bankruptcy during the Panic of 1837, and she never resumed formal schooling. Nor did she ever marry. She taught for a time, attended Unitarian religious services in Rochester, New York, to which her family had moved from Massachusetts, and found her way into the circle of women reformers. Her father was an early abolitionist, and other members of her family engaged in the social reform ferment of antebellum upstate New York. It was this region of the country that gave birth to the women's reform movement, the Oneida Community, the Church of Jesus Christ of Latter Day Saints, the Seventh Day Adventists, and a haven to runaway slave-abolitionists like Frederick Douglass.

In 1848, in the very town in which Anthony and Stanton later met, "A Convention to Discuss the Social, Civil, and Religious Condition and Rights of Woman" was held in the Wesleyan Chapel of Seneca Falls. For two days in the summer of 1848 a company of women and men listened to speeches and debated questions of the inequality of women in nineteenth-century law and society. A small coterie of friends who had met through their work in the abolitionist movement organized the event. In 1840 Stanton and Lucretia Mott had been irked by the refusal of the London World Anti-Slavery Conference to recognize formally the American women delegates, forcing them to observe the proceedings from the balcony of the hall. Their abolition work, and Stanton's domestic demands (she was new bride on her honeymoon when she met Mott in London), postponed their response, but they did not forget, or forgive, the slight. In 1848 the New York State legislature was debating a Married Women's Property Act, a reform proposal to expand a woman's right to her own property. (A married woman's property belonged to her husband.) The time seemed propitious to address all the oppression that women faced.

Over the next few months, the women organized the meeting, arranged for the venue, and devised a list of resolutions that conveyed to the public the legal and social reforms they advocated. They framed a "Declaration of Sentiments" roughly modeled on the "Declaration of Independence" issued by the Revolutionaries of 1776. Among the nineteen resolutions presented in Seneca Falls over those two summer days were a proposal to repeal all laws in "conflict, in any way, with the true and substantial happiness of woman." Another proclaimed "that woman is man's equal—was intended to be so by the Creator." Still another required that women be allowed to speak publicly at "all religious assemblies," and a later resolution extended the right of women to speak whenever "she addresses a public audience." The basic thrust of all the resolutions was that women should be treated as equal to men in every public endeavor. Among these pronouncements was the following: "Resolved, That it is the duty of the women of this country to secure to themselves their sacred right to the elective franchise." When the "Declaration of Sentiments" was presented for a vote on the second day of the convention, the suffrage resolution was the most controversial. It was the centerpiece of the women's complaints against the "tyranny" mankind had established over them throughout history: "He has never permitted her to exercise her inalienable right to the elective franchise." The men approved the Declaration by acclamation, save the suffrage "sentiment." It won by a bare majority.

Perhaps with the omen of the near failure of the franchise resolution fresh in their minds, Anthony and Stanton's attention that day in 1851 was focused on temperance. Stanton knew she had a potent ally. She recalled that Anthony's feminism first emerged at state teacher's conventions. There she "fought, almost single-handed, the battle for equality" and had "compelled conservatism to yield its ground so far as to permit women to participate in all debates, deliver essays, vote, and hold honored positions as officers." Anthony was a formidable force for moral improvement, and the condescension and discrimination toward her only stirred her to greater effort. Having won her battle within her professional organization, Anthony turned her attention to the temperance issue for which "she labored as sincerely." Indeed, Anthony's very first public address to any audience was a speech she delivered to the Daughters of Temperance at Canajoharie, New York, in 1849. She earnestly traveled the state speaking to groups and raising money for the cause.

For Anthony, Stanton, and many of their eventual colleagues in the woman suffrage movement, temperance was a woman's issue. Married women and their children were the victims of physical and economic abuse and neglect by drunken husbands and fathers. With the severe limitations on their ability to divorce, women were trapped in marriages with abusive alcoholic husbands. The temperance movement in the first half of the nineteenth century relied on the conscience and grassroots organizing of middle class women sensitive to their less fortunate sisters (though middle and upper class men could be just as besotted and abusive).

But the leadership of the temperance movement, like almost every reform movement at the time (and well into the twentieth century) was in the hands of men. Thus over and over again the women reformers ran into sexist attitudes among their male colleagues. Recalcitrant male legislators listened more closely to the farmers who raised the grain, and to the distillers who transformed the grain into spirits, than to the women who lobbied for restrictions on the manufacture of beer and hard liquor. It was, in fact, in the wake of their failure to command legislators' respect for their petitions on the temperance issue "that woman's moral power amounted to little as a civil agent," that Anthony, Stanton, and their close circle were convinced that they could effect no real change "until backed by [the] ballot."

Though these early feminists (a term they did not use) kept one eye on the entire woman's rights agenda throughout the decade of the 1850s, temperance and, to a lesser extent, abolition claimed the majority of their time and energy. It was also these concerns, as well as woman suffrage, that forged the alliances and friendships creating a sisterhood of women who would champion these issues for decades to come. The letters exchanged among these women documented this evolving network. Lucy Stone, Abby Kelley Foster, Martha Coffin Wright, Amy Post, and Paulina Kellogg Wright all initiated a correspondence with the brilliant and energetic Stanton. At first, Susan B. Anthony was only one of their number, but as the decade progressed and women's issues increasingly dominated their attention, the special relationship between Anthony and Stanton intensified, though the inequality or imbalance between them was reflected by the fact that in their letters Anthony always addressed the

older woman as "Mrs. Stanton," while the latter always called Anthony "Susan."

The women continued to face problems and discrimination with
regard to their public efforts. At the New York State temperance
meeting in June 1852, conservative clergymen protested the
women's participation, one arguing that "when a woman goes out of
her sphere . . . to make speeches . . . I say she unsexes herself." This
aggravated the women and they often scheduled women's rights
meetings after temperance gatherings. In 1852 and 1853 these
women's rights conventions began to claim more of their attention
as their temperance efforts were dismissed out of hand by male legislators, though temperance continued to dominate their efforts.

The turning point that seemed to shift their attention from temperance to woman suffrage came sometime between 1852 and 1854.
Anthony, Stanton, and the sisterhood had vigorously lobbied for a
bill in the New York State legislature that would replicate the so-
called Maine law prohibiting the manufacture and distribution of alcoholic beverages within the state. Stanton complained loudly about
their frustration in petitioning male legislators. "Let woman never
again be guilty," she proclaimed in an appeal to women temperance
supporters, "of the folly of asking wine and beer-drinkers to put
down the liquor traffic." She foresaw a much greater role for women
in New York politics: "Our position is every year assuming greater
importance." Though rebuffed by the state legislature on the temperance bill, she optimistically predicted that within ten years, under
the new married woman's property law, women would own a majority of the property in the state and that "money is power, and
Women will see the necessity then, if not before, of protecting their
property by vote." At a meeting of the Women's New York State
Temperance Society in October 1852, at which Lucy Stone offered
the principal address and the group endorsed the Maine law for New
York, Anthony also addressed the assemblage. She exhorted her audience that "woman must carry these temperance principles into politics. If we cannot vote we can influence voters. If man assumes to
vote for us, it is time we instruct him how we want voting done."

Stanton missed the meeting because she delivered her fifth child
only a few days later. After four sons, she was overjoyed to finally
give birth to a twelve-pound, healthy baby girl. She was ecstatic

when she announced the event to Lucretia Mott: "I am at length the happy mother of a daughter." This was not just a personal joy, for Stanton the birth of her first daughter was a historic moment. She exclaimed to Mott: "Rejoice with me all Womankind, for lo! A champion of thy cause is born." Before the girl was even two days old Stanton claimed that she "dedicated her to this work from the very beginning" and confided that all the time she carried her in her womb she believed she "was cherishing the embryo of a mighty female martyr."

Anthony was less impressed by Stanton's latest progeny. Writing to Lucy Stone, she complained, "oh dear, Lucy, what can she do with *five* children." Yet the thrust of Anthony's letter was to thank Stone for her attendance and speech at the temperance meeting and to beg the frequently frail Stone to "live a *long* life [because] There is a vast deal of work for you to do; therefore be prudent that you may have strength to accomplish it."

The increasingly close-knit group of women continued to alternate between canvassing for temperance and giving speeches on women's rights. In first half of 1853, Stone delivered two lectures on women's rights in New York City, while at the same time Anthony hosted temperance meetings upstate in Utica and Syracuse. Antoinette Brown, who had joined Anthony on the road trip, wrote her in August 1853 "that you *must* speak at N.Y. both at the Temperance & Woman's Rights Conventions." Through private correspondence and public appearances the women's circle grew. They supported one another in letters and by appearing at one another's talks. But the obdurateness of the legislators was taking its toll. More and more the women's faces turned toward suffrage, for only by exercising the franchise could they gain leverage over the men sitting in the assembly seats. By 1855 the die had been cast.

Anthony, according to Stanton, had been indefatigable and, even more important, highly successful in raising funds and distributing literature for the new cause. In meetings at Saratoga and Albany, New York, in 1855 the emphasis was on gaining the vote. The next year Anthony was busy circulating petitions, but the legislators preferred to read the "buffoonery" of those who mocked the women (men should wear petticoats and women pants before the legislature granted the women the right to vote) than the petitions the women signed.

A few men supported the women. Abolitionist reformer Wendell Phillips told gatherings that women should not be concerned about losing the "protection" of men if the women gained full civil rights. Whenever women exercised these rights, civilization prospered. Other abolitionists seconded Phillips's views. It appeared that a quid pro quo had been struck between the most earnest advocates of abolition of slavery and the most persistent advocates of women's rights.

John Brown's raid on the Harpers Ferry, Virginia, federal arsenal and the coming of the Civil War cast the women's campaign for the franchise into the shade, but after five years of Civil War, victory brought with it the promise of genuine reform. If the crusading spirit of the war could end the entrenched evil of black slavery, surely it would see the end of the denial of basic citizenship rights to women—particularly when women like Susan B. Anthony had supported the abolition of slavery. As Anthony had asked a gathering on the eve of the war, "Where, under our Declaration of Independence, does the Saxon man get his power to deprive all women and Negroes of their inalienable rights?" She refused to support Abraham Lincoln's candidacy because he was not an abolitionist. No compromise with slavery was her motto, a stance that she duplicated when it came to woman suffrage.

The Woman Who Dared to Vote

CHAPTER I

"We Represent Fifteen Million People"
Summer 1865–Fall 1869

With the end of the Civil War and the passage of the Thirteenth Amendment, the women's rights advocates who had worked so diligently for the abolition of slavery and the preservation of the Union had reason to believe that the political door had been opened for the cause of women's rights. And by "women's rights" they increasingly meant "woman suffrage." As historian Ellen DuBois points out, "The fact that the debate on the ex slaves' legal status focused on Black suffrage helped to destroy whatever doubts remained among feminists that the suffrage was the key to the legal position of women as well." But if they believed that the men who supported the freedmen's right to the franchise would reward the women for their service to the cause of abolition and the Union with their support for extending the franchise to women, the feminists were doomed to bitter disappointment. Woman suffrage was not included in these men's priorities after the war, if, indeed, the men had ever truly supported the women's cause.

In the closing stages of the war, the women's male allies turned to the procurement and guarantee of civil and political rights for male freedmen. It is not too much of a leap to speculate that when Congress added the word "male" to the Fourteenth Amendment and omitted "sex" from the Fifteenth Amendment, its members did so specifically because women had begun to petition and mobilize for woman suffrage. The issue had gained prominence among the reform women's groups but was not popular among men's reform groups. Indeed, the opposite was true, for they assumed that the uphill campaign to gain full civil rights, including the vote, for the freedmen would be burdened by any commitment to white women's voting.

The Center Holds, for a Time

In the immediate aftermath of the war, the coalition among the abolitionist leaders held. All had labored tirelessly in the decades before the Civil War in the American Anti-Slavery Society (AASS). After the Union's triumph over the Confederacy, and particularly after the passage of the Thirteenth Amendment abolishing slavery, the future for the AASS seemed dim. There was a sense that abolitionists had accomplished their goals. But there was also a sense that the AASS had been so successful in its aims that it was too valuable a coalition to abandon.

Wendell Phillips, a tireless advocate for freedmen's rights, argued against dissolution, primarily because he believed that the safety of the black man had not been secured. Susan B. Anthony agreed that it was premature to dismantle the AASS. As she recorded in her diary, "The disbanding of the American A.S. Society is fully as untimely as Gens. Grant and Sherman's granting Parole & Pardon to the whole rebel armies." On May 9 all the officers of the AASS gathered in New York City for the regularly scheduled business meeting, but everyone knew that the meeting was anything but routine. It would decide the organization's fate. At a closed-door session, Phillips told the members to continue the society's operations until the "liberty of the negro [was] beyond peril." William Lloyd Garrison's resolution to dissolve was rejected by a vote of 118–48. Phillips then replaced Garrison as president. At the public session of the society, the newly elected "Phillips called for land, the ballot, and guarantees of citizenship for African American [but] He would not, he said, yet ask for woman suffrage." Then Phillips gratuitously proclaimed, "One question at a time. This hour belongs to the negro."

During the summer that followed, guarantees for black male suffrage were much discussed among the former abolitionists. Ensuring the right to vote for the freedmen would protect the former slaves from those who had not accepted the demise of slavery and would insulate the Republican majority in Congress from state delegations dominated by ex-Confederates. But there was resistance to universal black male suffrage, even among the abolitionists, and proposals to limit the franchise based upon literacy or property holding were floated. In reply, on July 29, 1865, Elizabeth Cady Stanton published an appeal for true "Universal Suffrage" in the *National Anti-Slavery Standard.* She argued for an "impartial" standard for suffrage that would not discriminate on the basis of class. "We have tried class legislation and found it a dead failure," she wrote. She castigated her fellow abolitionists that "all this talk about education and property qualification is the narrow assumption of a rotten aristocracy." Although she claimed that "no country ever has had or ever will have peace until every citizen has a voice in the government," she did not explicitly call for woman suffrage.

By the fall, however, Susan B. Anthony was starting to believe that the question of woman suffrage could not be postponed. On October 13 she and Lucretia Mott called upon Andrew James Colvin, an ally in Albany who had helped get the New York State Married Women's Property Act passed in 1860. They discussed the prospects for woman suffrage in New York. Bearing in mind that the states still determined voting qualifications, and with the state constitutional convention looming, he urged her to campaign for woman suffrage but to keep this lobbying effort separate from the effort to excise the property qualification for black voters. Anthony realized that there was a growing divergence between the abolitionists who believed in prioritizing black men's right to vote and those who wanted to push for national protections for a universal suffrage that included both men and women.

On December 4, 1865, the first session of the thirty-ninth Congress commenced. Republicans in Congress assigned the question of black male suffrage to a Joint Committee on Reconstruction. Numerous proposals for amending the Constitution were immediately introduced. A friend of the women's rights supporters, former Indiana congressman and reformer Robert Dale Owen, kept Anthony and others abreast of the closed-door debates over a proposed Fourteenth Amendment to the federal Constitution. He told them that "one of the Committee proposed 'persons' instead of 'males.' 'That will never do,' said another, 'it would enfranchise all the Southern wenches.'" Not all the resistance to including women in the reforms Congress contemplated arose from anti-Southern sentiment or generalized sexism. Many probably agreed with another anonymous lawmaker quoted by Owen, who told his colleagues that "suffrage for black men will be all the strain the Republican party can stand."

The focus on constitutional solutions to the problem of black male suffrage spurred women to change their strategy in their struggle for woman suffrage. They moved their campaign from state capitals to Washington, D.C. As the authors of the *History of Woman Suffrage* (Anthony, Stanton, and Matilda Gage) explained, "Up to this hour we have looked to State action only for the recognition of our rights . . . but now, by the results of the war, the whole question of suffrage reverts back to Congress and the U.S. Constitution."

On Christmas Eve 1865 Anthony and Stanton addressed the very first petition to Congress on behalf of woman suffrage. Above the signatures of Stanton, Anthony, and Lucy Stone, the petition was sent from the *National Anti-Slavery Standard* office in New York to members of the National Women's Rights Committee. They also "decided to scatter a thousand copies of the form of petition, and get it published in as many newspapers as possible—and thus leave every representativ[e] woman to lead off in her own neighborhood and send a few names on each into Congress at the earliest day possible."

Anthony and the woman's rights advocates were by now veterans of grassroots organizing. In the cover letter distributed with the petition they pointed out that, "as the question of Suffrage is agitating the public mind, it is the hour for woman to make her demand." Time was of the essence. They alerted their correspondents that "propositions have already been made on the floor of Congress to so amend the Constitution as to exclude Women from a voice in the Government." The petition itself "respectfully" asked for "an amendment of the Constitution that shall prohibit the several States from disf[r]anchising any of their citizens on the ground of sex." They rested their case on the basis of fairness and equality. "In making our demand for Suffrage, we would call your attention to the fact that we represent fifteen million people—one half the entire population of the country." Women were worthy of the vote because they were "intelligent, virtuous, native-born American citizens." Experience has shown, they claimed, "all prove the uncertain tenure of life, liberty, and property so long as the ballot—the only weapon of self-protection—is not in the hand of every citizen." In other words, they used the same arguments on behalf of women that the Republican-controlled Congress was at that very moment employing to introduce legislation and a constitutional amendment on behalf of the freedmen.

In Congress, friends of the rights of the freedmen had welcomed the women's agitation and petitions in support of universal suffrage, but read these petitions through the lens of freedmen's rights. The *History of Woman Suffrage* recorded how Massachusetts Senator Charles Sumner, when the Thirteenth Amendment was debated, told the women that they "are doing a noble work" and urged them to "send on the petitions [because] they give me opportunity for speech." The bombastic Sumner, a zealot for his own causes, was grateful for the women's efforts not because he was committed to furthering their cause, however, but because he could exploit their work on behalf of his own. The women kept their end of the implied bargain. They worked tirelessly for the Thirteenth Amendment, generating more than 300,000 petitions to Congress during the drive for its passage. "But," according to the *History*, "when the proposition for the Fourteenth Amendment was pending, and the same women petitioned for their own civil and political rights, they received no letters of encouragement from Republicans nor Abolitionists," including Sumner.

After collecting signatures, during the second week in January 1866, Anthony forwarded the women's franchise petition to Pennsylvania congressman Thaddeus Stevens, chairman of the Joint Committee of Fifteen hammering out the language for the proposed Fourteenth Amendment. But Stevens, one of the most vociferous of abolitionists, did nothing about the petition. Anthony appealed to Democratic Congressman James Brooks, "Will you sir, please send me whatever is said or done with our petitions? Will you also give me names of members whom you think would present petitions for us?" Brooks did much more. First, according to Ann Gordon, "Brooks used his congressional frank to mail out the woman's rights petitions." Then, on January 23 he "asked the Clerk of the House to read aloud Anthony's letter and petition, and he announced his intention to amend various proposals before the House to read that congressional representation would be reduced if the elective franchise were denied 'on account of race or color or sex.'"

Stevens apparently doubted Brooks's sincerity in support of woman suffrage. He probably thought the Democrat Brooks was introducing the issue as a kind of poison pill to thwart efforts to guarantee the franchise for the freedman, much as opponents of the Civil Rights Act of 1964 added "sex" to the list of impermissible categories of discrimination. And to some extent Stevens may have been right, because when pressed Brooks told Stevens that "I am in favor of my own color in preference to any other color, and I prefer the white women of my country to the negro." Nevertheless, Stevens finally formally introduced the woman suffrage petition on January 29.

While the American Anti-Slavery Society had resisted dissolution the previous May, the political ground had shifted in the months following. Debates over "universal" or "impartial" suffrage had come to dominate both Congress and reform journals. Would all men, black and white, not just elite, well-educated, property-holding men, be guaranteed the franchise by a constitutional amendment? Would women be included in the move for full citizenship rights? On December 27, while Anthony and her colleagues were probably still busy mailing out their petitions, Theodore Tilton, editor of Henry Ward Beecher's strongly abolitionist weekly newspaper, the *Independent*, and "a man of unquestionable charm . . . wit . . . personal magnetism . . . physical beauty and rare culture," according to one biographer, stopped by the New York Anti-Slavery Society office and "talked of an 'Equal rights' Committe[e] or Society" with the society's "the 'National Standard' [as] its organ." Perhaps inspired by Tilton's suggestion, Anthony and close AASS colleague Parker Pillsbury sent letters that very day to the Pennsylvania Anti-Slavery Society about "the expediency of so altering the name of the [American Anti-Slavery] Society as to be more in accordance with the changed character of slavery and to add suffrage for women as one of its objects."

When Tilton had visited the AASS office and made his suggestion to Anthony, he had probably already written an editorial that he published that same day. It called for the founding of a new national organization "demanding suffrage for black men and women alike." For this experimental coalition for universal suffrage, he called upon abolitionist allies like Wendell Phillips, currently president of the

AASS, and his own minister and *Independent* colleague, Henry Ward Beecher, to play prominent roles in the new organization.

Founding the AERA

By the third week of January 1866, Anthony, Stanton, Lucy Stone, Tilton, and Frederick Douglass decided to found the New York State American Equal Rights Association. As Anthony wrote to a friend, "The time for Neg[r]o or Woman specialties is passed—and we proposed to step on to the broad platform of equality & fraternity." The plan to convert the AASS into a new organization devoted to universal suffrage for all men and women came up at a Boston meeting of the society near the end of January. The recommendation was introduced by Tilton and Stephen Symonds Foster. Foster's wife, Abby Kelley Foster, and Charles Remond immediately raised objections. They wanted the society to continue its name and focus on the plight of black suffrage. Wendell Phillips repeated his opposition to "engraft[ing] female suffrage" onto the platform of the Anti-Slavery Society.

Thus when the American Anti-Slavery Society held its annual meeting on May 8–9, 1866, the woman suffrage proponents ran into a brick wall. A resolution was proposed, addressing the people of New York State, that would have urged them to repeal the restrictive language of "white" and the "property qualification for colored voters as an urgent and unchristian, and a formidable obstacle to the progress of National reconstruction upon a just and true basis." Elizabeth Cady Stanton moved to amend the resolution "by inserting the words 'a republican form of government,' which would strike out the words male and white." She wanted to know why the women of the society should "go about this State and ask for suffrage for the negro, and not demand it for herself?" Abby Kelley Foster objected to Stanton's amendment. "She did not think such a subject should be introduced into an Anti-Slavery meeting." Foster supported woman suffrage and told Stanton and the rest of those assembled that "just as soon as the civil rights of the negroes are secured in the South, we cease to be an Anti-Slavery Society, and then I am ready for an organization for universal suffrage." Phillips went even further and, "with some acerbity, said Mrs. Stanton's amendment was out of order, because it was not consistent with the constitution." It was obvious that the American Anti-Slavery Society, as presently constituted, would not encompass the aspirations of the woman suffragists.

On May 10, the Eleventh National Woman's Rights Convention assembled for its own meeting, in the very same building—the Church of the Puritans—that the antislavery society had filled a day earlier. Anthony introduced a resolution stating "that the time has come for an organization that shall demand *Universal Suffrage*, and that hereafter we shall be known as the '*American Equal Rights Association*.* . . . Therefore, that we may henceforth concentrate all our forces for the practical application of our one grand, distinctive, national idea—*Universal Suffrage*—I hope we will unanimously adopt the resolution before us, thus resolving this Eleventh National Woman's Rights Convention into the '*American Equal Rights Association*.'" The resolution was unanimously adopted. The women had effectively usurped the cause of the antislavery society and merged it with their own, as well as co-opting many of its members. The AASS was doomed to extinction four years later, but the AERA was doomed as well and would implode even before its predecessor. The worm in the bud was the antislavery and women's rights supporters who followed Anthony and Stanton into the new organization, but did not believe, as they did, that the woman suffrage cause should be pushed with the same fervency as black male suffrage.

After the vote that converted the National Woman's Rights Convention into the first meeting of the American Equal Rights Association, the group adjourned so that Stephen Foster could write a proposed constitution for the new organization. This was an important exercise because it was on the basis of the AASS constitution that Phillips had dismissed Stanton's woman suffrage proposal. But the ideals of the organization were not fully encompassed in the businesslike provisions of the constitution. It identified officers and the mechanics of how local groups could affiliate with the national organization but lacked a clear statement of purpose. "An interesting discussion" arose at this point about the need for a "Preamble."

Lucretia Mott, the seventy-three-year-old abolitionist veteran who had helped found the Pennsylvania Anti-Slavery Society and organize the Seneca Falls women's rights meeting in 1848, "expressed herself specially desirous that there should be a preamble," and a majority of those attending seemed to agree. Mott particularly wanted it made clear "that it should state the fact that this new organization was the outgrowth of the Woman's Rights movement." She wanted no misunderstanding that "equal rights" referred only or even primarily to the rights of freedmen. Stanton "gave her idea of what the preamble should say," and the organization immediately voted to have her reduce it to writing. She called on spiritual imagery and natural rights exhorting her audience that the country had been "purified and exalted through suffering," and that from the carnage and destruction they had emerged "with a holier vision that the peace, prosperity and perpetuity of the Republic rest on *Equal Rights to All.*" The critical statement Mott had requested came at the end of the preamble when Stanton dramatically proclaimed on behalf of everyone that "we, to-day, assembled in our Eleventh National Woman's Rights Convention, bury the woman in the citizen, and our organization in that of the American Equal Rights Association." Stanton's eloquence was rewarded by the new organization when she was nominated as its first president. She declined, however, in favor of the older and deeply respected Mott. The new organization was now formally created.

All the dissension that had been present at the AASS meetings over the past year now seemed happily resolved. Stanton rose to speak and told the men and women of the new AERA that "it had been the desire of her heart to see the Anti-Slavery and Woman's Rights organizations merged into an Equal Rights association, as the two questions were now one and the same." Her sentiments were seconded by James Mott, who said that "he rejoiced that the women had seen fit to reorganize their movement into one for equal rights to all." Stephen S. Foster joined in the positive expressions of support and implicitly criticized the leader of the AASS, Wendell Phillips, when he told the meeting that "many seemed to think that the one question for this hour was negro suffrage." He believed that was an incorrect framing of the issues facing the nation. "The question for every man and woman, he thought, was the true basis of the reconstruction of our government, not the rights of woman, or the negro, but the rights of all men and women."

The group then passed resolutions that supported extending suffrage to men and women for whom the ballot "means bread, education, self-protection [and] self-reliance." But there was also a sense of admonishment in the resolution. "That while we are grateful to Wendell Phillips, Theodore Tilton, and Horace Greeley, for the respectful mention of woman's right to the ballot in the journals through which they speak, we ask them now, when we are reconstructing both our State and National Governments, to demand that the right of suffrage be secured to all citizens—to women as well as black men, for, until this is done, the government stands on the unsafe basis of class legislation." In other words, the women were telling their male colleagues that the time had come to put up or shut up.

Despite the lofty intentions of its founders, lines were beginning to be drawn even at this very first meeting. During the debates over the resolutions, Massachusetts' Charles Lenox Remond, the mulatto son of a free man who had immigrated to New England from Curacao and had been an antislavery activist since the 1830s, objected "to the last of the resolution" because, in part, "it might be that colored men would obtain their rights before women," but, if so, he was confident they would "heartily acquiesce in admitting women also to the right of suffrage." Mott, presiding over the meeting, expressed skepticism. She told the assemblage that "women had a right to be a little jealous of the addition of so large a number of men to the voting class, for the colored men would naturally throw all their strength upon the side of those opposed to woman's enfranchisement."

The black men at the meeting took umbrage at the women's objections to the Fourteenth Amendment on the basis that it protected the ballots of only black men. George T. Downing, a black man and successful restaurant and hotel entrepreneur, rose to question "whether he had rightly understood that Mrs. Stanton and Mrs. Mott were opposed to the enfranchisement of the colored man, unless the ballot should also be accorded to woman at the same time." In other words, Downing and the black and white men in the audience wanted to know, would the women stand in the way of extending suffrage to black men if the Fourteenth Amendment's "male inhabitants" language was retained. Congressional passage of the amendment was only a month away and Republican victory, they thought, was not assured. Would the desperately needed guarantees that they hoped the amendment would afford for the safety of the freedmen in the unsettled South lose the stalwart support of women? Stanton responded for some, if not all, of the woman suffragists that "we do not take the right step for this hour in demanding suffrage for any class; as a matter of principle I claim it for all. But . . . when Mr. Downing puts the question to me, are you willing to have the colored man enfranchised before the woman, I say, no." Like Mott she bluntly stated that "I would not trust him with all my rights . . . I desire that we go into the kingdom together, for individual and national safety demand that not another man be enfranchised without the woman by his side." Stanton had stirred the hornet's nest. Stephen Foster reacted strongly to Stanton. He told the convention that "even, therefore, if the enfranchisement of the colored man would probably retard the enfranchisement of woman, we had no right for that reason to deprive him of his right. The right of each should be accorded at the earliest possible moment, neither being denied for any supposed benefit to the other." The men claimed they supported woman suffrage but were simply being pragmatic. As Remond summed it up, "if he were to lose sight of expediency, he must side with Mrs. Stanton, although to do so was extremely trying; for he could not conceive of a more unhappy position than that occupied by millions of American men bearing the name of freedmen while the rights and privileges of *free* men are still denied them."

Back and forth the conversation went, becoming more and more heated. It was finally up to Stephen Foster's activist Quaker wife, Abby Kelley Foster, to explain why she objected to adding woman suffrage to the project of the immediate protection of the black men's franchise. "Were the negro and woman in the same civil, social, and religious status to-day, I should respond aye, with all my heart to this sentiment." She bluntly pointed out what she thought were the salient facts of the case. "You say the negro has the civil rights bill, also the military reconstruction bill granting him suffrage. It has been well said, 'he has the title deed to liberty, but is not yet in the possession of liberty.' He is treated as a slave to-day in the several districts of the South." Presidential Reconstruction had failed the freedman. "Without wages, without family rights, whipped and beaten by thousands, given up to the most horrible outrages, without that protection which his value as property formerly gave him." The Black Codes passed by the former Confederates who dominated the Southern legislatures threatened former slaves "without farther guarantees, to be plunged into peonage, serfdom or even into chattel slavery."

Foster appealed to her woman suffragist friends: "Have we any true sense of justice, are we not dead to the sentiment of humanity if we shall wish to postpone his security against present woes and future enslavement till woman shall obtain political rights?" Foster's appeal was, perhaps, the first signal of the coming rift among the longtime women's rights supporters of suffrage. But the center would hold for a while longer. Anthony appealed for unity despite their ideological differences. "The question," she told the meeting very near its end, "is not, is this or that person right, but what are the principles under discussion. As I understand the difference between Abolitionists, some think this is harvest time for the black man and seed-sowing time for woman. Others, with whom I agree, think we have been sowing the seed of individual rights, the foundation idea of a republic for the last century, and that this is the harvest time for all citizens who pay taxes, obey the laws and are loyal to the government." The sentiment espousing the universal principle of equal rights prevailed for the moment.

In order to secure the civil rights of the newly freed black men in a postwar era fraught with danger for the former slaves, legislation and perhaps another constitutional amendment would be required. The proposed Fourteenth Amendment secured civil rights to the freedmen first by nationalizing the concept of citizenship and then enforcing violations with penalties, including reducing a state's representation in Congress that impinged on its male citizens' rights.

But according to the *History of Woman Suffrage*, "Miss Anthony and Mrs. Stanton . . . were the first to see the full significance of the word 'male' in the 14th Amendment, and at once sounded the alarm." Their efforts included impassioned petitions to Congress. They told the lawmakers that "as you are now amending the Constitution, and, in harmony with advancing civilization, lacing new safeguards round the individual rights of four millions of emancipated slaves, we ask that you extend the right of Suffrage to Woman—the only remaining class of disfranchised citizens." At the very least, Anthony and her suffragist friends hoped that if the second section of the Amendment did not specify "male inhabitants," the cause of woman suffrage would not be impeded, as Theodore Tilton editorialized in his *Independent*, "If the present Congress is not called to legislate *for* the rights of women, let it not legislate *against* them."

With a bare nod to the women's herculean efforts expended on behalf of the Union and abolitionism for most of the previous decade, Phillips consoled the woman suffragists. He admitted that the phrase in the proposed Fifteenth Amendment that guaranteed the franchise against interference based only upon grounds of "race, color, or previous condition of servitude" was unfortunate. He told them, "I hope in time to be as bold as [John] Stuart Mill and add to that last clause 'sex!!'" But at the same time he counseled the women to postpone their ambitions, for "this hour belongs to the Negro." In the Senate, Sumner, who had so gratefully acknowledged the women's work for black emancipation during the debates over the Thirteenth Amendment, now balked at representing the woman suffrage cause during the debates over the Fourteenth. They later recalled in their *History* that "even such Republicans as Charles Sumner presented [the woman suffrage petitions], if at all, under protest. A petition from Massachusetts, with the name of Lydia Maria Child [Sumner's close friend and ardent supporter] at the head, was presented by the great Senator under protest as 'most inopportune!'—as if there could be a more fitting time for action than when the bills were pending."

On May 14, 1868, the American Equal Rights Association held its third annual "Anniversary" meeting with the coalition of leaders intact. Lucretia Mott continued to serve as president and a panoply of eminent former abolitionists served as vice president, including Elizabeth Cady Stanton, Frederick Douglass, Henry Ward Beecher, Antoinette Brown Blackwell, and Olympia Brown. On its executive committee appeared the names Lucy Stone, Elizabeth Tilton, Ernestine Rose, Theodore Tilton, and Susan B. Anthony.

Meeting again in New York City, the association continued to struggle with the question of whether woman suffrage had to wait upon the ballot first being guaranteed to black men. Though the Fourteenth Amendment had succeeded in Congress the month after that first contentious meeting of the AERA, the fight in the states over its ratification continued. Members of the association, including its prominent women members, had canvassed state after state for both legislative ratification and simultaneous bills for laws or state constitutional amendments that would grant the right to vote to women. Anthony and Stanton themselves had worked hard in Kansas to get public referenda on black and woman suffrage passed, though to no avail. Feelings were running high and the debate reflected the members' frustrations and fears.

Reverend Olympia Brown broached the problem by castigating "some of our leading reformers work for other objects first; the enfranchisement of the negro, the eight hour law, the temperance cause; and leave the woman suffrage question in the background." She predicted that "woman will be enfranchised in spite of them." She wasn't willing to postpone the woman suffrage question. "It is no use to tell us to wait until something else is done. *Now* is the accepted time for the enfranchisement of woman." She was particularly vehement about the Republican Party's abandonment of its women supporters both on the national stage and in the recent battle over the referenda in Kansas. "The Republican party controlled Kansas, and yet repudiated woman's rights in the canvass of last year."

Frederick Douglass took issue with Brown's complaints "that one good cause was in opposition to another." Douglass attempted to build a bridge over the troubled waters between the supporters of woman and black suffrage. He told the delegates that "I have always championed woman's right to vote," but he agreed with the supporters of black male suffrage that "the present claim for the negro is one of the most *urgent* necessity." He believed that yoking the two together would lead to the defeat of both, an outcome he found intolerable. The situation was totally different for black men than for women. "The assertion of the right of women to vote meets nothing but ridicule; there is no deep seated malignity in the hearts of the people against her." Women were not endangered by those who opposed their right to vote. But, he argued, "name the right of the negro to vote, all hell is turned loose and the Ku-klux and Regulators hunt and slay the unoffending black man." His contrast between the two programs did not stop there. "The government of this country loves women. They are the sisters, mothers, wives and daughters of our rulers," an argument long offered by men to defend their refusal to grant civil and political rights to women.

Lucy Stone, no supporter of Stanton's strong stance against the Fourteenth Amendment (because it contained language that limited the enforcement of the franchise only to the votes of "male inhabitants"), nevertheless refuted Douglass's claim for the benign attitude of those in government toward their women. She "controverted" his "statement that women were not persecuted for endeavoring to obtain their rights, and depicted in glowing colors the wrongs of women and the inadequacy of the laws to redress them." Douglass concluded his remarks by chiding that "women should not censure Mr. Phillips, Mr. Greeley, or Mr. Tilton, all have spoken eloquently for woman's rights," though their practical support for the women's cause since the proposal of the Fourteenth Amendment had all but disappeared.

By the time the American Equal Rights Association met for its annual meeting in May 1869, the rift that had emerged over the language of the Fourteenth Amendment had developed into a major schism with congressional passage of the Fifteenth Amendment only three months before. With ratification of that amendment pending, the woman suffrage leadership was up in arms. The New York "radical" suffrage faction of Anthony and Stanton wanted the amendment defeated because it failed to include sex in the protected categories for voting rights, while the Boston "moderate" faction of Lucy Stone, along with the many black and white males in the AERA, supported the amendment's immediate ratification.

As the *New York Times* reported, "Steinway Hall was nearly filled. . . . The majority of the auditors were females." Summing up the proceedings in the newspaper's typical understated fashion, the subheading to the paper's story informed the public that there was a "Spirited Debate on the Questions of Reform." A spirited debate, indeed. The next subheading, loosely quoting from a speech by Elizabeth Cady Stanton, hinted at how spirited: "Manhood Suffrage, National Suicide—Female Enfranchisement Our Only Safety."

Stanton presided and in her opening remarks she vividly claimed that "there had been for a long time an aristocracy of caste, and there yet existed an aristocracy of sex." In other words, she implied that the Thirteenth Amendment had ended white over black supremacy, but women had not yet been emancipated from male supremacy. A short time later the eloquent radical minister of the Independent Liberal Church in New York, the Reverend Octavius Brooks Frothingham, ascended the podium. Frothingham was a pioneering abolitionist within the Unitarian church, but when his transcendental and rationalist inclinations forced him out of the Unitarian movement he became the leader of a group of religious radicals who advocated an anti-Christian Unitarianism. His congregation met in Lyric Hall in New York City and he was considered a crowd pleasing orator, one of the finest of the age. On this day at the AERA convention, and despite the fact that his own record of support for woman suffrage was less than impeccable, he proclaimed to this faithful audience that woman suffrage "is the important question of the age." He went on, however, to incautiously comment that "people thought that the Government of this State might be better if some 40,000 or 50,000 voters could be disfranchised, and as many women enfranchised in their stead." Who, exactly, he thought should be culled from the New York voter lists was not clear.

Even so, Stanton rose to differ "with Mr. Frothingham as to disfranchisement. She did not believe in taking away from any one the right of suffrage to bestow it on another. All should be enfranchised, without distinction as to color or sex." Whether he had intended to or not, Frothingham had opened a festering wound within the universal suffrage movement. Stanton's reply had, for the time being, acted as a bandage but she would shortly later undo much of the good she had applied.

Stanton attempted to rally the organization behind an amendment to guarantee woman suffrage. She called upon the organization to celebrate the date March 16, 1869, which, "she said, will be memorable in all coming time as the day when Hon. Geo. W. Julian submitted a joint resolution to Congress to enfranchise the women of the Republic by proposing a Sixteenth Amendment to the Federal Constitution."

The wording of this early version of the woman suffrage amendment differed significantly from what would be passed as the Nineteenth Amendment in the next century (see the postscript). Influenced by the language of the Fourteenth and soon-to-be-ratified Fifteenth Amendments, it read: "The right of suffrage in the United States shall be based on citizenship, and shall be regulated by Congress; and all citizens of the United States, whether native or naturalized, shall enjoy this right equally without any distinction or discrimination whatever founded on sex."

Stanton hoped for a resolution from the AERA supporting the proposed amendment. After all, hadn't that been the group's objective when the organization had been founded out of the National Woman's Rights Convention? She "demanded" the amendment's adoption for several reasons. The *New York Times* summarized her arguments as a kind of battle between the sexes and that "manhood suffrage is national suicide and woman's destruction. Every consideration of patriotism, as well as personal safety, warns the women of the Republic to demand their speedy enfranchisement . . . because the history of American statesmanship did not inspire her with confidence in man's capacity to govern the nation alone with justice and mercy."

While Stanton may have upset the few men in the audience with her fulminations against their sex, many who supported woman suffrage might understand her invective. But Stanton's rant did not stop there. Expressing the pent-up frustration of many "educated, refined women" who saw the Fifteenth Amendment enfranchise far less able men, she complained that it created "an antagonism" between women and "the lower orders of men, especially at the South, where the slaves of yesterday are the lawmakers of to-day. It not only rouses woman's prejudices against the negro, but his hostility and contempt for her."

Up to this point, Stanton and Anthony's antipathy to ratification of the Fifteenth Amendment, expressed by Stanton at the convention in fairly diplomatic terms, and in their journal the *Revolution* in more stark terms, had not resulted in open warfare at the convention. But when the slate of new officers for the AERA was presented by the organization's nominating committee, "before the result could be announced, Mr. S[tephen] S[ymonds] Foster rose and objected to the names of Mrs. Stanton and Miss Anthony on the ground that the paper published by them (*Revolution*) stigmatized the Fifteenth Amendment as 'infamous,' and advocated 'educated,' not impartial suffrage."

Foster was undoubtedly reacting to Stanton's essay in the *Revolution* the previous December entitled "Manhood Suffrage." It was an angry diatribe in which she imprudently cast ethnic aspersions on some potential male voters. "Think of Patrick and Sambo and Hans and Uyn Tung who do not know the difference between a Monarchy and a Republic, who never read the Declaration of Independence or Webster's spelling book, making laws for Lydia Maria Child, Lucretia Mott, or Fanny Kemble." With words like these echoing in his head, in less than three years, Foster, the optimistic and fervent supporter of Stanton at the founding of the AERA, had turned into her enemy.

————

Out in the Cold

Stanton and Anthony had for decades been undisputed leaders of the women's rights movement, but Foster's objection represented the "moderates" and loyal Republicans' attempt to unseat the two women. It was a clash of ideologies: should the post–Civil War window of opportunity for human rights include a push for women's rights, now seen through the primacy of the campaign for woman suffrage, at the same time as the push for the rights of freed black males? Or should the black man's necessity be prioritized over the less urgent, or so it seemed, rights of women?

Anthony and Stanton, though strong abolitionists before and throughout the war, now decided that their full energy should be dedicated to the woman's cause. They believed that the postwar window of opportunity to achieve their goal would be lost for decades if the politicians explicitly prioritized black men over women. Just as Stanton had declared in her dissent from Reverend Frothingham's comments, they believed in universal suffrage and civil rights. But they steadfastly argued that compromise and the ranking of one group's interests over the other's was disastrous, and they decided to take a hard line in opposing the Fifteenth Amendment. The "moderates" supported the Republican Party and its decision to secure the rights, and safety, of the freedman. They viewed Stanton and Anthony as dangerous "radicals" and believed they had to discredit and oust them from their public position at the head of the woman suffrage movement.

Foster's attack on Stanton and Anthony at the AERA convention was not the first salvo the "moderates" had launched against them. According to at least one Anthony biographer they had been deliberately sabotaged during their canvass of Kansas during the drive up to that state's public referenda on woman and black suffrage. One of the Republican stalwarts had sent the eccentric and racist George Francis Train to join them on their railroad trip throughout the state. Desperate for any aid whatsoever during that grueling, and ultimately futile, campaign, Stanton and Anthony had allowed Train to stump with them. Train had also volunteered to help fund the publication of the *Revolution*. The always impecunious Anthony decided to accept his financial assistance, and in return they published some of his articles. Anthony and Stanton found Train's racism distasteful but decided they could not reject his overtures. The joint venture did not last long since Train failed to donate the funds he had promised. Nevertheless, Foster now raised their association with Train as one of the reasons why the AERA should repudiate them.

Another accusation Foster used to impugn Anthony was to repeat a false charge that she had misused, even embezzled, some of the organization's funds that had been allocated for her use in the Kansas campaign. Anthony rose to answer this allegation by pointing out that she had accounted for her expenditures "item by item, to the Committee of Auditors in Boston, who had pronounced the account correct." Stanton was even more incensed at Foster's slurs against Anthony and herself. According to the *New York Times*, "Some excitement arose at this point, Mrs. Stanton declaring Mr. Foster out of order." She demanded a vote on whether Foster "should be allowed to proceed," and when the vote went against him, "Mr. Foster sat down, having previously declared his determination to retire from the meeting." For the moment, the anti-Anthony and Stanton forces retreated. The committee's ticket of nominees for officers for the next year, including Elizabeth Cady

Stanton and Susan B. Anthony "was then elected, there being only one vote in the negative."

The controversy did not abate with the vote on the AERA's officers. Immediately afterward, Frederick Douglass arose to address the audience. He claimed that "he came there . . . not so much to speak as to listen," but apparently what he had heard moved him to come forward. He began by praising Mrs. Stanton for that portion of her statements "wherein she declared herself in favor of not partial, but universal suffrage." He told the assemblage, referencing Foster's unpopular attempt to oust her from the organization's leadership, that "for this declaration if for no other reason, she deserved the highest position in this movement, and she would have it whether elected or not." Indeed, he went on, "in the eyes of the whole country she would always occupy it." Douglass did not accord any accolades in his comments for Anthony, only Stanton.

But he protested Stanton's disparagement of the "lower orders" of men, including the newly freed black men, Douglass again referring to Stanton's *Revolution* article. He reiterated some of the arguments he had made in prior years that "with the negro the right to exercise the suffrage was a matter of life and death; his existence depended upon it." Douglass then provided a litany of horrors to which the former slaves had been subjected: sometimes "hunted like a wild beast" and "torn from his home and hung to the lamp-post by an infuriated mob," and how "the negro mother had seen her babe torn from her breast and its brains dashed out against the lamp-post."

He drove home his point: "All this was done to the negro simply because he was black. Woman had suffered nothing of this kind. When she is shot down by the Kuklux, or hung to a lamp-post at every turn, simply for being a woman, then he was willing to admit there would something like an equality of urgency between her and the negro in the matter of having extended to them the right of suffrage." Someone in the audience, it is not clear who, demanded of Douglass, "if everything he had said of the outrages toward the negro was not equally true of negro women?" Douglass admitted that it was but retorted that "it was not because they were women, but because they were black."

Douglass discounted the idea that black women were subjected to assaults because they were women and seemed to believe that black women's safety would only need black men's votes to protect them. What Douglass most reviled in Stanton's remarks, both at the convention and her even more vituperative articles in the *Revolution*, was her outrage at the granting of the ballot to prospective freedmen and ignorant immigrant laborers before the "daughters of Washington and Jefferson."

Anthony rebuked Douglass. She argued that "the question of precedence has no place on an equal rights platform. The only reason why it ever found a place here was that there were some who insisted that woman must stand back & wait until another class should be enfranchised." It was only because others had raised the issue of prioritizing black men over women that "my friend Mrs. Stanton & others of us have said, If you will not give the whole loaf of justice to the entire people, if you are determined to give it, piece by piece, then give it first to women, to the most intelligent and & capable portion of the women at least."

Lucy Stone tried to cool the emotional temperature in the room. She said that she "thought the question of priority should never have been introduced into this discussion." Despite the male-centric language introduced into the Constitution by the Fourteenth and Fifteenth Amendments, "She did not believe . . . in taking a mournful view of the matter." Indeed, recent events had given her optimism. Referring to the enfranchisement of women, "She thought the day of woman's independence was breaking; that in some States, at least, women would vote for President in 1872. Success was sure to crown woman's effort to obtain the ballot, because her demands were founded on the principle of eternal justice." But the damage had been done. Another two days of wrangling followed, exacerbating the now irreconcilable breach between the two factions. The AERA, a doomed experiment in forging a coalition to effect universal suffrage, had come to an end.

The National Women's Suffrage Association

On May 15, two days after the American Equal Rights Association meeting had adjourned, Stanton and Anthony presided over a Saturday evening reception for visiting women delegates to the convention at the Woman's Bureau, a headquarters for suffrage activity, and a refuge for women activists, lodged in an elegant New York City brownstone. Whether planned in advance, as Henry Blackwell later asserted, or the idea had sprung spontaneously out of the assembled women's complaints and conversation over refreshments, the reception turned into a meeting to form an independent woman suffrage organization: The National Women's Suffrage Association (NWSA).

As Stanton later recounted, "A general dissatisfaction had been expressed by most of the women attending the [AERA] Convention with the name and latitude of debate involved in an 'Equal Rights Convention.'" Stanton, and more particularly Anthony, had encouraged women attending their various woman suffrage speaking engagements throughout the midwestern and western states to come east for the annual meeting of the AERA. A good showing of these women had heeded their call but had assumed that the AERA was a woman suffrage organization.

When they heard the debate over prioritizing black male suffrage over woman suffrage, they were frustrated and angry. According to Ann Gordon, "Ernestine Rose had first voiced the hope that a woman suffrage association might replace the Equal Rights Association, in her final speech at the anniversary on May 13." But "when her suggestion was taken up for debate [Stanton] ruled that the association's constitution required prior notice of an intent to change the name." Mary Livermore probably spoke for many present when she recalled that "I would not have come on to the anniversary, nor would any of us, if we had known what it was. We supposed we were coming to a woman suffrage convention." Under the circumstances, it is not surprising that the women at the Woman's Bureau reception decided to create a new organization dedicated to the woman suffrage issue. There was one area in which a lively debate arose. With their recent experience in mind, some women wanted the new organization to exclude male members. In the end, NWSA allowed men to join but did not allow them to serve as officers. They decided that women would lead this woman suffrage movement.

Their objective, as Stanton wrote in her *Revolution* article five days later, was to "make the Sixteenth Amendment the sole object of its future work and consideration." The strategic plan resembled all the work they had undertaken since the early days of the woman's rights movement. They proposed to make "a thorough canvass of the several states with conventions, tracts, petitions," and planned "that at the opening of Congress, we may send in the largest petition that has ever yet been presented at the national capitol." In other words, they would continue to petition, plead, and rely on their male representatives to "do the right thing" in the same way they had for decades.

Just Vote

The first glimmer of a new strategy emerged out of a woman suffrage meeting held in St. Louis, Missouri, in October 1869. A local attorney named Francis Minor and husband to the president of the Missouri Woman Suffrage Association, Virginia Minor, presented several resolutions later published in *Revolution*. The crux of his argument, adopted in the Missouri "Resolutions," was that under the Fourteenth Amendment's "privileges or immunities" clause, women, as citizens of the United States, had the right to the elective franchise. Though the Constitution "leaves the qualifications of electors to the several states, it nowhere gives them the right to deprive any citizen" of the right to vote. Minor told Stanton and Anthony that "if these resolutions are right, let the question be settled by individual determination." The strategy Francis Minor recommended was for the women suffragists to attempt to register and vote, to assert their constitutional right, and, if denied (as they almost certainly would be), to bring a civil rights lawsuit against the state officials who had obstructed them. It was a daring and assertive strategy. They would take their claim for suffrage all the way to the Supreme Court, and they believed the justices would vindicate them. If they succeeded they would not need any tedious petitions to Congress for a constitutional amendment or the slow lobbying of state legislatures for its ratification. The judicial route could be a shortcut to woman suffrage.

Only a few days after Francis Minor wrote to the *Revolution* with his proposal for a radical new strategy for the woman suffrage campaign, Elizabeth Cady Stanton received a letter from her old friend and ally in the women's rights movement, Lucy Stone. Stone was writing to Stanton as a courtesy to tell her that she and many of her Boston woman suffrage colleagues had issued a "call for a Convention to form an American Woman Suffrage Association," in direct competition with NWSA. Stone tried to reassure Stanton that, "so far as I have influence, this soc. shall never be an enemy or antagonist of yours in any way." But in the next breath she criticized Anthony and Stanton's NWSA and admitted the natural rivalry. The new AWSA, Stone declared, "will simply fill a field and combine forces, which yours does not." By combining forces, Stone meant that her organization would absorb all the ardent abolitionists who fought for the black male suffrage guarantees of the Fifteenth Amendment. Though the Boston woman suffrage activists objected to Anthony and Stanton's rejection of support for the Fifteenth Amendment as long as it only protected men's suffrage and not women's, Lucy Stone was not entirely unsympathetic with their position. In May 1867, when they had all been stumping for woman suffrage in Kansas, Stone had written to Anthony in frustration that "the Negroes are all against us. There has just now left us, an ignorant black preacher named Twine, who is very confident the women ought not to vote—These men *ought not* to be allowed to vote before we do, because they will be just so much more dead weight to lift." Apparently, Stone's frustration had abated. She now no longer believed the black man's franchise should wait upon woman's.

Stanton was unimpressed with Stone's letter informing her of the AWSA convention, and in an article for the *Revolution* dated October 28, nine days after Stone's letter, she claimed that she had only learned of the upcoming AWSA convention in Cleveland, Ohio, in November "from the daily journals." She attributed the impetus for the meeting to "a few dissatisfied minds," and she opined to her readers that at "the present stage of the Woman's Suffrage movement in this country a division in our ranks is rather to be deplored." She sincerely worried about what effect the rivalry would have upon the movement, "for when friends disagree new-comers hesitate as to which side to join; and from fear of being involved in personal bickerings they withhold their names and influence altogether." As angry as she may have been at Stone and the others for creating a competitor to NWSA, Stanton felt anguish about "the result to the old friends themselves, when, instead of fighting the common enemy, prejudice, custom, unjust laws and a false public sentiment, they turn, as the old Abolitionists in their divisions did, and rend each other." Finally, Stanton pointed out that allies in reform movements had a long history of dissension, dissolution, and reforming into new groups. One need not look as far back as the 1840 Garrisonian Anti-Slavery Society versus Liberty Party split, as Stanton had pointed out. After all, only three years earlier reformers witnessed the American Anti-Slavery Society's acrimonious evolution into the American Equal Rights Association. Stanton claimed she had tried to prevent the schism in the woman suffrage movement. She recounted how "when the Boston malcontents" (not a description to encourage reconciliation) "first consulted me on this point, I said, if your hostility to the National Women's Suffrage Association is one of leadership alone, as it seems to be, and any other woman desires to be the President of the Association, I will gladly resign at any moment."

Despite her claimed attempt at reconciliation, Stanton was deeply bitter and angry at the former friends and allies she believed had betrayed her and Anthony. She pointed to the circular letter's claim "that there is no antagonism between the new and the old, yet the contrary is well known to every worker in the movement." The signatories of the letter calling for the new organization, Stanton claimed, "have been sedulously and malignantly working for two years to undermine certain officers [herself and Anthony] in the National Association and their journal, in the minds of all those who affiliate with them." She argued that numerous individuals who had signed the document would not have joined Stone and company if they "had known the animus of the persons" behind the call for AWSA. She warned her readers that the "fifty grave and reverend gentlemen who have signed the call for a new Woman's Suffrage Association" were not true supporters of the cause but had a different agenda. For most of them "they go there to make a Republican or Abolition platform."

Susan B. Anthony heard from many loyal supporters who opposed the formation of a new woman suffrage organization. Some wanted to attend the Cleveland meeting so they could speak out against it. Anthony wrote to one that "you guess rightly about Mrs. Stanton—she will *not* go to Cleveland . . . nor will S. B. Anthony.

But, for persons *not members* & *officers* of the National to be there & speak & vote *against* forming a *new* & inevitably antagonistic society might be well enough." Well enough, indeed, for sometime between November 8, when she wrote to her friend that she most emphatically would not attend the Cleveland meeting, and November 24, when the rival faction convened their meeting, Susan B. Anthony changed her mind.

According to Ann Gordon, Anthony's surprise arrival at the AWSA meeting caused considerable discombobulation. "James Bradwell of Chicago asked the convention to honor her with a seat on the platform," as was customary when a dignitary in the movement was present at such a public meeting. His suggestion seemed to take T. W. Higginson, presiding at the podium, aback. Gordon, quoting from a local newspaper account of events, relates that he "hesitated, stumbled in speech, and it was fully three minutes before he could utter the name of Susan and invite her to the place of honor." When Anthony, deep behind enemy lines, rose to ascend the dais, "she was greeted with loud applause." Her remarks, according to the *Cleveland Plain Dealer*, was "the speech of the evening." According to the newspaper account, Anthony assured the AWSA audience: "don't be scared. Our situation is most hopeful and promising. These independent and separate movements show that we are alive." She also expressed the hope that "this new association would be abundantly successful, and urged all present from the twenty-one states represented to go home, organize societies, and ally themselves either with the American Association at Cleveland or the National Association at New York."

Anthony was showing the world that she was gracious and dedicated to the cause—above any petty jealousy. The press certainly took note, and undoubtedly the Cleveland audience was equally impressed. She then made a substantive plea for everyone to go home and work for the proposed Sixteenth Amendment. Anthony told the AWSA delegates that "for herself she didn't propose to waste time now on state legislatures." In essence, her graciousness was the preamble to her plan to urge the rival convention to undertake the NWSA strategy rather than its leaders' own.

How much Anthony's presence at and remarks to the founding meeting of the rival AWSA influenced woman suffrage groups to join her, rather than Stone's, organization is not clear. But the conflict between the two groups had an impact, as Elizabeth Cady Stanton had predicted, on the woman suffrage movement. For example, while the San Francisco County Woman Suffrage Association affiliated with NWSA, the statewide group voted to join neither organization, at least for a year, waiting to see how the dust would settle and which national organization would survive. Despite the turmoil, the National's convention the following January in Washington, D.C., was a tremendous success. Anthony cheerfully noted in her diary that they had a "splendid audience" on the first day in Lincoln Hall, and on the second day they had "larger audiences still," so much so that they "voted to continue another day." Happily, she recorded the next day that "audiences still increased to the evening session—when the hall was packed."

Anthony's good mood about NWSA and its work was reinforced the following month when her colleagues at the Woman's Bureau threw a fiftieth birthday party for her. By now, Anthony and her allies were masters of public relations and used the event to bring woman suffrage again to public attention by inviting the influential New York press to cover the celebration. Even the staid *New York Times* lauded Anthony on the occasion. They reported that "Miss Anthony . . . bears her fifty Summers lightly." The *Times* had never editorialized in favor of woman suffrage but could not deny that Anthony deserved admiration. "Whatever our sentiments may be as to the cause she advocates," they wrote, "we do full justice to her restless energy and activity and unswerving fidelity to her principles." For her part, Anthony, always single-minded on behalf of woman's right to vote proclaimed to the assembled press and friends that she would not be content until a Sixteenth Amendment for woman suffrage was passed. Only "When the Secretary of State shall proclaim that twenty-eight States have ratified that amendment then Susan B. Anthony would stop work, and not before."

The following month brought an effort by a number of woman suffrage supporters, individuals who considered themselves friends of both Anthony and Stanton, as well as Lucy Stone and Henry Blackwell, to reconcile the competing suffrage organizations. Spearheaded by Theodore Tilton, they addressed an "Appeal for a Union of the Woman Suffrage Associations" to Elizabeth Cady Stanton, president of NWSA, and the Reverend Henry Ward Beecher, the president of AWSA. They wrote to the two groups as "co-workers like yourselves in the cause of Woman's Enfranchisement, but not members of either of the Societies you represent." The appeal tried to point out how much NWSA and AWSA had in common by setting up two columns and comparing various articles from the organizations' constitutions. The appeal concluded that anyone comparing the two could "detect at a glance . . . that these two constitutions differ only in language, not in purpose."

The appeal went further. A comparison of recent advertisements for each of the organization's upcoming annual meetings showed that the "two national societies for Woman's Enfranchisement—both having an identical object, both founded on similar constitutions . . . and both appealing to one general constituency for support—have recently advertised their approaching May meetings to be held in the same city, on the same days, at the same hours, and in two halls hardly a stone's throw apart." The rivalry was threatening the cause itself. Resources and personnel needed for the fight for woman suffrage were being split between them. The juxtaposition of the two competing conventions not only highlighted that inevitable conclusion but also presented a divided front ripe for ridicule by their enemies and journalists.

There was also the tragedy of women loyal to the cause being forced to choose between two sets of friends and colleagues. The appeal was a heartfelt document expressing sincere and serious concerns of many in the movement. "In view of this striking want of co-operation between these two societies . . . dividing into rival parties the great body of life-long co-workers in the common cause; creating an embarrassment to hosts of new friends who, in flocking to the standard of Woman's Suffrage, are perplexed to choose between two organizations:—in view of these regretful facts, we use our prerogative of friendship and good will (cherished equally toward both bodies) to express our belief that no sufficient reason exists to justify the future permanence of the disunion which we at present deplore."

The appeal was taken seriously by both the Anthony-Stanton and Stone-Beecher camps, though neither responded immediately with unalloyed support for unification. Anthony wrote to Stanton that she had immediately replied to Tilton claiming that "the responsibility of Division rests with & on the Americans [AWSA]." She was particularly incensed over AWSA's plan, as Tilton had pointed to in the "appeal," to hold their convention at Steinway Hall in New York City—the home town, as it were, of the National—on the very same day, May 11, that Anthony's association had planned to hold their own convention in Irving Hall in the same city. Indignantly, Anthony told Stanton: "They call a *mass Convention*—in same City on same days that the New York *National holds its regular annual meeting* they cant blind peoples eyes to that fact." She related that she had "told T[heodore] T[ilton]" that unlike AWSA, the National had not "in anywise trespassed or trodden upon any friend or existing association . . . but stood ready to receive and accept any & every proposition from the seceders that savored of justice & right."

Anthony's characterization of the AWSA leaders as "seceders" was both inflammatory, considering the late Civil War history, and inaccurate; though AWSA had been founded after NWSA, Lucy Stone, Henry Blackwell, and Henry Ward Beecher and their friends had never been members of the latter. Over the coming months it would become increasingly clear that there was a clash of personalities at work here as much as ideologies. Anthony was decidedly wary of the meeting Tilton and his group proposed to hold in April. "In heavens name I hope *you have* not given any other answer if the Call for a *truce meeting* has met you on the way." She was clearly agitated and suspicious when she told Stanton "it is proposed for the *6th of April*—when neither you nor I can possibly be in New York." Anthony related that she had written Tilton that "there is but one true way—that is for the *seceders* & *neutrals* to *come* individually or collectively into the National's annual meeting & then & there speak & vote as to officers & Constitution . . . and *abide* by the *decision* of *the Majority*."

In other words, she wanted home court advantage. And she was confident that she and Stanton would prevail over their rivals in any vote. She had told Tilton that "we could not honorably and should not accept any proposition that ignored—Stanton & Anthony." Finally, Anthony had told Tilton that "we can have no *national cooperation on any other plan.*" Lucy Stone had a very similar response to the Tilton "appeal." In her *Woman's Journal*, according to Ann Gordon, Stone had told Tilton, "For ourselves, we are satisfied with the organization of the American Woman Suffrage Association," and "its friendly door is wide open for any who wish to join it. Do we need any other?"

Prospects for détente between NWSA and AWSA did not appear rosy. Anthony's suspicions, personal enmity, and anger only grew as the days passed. She wrote to another friend and ally shortly after her missive to Stanton: "Here is Theodores *Poultice* for the '*sore-heads*' of the Boston-Cleveland secessionists. . . . You see *his* plan is to bring the *National* to *confer with secession* as *equals*." NWSA seemed at this point a far more popular organization, if only because it was more democratically organized. Membership was open to anyone who wished to affiliate with it; it was a grassroots organization. The American group, however, was far more hierarchical, its membership open only through affiliated state groups and representation apportioned therefrom. Anthony accused the Boston dominated leadership of AWSA of trying to steal the woman suffrage movement away from her. "Now that the idea of '*Thief*' has its *root* in *Lucy Stone* and Co's movement to overthrow *me personally* . . . am I to be compelled to *concede* my position *to her* & *to Boston?* . . . I stand *plaintiff* not *defendant*—before that woman & the Boston clique."

CHAPTER 2

"Entitled to the Unabridged Exercise of Privileges and Immunities"

Fall 1869–Fall 1872

During all the tumult over the rivalry between NWSA and the AWSA, Anthony had been stumping throughout the Midwest and the West generating support among women for the suffrage cause. Triumphantly, she wrote a letter to the *Revolution* from a stop in Jonesville, Michigan, penning that "the west will be largely, gloriously represented at our May Anniversary." But her meetings with women far and wide had met with one consistent entreaty, a *"demand [for] union every time."*

For the month past she had repudiated and rejected Tilton's appeal, but in the face of such broad support for the idea of unification everywhere she stopped on the road, Anthony realized she would have to revise her position. She concluded that the status quo was having a deleterious impact on the cause of woman suffrage. Anthony would do anything to save it. "All the differences and disagreements of parties and persons," she wrote to the readers of the *Revolution*, "must be put in the background." She had been heartened by the enthusiastic crowds she had met in "Quincy, Farmington, Elmwood, Mendota, Peru and LaSalle—Batavia, Peoria and Champaign in Illinois, and in Sturgis, Jonesville, Michigan." The push for the Sixteenth Amendment guaranteeing woman suffrage had picked up steam, and she believed she was close to the goal: "I can tell you with emphasis the fields are white unto harvest—waiting, waiting only the reapers." Only the division between the suffrage leaders could jeopardize their movement. "And it is a shame—*it is a crime*—for any of the old or new *public* workers to halt by the way to pick the *'motes'* out of their neighbors' eyes." Anthony ended her missive to her *Revolution* loyalists with a plea and implied accusation: "How any one can stand in the way of a *united national organization* at an hour like this, is wholly inexplicable to [signed] *Susan B. Anthony.*"

Unification Assayed

Anthony and NWSA now adopted an official position in favor of a new woman suffrage organization created out of a merged NWSA and AWSA. They took the high road in response to the popular demand for unification. At Tilton's April 6 meeting in New York they supported the proposal for the new combined organization and stepped in to help write a proposed constitution. Lucy Stone's AWSA "professed to 'desire harmony,'" according to Ann Gordon, "but opposed the creation of a new organization, and . . . withdrew from the conference."

There was barely a month before the scheduled competing conventions in New York City. But over that time, the debate over unification escalated. AWSA, through its organ, the *Woman's Journal*, condemned "Mr. Tilton's Movement." The National, through the *Revolution*, accused its rival of ignoring all the women across the country who demanded a unified woman suffrage movement. If Anthony's abrupt change of course on the merger question had aimed to win the public relations campaign on behalf of her group, the strategy was succeeding. Ann Gordon recounts that "other editors weighed in." The *Springfield* [Massachusetts] *Republican*, a paper in the AWSA leaders' backyard, condemned "Lucy Stone, and Garrison and Higginson, and the rest of the Boston obstinates and monopolists."

When Anthony's NWSA met in Apollo Hall in New York City on May 10, 1870, the primary item on its agenda was unification. Before an audience representing nineteen states and territories, Elizabeth Cady Stanton called upon Theodore Tilton to present "the proposition to unite all the friends of Woman's Suffrage into one society with officers from both the National and American Associations." The convention was now a "Meeting to Dissolve the National Woman Suffrage Association" to create the new unified suffrage organization. During the discussion over the proposal many "younger workers" expressed their opposition "against any association that did not put either Mrs. Stanton, or Miss Anthony at its head." In an attempt to forestall a rebellion from their own constituents over leadership when it was obvious that AWSA would balk at their heading up a combined group, "both Mrs. Stanton and Miss Anthony" told the audience "that they would neither of them accept the position" as president of the new organization.

With their assurance that it was their choice not to head the proposed organization, the assembled women "voted to accept Mr. Tilton's proposition to call the new society the Union Woman's Suffrage Society" and "adopt the constitution [primarily drafted by representatives of NWSA] offered by Mr. Tilton." Theodore Tilton was then "elected President and a committee was appointed to prepare a list of officers," and the result was "reported at the Wednesday morning session." NWSA had heard and conceded to the clamor of the rank-and-file woman suffragists.

The next battleground for the unification juggernaut was the American Equal Rights Association meeting the week following the NWSA convention. The AERA had barely survived the disastrous meeting in 1869 at which the women suffragists had found themselves shut out, and following which they had created NWSA during the Women's Bureau reception. At its executive committee meeting in March 1870, after the last state necessary had voted for ratification of the Fifteenth Amendment the previous month, the Lucy Stone and Henry Blackwell group had successfully blocked a move to convert the AERA into a woman suffrage organization. Now, in mid-May 1870, at the AERA business meeting, they were easily outvoted.

Stone and Blackwell were the *only* two votes against the AERA's merger with the newly formed Union Woman Suffrage Association, though they consumed "two hours of valuable time in the mortal life of two-and-twenty human beings." Stanton was elated. She exulted to Martha Coffin Wright that "I have not time to tell you all our performances this week . . . but we have had grand times in getting the National & Equal Rights both merged into the Union movement." Stanton and Anthony's outmaneuvering of the AWSA leaders had been incredibly effective. Stanton told Wright that "Boston is *awful* sore." Stone and company were now boxed in.

"Unless Boston comes into Union she [Lucy Stone] will stand alone in the cold." She was happy to report that AWSA was steadily losing support and allies. "Beecher says he will resign [as president of AWSA] at the end of year he is sick of the pettiness he has seen." But "Lucy is as hostile as ever cannot be mollified."

If Lucy Stone was looking to rally her forces against the Union led by Anthony and Stanton (despite the fact that Tilton served as titular head of the organization), she found it in a speech Stanton gave only days after her cry of triumph to Wright. The impetus for Stanton's speech were events just concluded in a notorious murder case involving a love triangle, the acquittal of the accused killer, and a bizarre conflict between two states' divorce laws. The former wife of the defendant, who had secured a divorce in Indiana, was prevented from giving testimony in the New York trial when the court allowed the defendant's objection invoking the rule of spousal privilege, because as far as New York law was concerned the witness and accused were still married. Stanton presented an impassioned and eloquent diatribe to a mass meeting of women in New York gathered to protest the outcome of the case.

The object of Stanton's remarks was criticism of divorce laws that imprisoned couples, particularly women, in loveless and abusive marriages. This had been a favorite subject of Stanton's for several decades, and she welcomed a new opportunity to address an audience with her arguments. While she was far from endorsing anything like "free love," she nevertheless strongly endorsed the liberal freedom to divorce. Stone's *Woman's Journal* jumped on Stanton's "loose notions of marriage and divorce," calling her speech "demoralizing" and claiming her ideas would "destroy the purity and stability of marriage" and would "abrogate marriage, and we have then the hideous thing known as 'free love.'" The *Journal* warned its readers: "Be not deceived—*free love means free lust.*" As Ann Gordon points out, the *Woman's Journal* editorial against Stanton "set in motion" (quoting a headline from the *New York Tribune*), a "war in the Woman Suffrage Camp." Though this war had been under way for some time, Stanton's stand on liberal divorce enabled the Stone faction, practically on life support after the AERA's defection to the National-dominated Union, to find new life. Gordon summed up the outcome of the brouhaha between Stanton and AWSA, saying it "sharpened differences between the Union and American associations just before the latter's annual meeting. By the time that meeting convened, the *Revolution* no longer hoped for union but prepared its readers to 'go a solitary path.'"

Only fifty people attended AWSA's annual meeting in Cleveland in late November 1870. One newspaper observed that the gathering "was, in point of attendance a failure. The audience at no time more than peppered the great hall, and the delegates were comparatively few." Indeed, the paper noted that "there was nothing of that fervor of interest which last year made the formation of the Society attractive even to outsiders." The organizers blamed the poor showing on the fact that the meeting coincided with "Thanksgiving and bad weather." In addition, a leader of the association interviewed by the paper commented, "As for the decided decrease in public enthusiasm during the last six months . . . 'tis but the chimera of empty and malicious brains like those which do parade their doctrines in the horrid columns of the *Revolution*." The western delegates, as Anthony had realized in the course of her own travels in the region, "recognize the stagnation of The Cause, [and] declare rebelliously that it is all because of the quarrels, the envies, and jealousies between the two factions, and insist upon reconciliation and consolidation."

The Boston group led by Lucy Stone did not seem to get that message, and the newspaper picked up on their obliviousness, declaring that "the infantine ignorance on the part of the Boston division, of the existence of any quarrels, envies, and jealousies, is a thing charmingly instructive to observe as a work of moral art." Anthony did not hesitate to admit to the journalist covering the meeting "the fact of war, and declares that it is the result of a struggle for leadership, of a dreadful plan deep laid in the vindictive bosom of Massachusetts." Even the reporter professed astonishment at Anthony's "candid declaration." Prospects for reconciliation and union were not good.

Nevertheless, the proposal for merging with the Union Woman Suffrage Association was the primary item on the AWSA meeting agenda. Though Lucy Stone and her closest allies resisted the idea, there were many prominent delegates who supported it, including Frederick Douglass. But many members had sent letters to the meeting strongly opposing any union with an organization with Stanton in a leadership position. Though she probably knew her efforts were in vain, Anthony attended the proceedings as an envoy from the Union to present a letter with the formal merger proposal. Judge James Bradwell, a "tall, big-shouldered lawyer," and member of AWSA, fervently endorsed the proposal, proclaiming that "Union is strength . . . in this contest a union in behalf of all is desirable; let us have union." He then "straightway" presented "for the approval of the Convention" the Union's resolutions for merger.

According to one newspaper report, "There was a sensation in the small audience . . . [though] Lucy Stone, always sweet-faced, tender-voiced, and exceedingly shrewd, looked more placid than ever." Her rival, "Miss Anthony, sitting solitary below [Anthony was not accorded the honor of sitting on the dais] became rather grim." One voice from the audience, "a snapping, bright-eyed, clear headed little Western woman . . . made an extemporaneous speech," in which she wanted "to know why the leaders of the cause couldn't have their own private views without having the associations to which they belonged held responsible for them." She expressed the growing sentiment "that the feeling of union was fast gaining ground in the West, and deprecated personal differences among the leaders." In response, "A man from Chicago rose in his might, and said that Mrs. Stanton had shocked people from Maine to Wisconsin." This gentleman was against the union proposal and told the gathering that Tilton's Union Woman Suffrage Association "was about falling to pieces, and that was the reason it came to them begging for union."

Stone made her position clear on the proposal. She claimed that she "wishes it to be understood that the division [between the two factions] is simply a division in methods and principles, and that there's no quarrel." But with her next breath she raised the incendiary issue of Stanton's position on liberal divorce. There was no quarrel, "nothing but a difference on the subjects of marriage and divorce."

At last, Anthony participated in the debate. "Judge Bradwell implored the Convention, in a moving manner, not to treat Miss Anthony 'as a publican and a sinner,' but to permit her to present her opinion on the subject of union." Anthony had listened to the letters that had been read out loud, the comments from the audience, and Stone's implied slur against the Union (and Nationals) about their endorsement of Stanton's liberal views on divorce. The newspaper reporter described the scene: "She "rose with what Mr. Pumble-chook [a character from Dickens's *Great Expectations*] would call 'a Countenance.'" Anthony had taken umbrage at the condemnations of friends and their organization. She loudly protested, "I do not want you to talk blind any longer! Talk plain and say what you mean!"

Anthony did not repudiate her friends' position. "If you oppose this union because Mrs. Stanton advocates the right of woman to free herself from a marriage relation that is worse than slavery, say so." She pointed to all the inequities married women faced within marriage and the impediments that prevented them from freeing themselves from their predicament. Anthony then tried to impeach the American's leader in order to defend Stanton: "The *Woman's Journal* is the last paper in the world that ought to speak against greater freedom for women in marriage and divorce, for one of its editors—I refer to Lucy Stone—at her wedding, refused to submit to the legal form of marriage, which on her part, was only a condi-tional one. . . . If you are going to keep on hounding Mrs. Stanton upon this subject I want to know it."

If Anthony's purpose was to try to undermine Stone's moral standing, her attack only incensed the already wary AWSA audi-ence. Thomas W. Higginson, who presided over the meeting in the absence of Henry Ward Beecher, indignantly responded, "I cannot allow one who is admitted to the floor of this Convention by cour-tesy to attack the character of a prominent officer of this society, and go unrebuked." Higginson, like many in the audience, misinter-preted Anthony's statement. She was trying to say that Stone, who had rewritten her marriage vows to eliminate inequalities and had retained her own name, certainly understood better than most the points Stanton had tried to make and was thus being hypocritical in leveling harsh attacks against Anthony's friend. Higginson thought Anthony was suggesting that Stone's alteration of the marriage cere-mony meant she wasn't lawfully married—she was thus living in sin with Henry Blackwell and their daughter was illegitimate. That would have been a slander but that was not what she intended.

Anthony tried to defend herself. "No longer to be repressed," she "rose and apologized in a frank and womanly way." She insisted "that she didn't mean to assert that Mrs. Stone's marriage was illegal." Apparently this placated many in the audience who "seemed to approve of this apology." But she was interrupted by Higginson and not allowed to continue.

Stone's husband, Henry B. Blackwell, then added his voice to the discussion: "If I believed that a union of these two societies was possible, I should be in its favor. But it is impossible." The personality conflict may have influenced him, but his primary objection was that the Union had, in its organ, *Revolution*, endorsed the idea that the "'freedom to marry and to freely sunder a yoke they have freely bound'" meant more than "mere political equality" and that Blackwell contended such a standpoint "demands a wider platform than woman's enfranchisement."

After Blackwell's remarks, "A general squabble finished the discussion of the question of union. Everybody thought everybody else was wrong, and therefore combated energetically." Only a Mr. Whitehead from New Jersey, "a broad-shouldered, genial creature, said there were faults on both sides. He saw jealousy, envy, strife, in the leaders, which ought not to exist . . . paid glowing compliments to Miss Anthony, Mrs. Stone, Mr. Blackwell." Yet even this conciliatory gentleman insisted that he "asked for peace . . . not for union." It was no surprise, therefore, that on the second day of the convention that the proposal for "union with the Association, of which Theodore Tilton is the head," was defeated, though there is some dispute over the vote.

The official vote of everyone present, according to AWSA and dutifully reported in the Cleveland newspaper, was "113 to forty-seven against the union." But Anthony, writing to Isabella Beecher Hooker the following week, claimed that if one used AWSA's own one delegate per state representation rule, the vote "would have been overwhelmingly *for union*." Ann Gordon calculates that it was actually "twenty four to twenty-six against union, with delegates from Louisiana and Nevada abstaining." Whatever the calculation of votes, any prospect for unification was dead.

Victoria Woodhull and the New Course

It was now time for the resurrection of the National. The union was abandoned and plans for a meeting after the New Year were in full swing. Susan B. Anthony exultantly told Isabella Beecher Hooker on December 2 that it was "now ho for Washington. . . . The best Hall *Lincoln* is already engaged for the 11 & 12. . . . We must make that Convention ring around the world." Anthony's optimism that the January meeting would attract the nation's and the movement's attention back to her and the National was to be sidetracked by a new player in the woman suffrage movement: Victoria Woodhull.

Victoria Claflin Woodhull, "a woman of beauty and wit" according to Eleanor Flexner and Ellen Fitzpatrick, was a flamboyant and controversial figure. The daughter of a reputed con man and the fifteen-year-old bride of an alcoholic doctor, she had learned self-reliance early, and her experiences taught her the necessity for woman's rights. She and her younger sister made a fortune on the New York Stock Exchange. In 1870 the two women, with the assistance of the shipping and railroad magnate "Commodore" Cornelius Vanderbilt, opened their own brokerage house (the first such business owned by women) and then used some of their funds to found a newspaper, *Woodhull and Claflin's Weekly*, a journal famed for publishing articles about woman suffrage, marriage and divorce, spiritualism, and free love. Thus, within a year Victoria Woodhull had broken sexist barriers in business and thrust herself into the midst of the woman's rights movement.

Before the year was out, on December 19, 1870, Woodhull would send a "Memorial" to Congress claiming the right to vote based on her rights as a citizen of the United States under the Fourteenth and Fifteenth Amendments—the very argument Francis Minor had published in the *Revolution* a little over a year before. She did not petition for a Sixteenth Amendment; under her legal argument it was not necessary. All she requested of Congress was "to make such laws as in the wisdom of Congress shall be necessary and proper for carrying into execution the right vested by the Constitution in the citizens of the United States to vote, without regard to sex."

The House referred Woodhull's "Memorial" to its Judiciary Committee, and they were sufficiently impressed to call her to testify about the issues she had raised. According to Ann Gordon, Isabella Beecher Hooker had "abandoned her own hopes of a hearing before the Senate Committee on the Judiciary on a sixteenth amendment when she saw a notice that the House committee would hold a hearing on Woodhull's memorial." Pulling strings, "She arranged to reschedule that hearing to coincide with the opening of the Washington convention" on January 11, 1870.

When Anthony arrived in Washington on Tuesday, January 10, she confided in her diary that she "found papers full of Victoria C. Woodhull's Memorial to Congress." As Ellen DuBois points out, "Woodhull's dramatic appearance before Congress, the first ever by a woman on behalf of woman suffrage, took Anthony and Stanton by surprise." The *New York Times* reported that Woodhull's "contemporaries in the woman's rights or suffrage movement have heretofore ignored her, have frowned upon her as an interloper, and have denounced her as unworthy of the association and confidence of the pure and chaste advocates of the great cause. [But now] the cry is 'anthems to Woodhull.'" The intrepid *Times* reporter managed to snag an interview with Anthony, who complimented Woodhull's petition as "a fortunate and propitious idea, which, 'added to the charm of youth and all that sort of thing, you know . . . has carried conviction to the hearts of these men here.'" It is clear what the *Times* correspondent thought the plain fifty-one-year-old spinster Anthony believed was the appeal of the attractive and stylish thirty-three-year-old Woodhull's petition. While Woodhull's charm and attractiveness might have had some impact on the male preserve of the U.S. House of Representatives, the journalist failed to credit its legal and constitutional arguments.

When the hearing convened at 2 p.m. nearly the entire National leadership—"Mrs. I. B. Hooker, Rev. O. Brown, Conn.; Mrs. P. W. Davis, Miss K. Stanton, Rhode Island; Mrs. J. Griffing, and Mrs. Lockwood, D.C.; and Miss Susan B. Anthony"—joined the "goodly assemblage" (the *New York Times* dubbed it a "motley assemblage") crowded into the committee room. The next day's report in the *Times* vividly set the scene: "The Committee were ranged round the left side, head and foot of the table, and backed on the left by the male interlopers, while on the right side of the room were the women, some seated in chairs, others leaning against the book cases, in attitudes which very much resembled the customs of malekind."

The meeting was called to order by Ohio congressman John Bingham. Isabella Beecher Hooker introduced Victoria Woodhull. Woodhull then began by reading the "Memorial" she had sent to Congress. According to the *Washington Republican* newspaper (included in the *History of Woman Suffrage*), "It was the first time the lady had ever appeared in public, and her voice trembled slightly with emotion which only made the reading the more effective." Many of the leaders of the suffrage movement sitting in the room that day, Anthony in particular, had given hundreds if not thousands of public speeches over the past decades; it is highly probable that they experienced a certain amount of envy of Woodhull's sudden prominence and the distinction the House Committee had accorded her. At the same time, they were undoubtedly pleased that their cause was finally getting a hearing.

Though not the first woman called to testify before Congress, as some students of these events erroneously report, Susan B. Anthony got her turn to speak to the committee. She didn't rehearse the legal arguments Woodhull and attorney Albert Gallatin Riddle had made prior to her testimony. Rather, Anthony "demand[ed] that a report should be made by the Committee either for or against the petition, so as to provoke discussion in the House." She then "grew truly and rhetorically eloquent in her final appeal . . . [to] give [the women of the country] the rights granted to the freedmen of the South."

Woodhull's "Memorial" and the hearing before the Judiciary Committee marked a sharp turning point in the strategy of the National suffragists. When they finally convened their meeting the next day, it was clear that Anthony had enthusiastically converted to the strategy that Francis Minor had recommended earlier but now was brought to the fore by Victoria Woodhull. Anthony told "the immense audience in Lincoln Hall" that they "would try no more to effect an amendment, as under the amendments already made they had sufficient rights." It was time for the woman suffrage movement to adopt what *The History of Woman Suffrage* would use as the title for volume 2's chapter 23, and Ellen DuBois would popularize as the "New Departure" strategy.

The Washington Convention unanimously adopted a formal set of resolutions that Anthony presented outlining the new campaign. The preamble unambiguously stated that women were citizens of the United States and their individual states, as outlined by the Fourteenth Amendment, and thus were "entitled to the unabridged exercise of the privileges and immunities of citizens, among which are the rights of the elective franchise and to hold office." While the Fourteenth Amendment clearly used the expression "privileges or immunities," it did not expressly define what they were and certainly did not mention the "elective franchise" in that context. This would prove a problem for the suffragists when they finally reached a courtroom, and their first substantive resolution indicated they were aware of the issue. In that first resolution they urged supporters to present petitions to Congress to pass "an act declaratory of the true extent and meaning of said fourteenth article."

Petitions to Congress (or state legislatures) were nothing new. The women's movement had employed this supplicatory strategy as their primary modus operandi for decades. But the second resolution outlined a new and far more daring plan of action. "That it is the duty of American women in the several States and in the District of Columbia to apply for registration at the proper times and places for registration of voters, and in all cases, when [as they fully expected to happen] they fail to secure registration, that suits be instituted in the various courts . . . to the end that their existing franchises shall secure general and judicial recognition."

This was exactly the plan that Francis Minor had recommended back in October, 1869—civil suits against authorities who refused to allow women to register and vote. The woman suffragists did not anticipate that some friendly election officials might actually allow women to register and vote and that the federal government would then prosecute them in criminal court. Anthony was jubilant and rejuvenated. While still aboard the Chicago, Burlington & Quincy Railroad traveling from Chicago to Missouri only days after the Washington meeting, she wrote to Isabella Beecher Hooker that "I feel a new inspiration—spoke [at a stop in Grand Rapids, Michigan] as if the very gods were whistling through me." She excitedly told Hooker that "we surely are going to vote for the next President."

Anthony did not have to wait long for the report she had "demanded" the House Judiciary Committee prepare on Woodhull's woman suffrage petition. On January 30 the Committee issued a majority report, quickly followed by a minority report. Congressman Bingham, chair of the Committee, released the majority report, which, according to the next day's newspaper, "is regarded as disposing entirely of the constitutional questions which were lately raised by Miss [*sic*] Woodhull and adopted by the other leaders in the woman suffrage movement."

The majority laboriously covered prior case law, a thin record because the majority of Reconstruction-era Supreme Court opinions on the subject of the "privileges or immunities" of U.S. citizens would not be handed down for more than two years. Nevertheless, the majority concluded that "we are of opinion, therefore, that it is not competent for the Congress of the United States to establish by law the right to vote without regard to sex in the several States of this Union without the consent of the people of such States."

Nor did the Bingham report believe Congress "by a mere declaratory act shall say that the construction claimed in the memorial is the true construction of the Constitution . . . the right to vote is vested in the citizens of the United States, 'without regard to sex.'" In conclusion, the majority recommended the adoption of the resolution: "That the prayer of the petitioner be not granted, that the memorial be laid on the table, and that the Committee on the Judiciary be discharged from the further consideration of the subject." While the majority offered no immediate relief to the woman suffragists, ironically they endorsed the strategy recently adopted by Anthony and the National—namely, that "if, however, as is claimed in the memorial referred to, the right to vote is vested by the Constitution in the citizens of the United States, without regard to sex, that right can be established in the Courts without further legislation."

Two days later Massachusetts Representative Benjamin Butler and Iowa Congressman William Loughridge issued a minority report. The congressmen attempted to refute, point by point, each of the legal arguments in the majority report and "on the question of female suffrage, say that it is one of exceeding interest and importance, involving the constitutional rights, not only of the memorialists, but of more than one half of the citizens of the United States." They claimed that "from the very beginning of our Government the right of suffrage is a fundamental right of citizenship," a claim they believed was supported both "by the authorities and by reason." They concluded, therefore, that "it is perfectly proper . . . [f]or the House to pass a declaratory resolution . . . and that female citizens, who are otherwise classified by the laws of the States where they reside, are competent voters for representatives in Congress."

The *New York Times* reported that "a number of women, advocates of suffrage for their sex, have been in attendance at the Capitol for some days past," apparently trying to impress upon the Congress how seriously they took their cause. They had actually made "their headquarters the room of the House Committee on Education" and were lobbying the representatives, perhaps hoping that the full House would adopt the minority rather than the majority report from the Judiciary Committee. There was also a movement afoot to get the House to pass a resolution that would allow Victoria Woodhull an opportunity to address the full House in its chamber. But the suffragists were not alone on Capitol Hill. The *New York Times* also reported that "nearly five thousand" women "presented remonstrances to Congress 'against the oppression of having suffrage forced upon them,'" most notably Catherine E. Beecher, one of the celebrated Beecher family and half sister to Isabella Beecher Hooker, who had testified in favor of suffrage before the committee. Catherine Beecher, through a letter of support for the antisuffrage women, declared that "it is not true, as reported, that she is in favor of woman suffrage, nor is it true of a large majority of her family and personal friends."

Susan B. Anthony was not in Washington when the committee reports were issued. Once more she was on the road carrying the suffrage message, this time to women in Kansas and Nebraska. She heard of the developments in a letter from Victoria Woodhull and received copies of the reports by telegraph. She quickly replied, "Bravo! My Dear Woodhull," and in the same letter she applauded "Glorious 'Old Ben!'" Anthony was totally supportive of Woodhull's work in Washington and told her, "It will be a great triumph if you get the Representative house," with regard to the resolution to have

Woodhull speak on the House floor. Anthony was not discouraged by the Judiciary Committee's response to Woodhull's "Memorial." She remained completely committed to the new Francis Minor Woodhull strategy that she'd gotten the National to adopt the previous month. Indeed, she found tremendous support in the West for the approach. "Everybody here chimes in with the new conclusion that we are free already," she informed Woodhull. She confided how enthusiastic she was about the strategy: "I have never in the whole twenty years' good fight felt so full of life and hope." Woodhull's maneuvers in Washington and the strategy she had endorsed energized Anthony. Woodhull was Anthony's new best friend as she signed off her letter to the younger woman, "Go ahead! bright, glorious, young, and strong spirit, and believe in the best love and hope and faith of [signed S. B. Anthony]."

A New Departure?

The Woodhull glow began to dim over the coming months. Scandalous rumors were coming to the fore about her views on free love and her lifestyle—she reputedly lived together in one domicile with her husband, her alcoholic ex-husband, her children, and her lover. Even close friends and longtime associates tried to warn Anthony that Woodhull threatened to bring disrepute upon the woman suffrage cause. In a report on her work in Washington, D.C., and the plans for the upcoming National Woman Suffrage Committee meeting, which Isabella Beecher Hooker forwarded to Anthony, she passed on the disturbing gossip about Woodhull.

Hooker and others suggested it would be imprudent to prominently feature Woodhull on the dais and allow her to speak from the podium at the May meeting. Anthony vigorously defended Woodhull. She saw the attacks as an unfair application of the old double standard in sexual morality, "the same old game—to cut off Woman for offenses almost every man is guilty of." She told Martha Coffin Wright two months before the meeting, "I have *heard gossip* of *undue familiarity* with persons of *the opposite sex*—relative to [Henry Ward] Beecher, [Thomas W.] Higginson, [Benjamin] Butler, [Matthew Hale] Carpenter, [Samuel Clarke] Pomeroy—and before I shall consent to an arraignment of *Woodhull* or any other *earnest woman worker* who shall come to our Platform in Washington or elsewhere—I shall insist upon the *closest investigation* into *all* the *scandals* afloat about those men." She strongly objected to suggestions that Woodhull was unfit to participate at their meeting.

Anthony facetiously called for the same test for the men who had been invited, "When we shall require of the *men*, who shall speak— vote, work for us—to *prove* that they have never been unduly familiar with any woman . . . it will be time enough for us to demand of the *women* to *prove* that *no man has ever trifled with* or desecrated them." Anthony chided sisters in the movement who cast aspersions against her new friend: "Let *her* who has never had a *line in her history* but that she would be perfectly willing to have spread out to the gaze of the course, gross, brutal world—be the first to cast a stone at Mrs Woodhull." Stanton agreed with Anthony. She told Lucretia Mott that "I have thought much since leaving of *our dear Woodhull* & all the gossip about her & come to the conclusion that it is great impertinence in any of us to pry into her affairs."

Stanton's sympathy may have been aroused in part because of the infamy that had been laid at her door when she had spoken out in favor of liberalizing divorce law. She, like Anthony, deeply admired Woodhull, who, she told Mott, "stands before us to day one of the ablest speakers & writers of the century." The facts about Woodhull's dubious history had come to light, but Stanton tried to allay Mott's misgivings. "Does not the man & woman that can pass through every phase of social degradation, poverty, vice, crime, temptation in all its forms, & yet tower above all their kind, give unmistakable proof of their high origin, the moral grandeur of their true nature."

When the National met at Apollo Hall in New York City on May 11, 1871, Anthony, according to her biographer Kathleen Barry, "saw to it that Victoria Woodhull was seated on their platform between Elizabeth Cady Stanton and Lucretia Mott, giving her full legitimization." Isabella Beecher Hooker presided at the meeting. Hooker addressed the "numerously attended" audience and "urged every woman to vote or attempt to vote at every State and Federal election" under the new strategy the organization had adopted in January. Hooker understood that many women might be intimidated by election officials but "deprecated the fear which some women had of going to the polls." Isabella Beecher Hooker had clearly taken to heart the advice Anthony had given her in advance of the meeting to "make our May meeting bristle all over. . . . Don't let us be bored with mere theorizing in the propriety of voting."

Stanton was the featured speaker. Instead of the expected appeal for woman suffrage, Stanton delivered an educational speech on politics and government. It was a populous appeal for the direct election of senators and the president, term limitations, and a candid attack on the corruption of the Grant administration, though she was equally critical of the Democrats. Reading between the lines, Stanton seemed to be laying the groundwork for the creation of a third party spearheaded by women suffragists and their male supporters, something her new ally Victoria Woodhull had been campaigning for in her weekly journal.

The business of the meeting was the adoption of a slate of resolutions. First of these was a reiteration of the new strategy. There was no appeal for a Sixteenth Amendment, only an assertion that "as women are counted in the basis of representation, subjected to taxation and punishment for crime . . . under the Federal Constitution, they are citizens and . . . under the Fourteenth and Fifteenth Amendments the specified right of all citizens to vote is plainly declared, we demand of Congress a law that shall secure this fundamental right."

The remaining two resolutions went beyond the issue of suffrage. The second resolution asserted that "the woman movement means no less than the complete social as well as the political enfranchisement of mankind." This was echoed in the third resolution that boldly argued that "the evils, sufferings and disabilities of the women as well as men are social still more than they are political, and that a statement of women's rights which ignores the right of self-ownership is insufficient to meet the demand." While the resolutions echoed the Declaration of Sentiments of 1848, the expansion of the resolutions to emphasize social freedom, not just suffrage, seems to be both an extension of National's defense of Stanton's endorsement of liberalizing divorce laws as well as, perhaps, a defense of Woodhull. A moment of levity occurred as Anthony read out the resolutions. Someone requested that she "read a little louder," to which "a gentleman near the platform offered his services as a reader, which was indignantly declined. Miss Anthony said it was another piece of man's presumption in imagining that he could read louder than a woman." Her comment was met with "loud cheers."

Anthony was, in essence, the warm-up act for the next speaker: Woodhull. Woodhull roused the audience with the announcement that "they would try the question of woman suffrage in the Courts," and "if they failed there, they would seek redress from Congress." Woodhull's battle plan was far less ambivalent than the resolution Anthony had read to the audience moments before. She went even further. Women "must have their rights of the franchise . . . and if Congress refuses, [women] must adopt other means—to plant a government of righteousness instead of the Government imposed upon them—Without their consent." She was, in fact, endorsing the idea that the women should abandon the faithless Republican and antagonistic Democratic parties to strike out on their own. The audience knew that Woodhull harbored political aspirations and she tried to circumvent criticism when she told the assemblage that "she was charged with being influenced with unpardonable ambition, in announcing herself as a candidate for the next Presidency." But she denied that she was motivated by personal ambition, and in all modesty she claimed that "all that she had done was done for the sake of humanity."

By invoking her campaign for the presidency immediately after discussing the strategy she had helped promote before Congress in January to gain woman suffrage, Woodhull had cleverly linked the aspirations of National to her own political enterprise. An evening session followed Woodhull's remarks, over which Susan B. Anthony presided, and though she and Isabella Beecher Hooker tried to refocus the meeting strictly on woman suffrage, "the May meeting," as Kathleen Barry summed it up, "was a smashing success and became known as the 'Woodhull convention.'"

When it came time for the annual Washington, D.C., meeting in January 1872, Anthony asked Stanton to carefully craft the official call for the convention. Stanton was also probably responsible for having it published in the *New York Times* on January 8, 1872. The call is noteworthy for several reasons, but particularly the phrasing of the invitation to "all those interested in woman's enfranchise-ment" to attend the meeting in Lincoln Hall on January 10–12, "to consider the 'new departure' [namely] women already citizens, and their rights as such secured by the Fourteenth and Fifteenth Amendments of the Federal Constitution."

This is the first and only contemporaneous instance that this au-thor could find in which the term "new departure" was used to de-scribe the Francis Minor/Victoria Woodhull strategy. It was a strat-egy that required litigation rather than lobbying state or federal officials. Henry Blackwell used the expression in a letter to Eliza-beth Cady Stanton in June 1872, but he was not referring to the constitutional litigation strategy. When he told her that "this is the propitious moment for taking a new depart[ure] in the W S Move-ment," he only meant that the leaders of the movement try to tone down their rhetoric against men and support the Republican Party. Stanton used it again in 1881, as noted above, as the title for the chapter in which she discussed the adoption of the strategy in vol-ume 2 of *The History of Woman Suffrage*. But at this point in time it was the Democratic Party which had widely adopted the expression the "New Departure," using uppercase letters as a ruse to attempt to recapture political ground from the Republicans after 1870, particu-larly in 1871 in anticipation of the 1872 elections. Stanton, an ex-ceptionally savvy reader of political trends, was undoubtedly famil-iar with the term and borrowed it, thus the use of quotation marks and lowercase letters. Knowing her audience had read and heard of the House Judiciary Committee hearing the year before, she openly attributed the new departure strategy to Woodhull. "This view," she wrote, was "presented in the 'The Woodhull Memorial' at the last session of Congress was respectfully received, and a minority report of the Judiciary Committee made in its favor."

The third point was Stanton's forceful command that "the 15,000,000 women of this Republic rise up in their dignity and use these new-found liberties for their own personal freedom. . . . A united effort, now, and the day is ours." Stanton clearly envisioned a massive exercise in civil disobedience (from other speeches she wrote it is clear she had read Henry David Thoreau's *Civil Disobedi-ence*) that would carry the day for woman suffrage: "A united effort, now and the day is ours." She explained that "we shall not only vote for the next President, but, if true to ourselves, [we will] have a potent voice in determining who shall be nominated for that office." There was another threat inherent in her call to action. As she pointed out, "The times are auspicious, party ties are broken, politicians are losing their hold on the masses, who have clearer ideas of human rights than ever before." Republican politicians, in other words, who had used women in their campaigns in the past for grassroots organizing and canvassing could not rely on them this time; the women's party allegiance was up for grabs.

The women had learned the civil rights lessons of recent years and proclaimed that "of all the vital issues now looming up for the party of the not distant future, there is not one so momentous and far reaching in its consequences as woman suffrage." Both the Democrats and Republicans were on notice: ignore the woman suffrage issue at your peril. But, and this is another interesting point about the call from January 1872, there was no hint that the National supported an independent party presidential bid by Victoria Woodhull. Notable, as well, is the fact that the notice of the call submitted to the *Times* was "signed by Lucretia Mott, Elizabeth Cady Stanton, Susan B. Anthony, and many others." Woodhull, while given credit for her "Memorial" and its new departure strategy, was not prominently featured as one of the National's leaders. A close reading of the call to the convention supports Kathleen Barry's contention that Susan B. Anthony was beginning to have her doubts about Woodhull and had her in mind "as a potential threat" when she asked Stanton to be extremely careful in drafting the document, reminding Stanton that "*you*—E.C.S.—are *President* of the National W. S. Committee."

Anthony versus Woodhull

Susan B. Anthony's doubts about Victoria Woodhull's self-aggrandizement at the expense of the woman suffrage cause increased, according to Barry, "while she was lecturing in Kansas . . . in the spring of 1872 [and] a man handed her a copy of Woodhull's newly published paper," the most recent issue of *Woodhull and Claflin's Weekly*, in which appeared "a call for the National's May meeting" that proclaimed "this convention will declare the platform of the People's Party, and consider the nominations of candidates for President and Vice-President of the United States." Anthony's reaction was predictable. She "was furious, especially when she saw that the call had been signed with her own name," among other leaders of National. Anthony clearly saw Woodhull's plan to usurp the National's meeting in New York as a threat to the cause and to the influence of the National Woman Suffrage Committee. The movement had already been riven by the AWSA and National split, and now Woodhull threatened to drain its resources even further by her personal political ambitions.

According to Barry, Anthony did two things after her return to the East Coast. First "she rented the hall for their meeting" and then she "went directly to Tenafly [New Jersey] to confer with Mrs. Stanton." The first maneuver was intended to forestall Woodhull from dominating the meeting by "owning" the venue. The second was to enlist Stanton's support against Woodhull. In this last effort, Anthony would find herself disappointed. Again, according to Barry, "she found that her friend had complete confidence in Woodhull's plan and was just as sure that it presented no threat to the movement."

Confrontation was, perhaps, inevitable. When the National Woman Suffrage Association met in Steinway Hall on May 9, 1872, there was, according to the *New York Times*, "some slight want of unanimity prevailing among the leaders, the woman suffrage purely, and the party headed by Victoria Woodhull, but with the exception of a slight breeze toward the end of the session, the Convention terminated agreeably." One can almost hear the nineteenth-century equivalent of the NWSA spin doctors in characterizing events. Kathleen Barry is less restrained in her account. She relates that "after Anthony opened the meeting, [Victoria Woodhull] marched down the aisle and took the platform." She announced that this was not only the National Women's Suffrage Association convention but a meeting of the People's Party. This set off Anthony, who "countered . . . that she had rented the hall in her own name for the National meeting only [after which she] asked all those who were there for the meeting of the People's party to leave the hall." Undoubtedly, much to Anthony's surprise, Stanton and Isabella Beecher Hooker protested her expulsion of Woodhull from the hall.

At this point "Woodhull and her supporters left the hall, Stanton resigned from the presidency of the National, and Anthony was elected in her place."

This was not the end of the contretemps between Anthony and Woodhull. At the evening session, over which Anthony presided, after the "platform of the Convention [which had been] read in the morning session and laid over for discussion" had been adopted, a "Mr. Wolff, an advocate of the Victoria Woodhull doctrines, rose to protest against the platform, and was received with loud and continued hissing. . . . A scene of the utmost confusion ensued." According to Barry, the confusion included Woodhull ascending the platform, "where Anthony was presiding, and announc[ing] that the People's convention would meet the next day at Apollo Hall [and then] moved that the National meeting be adjourned." Anthony tried to rule her out of order, but Woodhull ran over her by calling for a vote "and received responsive 'ayes' from the audience." As Woodhull effectively stole the meeting out from under Anthony, Barry, apparently relying on the story Ida Husted Harper tells in her nineteenth-century biography of Anthony, recounts that Anthony "walked off the platform and out of the building. In a few minutes, the gas lights went out in the hall." Apparently, Anthony had "found the janitor [and] instructed him to extinguish the lights." In her diary that night, Anthony recorded that "the Woodhull Co. Bound to take possession of the Convention—but failed—& left in disgust."

While Anthony had won the battle to separate the National from Woodhull's presidential campaign, it was not immediately clear when the smoke settled who had won the war. When Woodhull's People's Party convened the next day at Apollo Hall, among those in attendance were several of Anthony's closest comrades, including Elizabeth Cady Stanton and Isabella Beecher Hooker. Anthony tried to continue with the NWSA convention in Steinway Hall, but even she had to admit they had only a "small audience." Anthony was thoroughly disheartened, and her diary entry the second night recorded "the fiasco perfect—from *calling* Peoples Convention— never did Mrs. Stanton do so foolish a thing—all came near being lost." On the Saturday after the convention concluded, Anthony and some friends "went over to Tenafly [Stanton's home]—I *never was so hurt with folly of Stanton.*"

The next day she entered in her diary that it was a "pleasant day—but sad to me—our movement as such is so demoralized by the letting go the helm of ship to Woodhull—though we rescued it—it was as by a hair breadth escape." As Barry puts it, "she remained self-assured and adamant in public [but] Anthony's confidence crumbled in private for the first time in her career." Anthony emotionally confided in Martha Coffin Wright less than ten days after the "fiasco" in New York, "I tell you Mrs Wright I am feeling to day that *life doesn't pay*—the way seems so blocked up to me on all sides."

A Splinter Rather than a Plank

Eighteen-seventy-two was a presidential election year. Almost immediately after the May NWSA meeting Anthony had to turn her attention to the political conventions of the two major parties. Her mission was to convince the Republican and/or Democratic parties to adopt a plank in their party platforms in the upcoming election that would support woman suffrage. First up was the Republican Party convention in Philadelphia. Anthony told a meeting of the Radical Club of Philadelphia that "she had been at the convention in the morning, but was not sanguine in regard to the speedy adoption of a female suffrage plank by the Republican party." The Republicans decided to throw the woman suffragists a bone. Henry Blackwell, in a June 8 letter to Elizabeth Cady Stanton after the meeting in Philadelphia, claimed credit. He told her that "I have done the best that *could* be done in Phila under existing circumstances. . . . Aided by the best men in the Republican party, I labored individually with the members of the platform Committee." The platform fell far short of endorsing the franchise for women. The Fourteenth Resolution, or plank, merely stated: "The Republican party is mindful of its obligations to the loyal women of America for their noble devotion to the cause of freedom. Their admission to wider fields of usefulness is viewed with satisfaction, and the honest demand of any class of citizens for additional rights should be treated with respectful consideration."

Blackwell told Stanton that he hoped that "this recognition of Woman's claim will prove the thin edge of the entering wedge of a complete endorsement of Woman Suffrage, if only we can concentrate the Woman Suffragists of the country in a hearty support of the Philadelphia nominations & platforms." Blackwell, a loyal Republican to his core, wanted to enlist Stanton and Anthony's support for the Republican ticket of Grant and Wilson (and Republican candidates for Congress). He assured Stanton that "9/10 of the men who favor W S are Rep[ublican]." There was no alternative for woman suffragists than to support the Republicans. After all, "Mrs W[oodhull] has gone off with her motley crowd of disrep[utable]s & visionaries upon a crusade of egotism" and "The Dems. Upon their low plane of appet[ite] & bigotry & ignor[ance] have spurned Miss A[nthony]. . . . They are *doomed* as a party & will probably go and hang themselves like the other Judas by nomin[ating] Greeley."

Anthony agreed with Blackwell's opinion of Greeley. In an interview with Anne E. McDowell for the *Philadelphia Evening Telegraph* a few days after the Republican convention concluded, she said, "he is utterly unfitted, by his credulity and lack of judgment, either for a successful statesman or wise President. In all questions where principle is involved he is fluctuating and unreliable." McDowell followed up on the suffrage issue, asking Anthony "but he was once the friend of this reform, was he not?" Anthony replied, "Yes, he once professed to favor woman's political enfranchisement, but for the last ten years he has been our persistent and uncompromising enemy, and has allowed the *Tribune* [Greeley's newspaper] to be used constantly to abuse and misrepresent us." McDowell ingenuously pressed Anthony, "Then it is safe to conclude that you will not give your support to the Greeley ticket?" Anthony answered unequivocally, "I would sooner cut off my right hand than use my influence in behalf of this enemy to the woman cause."

Anthony was far more kindly disposed to the Republican nominee, Ulysses S. Grant, and his wife, who was said to influence him greatly. He is "with us heart and soul," she said, pointing to his acceptance of the nomination, where he recommended "equal rights to all citizens." Recognizing that he was "a sop thrown to us women," however, she held no love for the man, frankly admitting that "I do not admire Grant, and do not care to see a 'fast man' at the head of the nation . . . [but] Principles to me are more than individual character."

When asked about Victoria Woodhull's "candidacy," Anthony was distinctly cool about her former friend and ally: "Of this woman's social and financial theories I have nothing to say." She admitted Woodhull had "done the woman's movement some service in the past." But as for Woodhull's independent party's bid for office Anthony told McDowell that "I regret very much that Mrs. Woodhull should have gone off to a party of discontented men, who, being devoid of money, reputation or social position, seek to vent their spleen and disappointment through her. But against Mrs. Woodhull personally I have nothing to say."

Despite Anthony's antipathy for Horace Greeley, she allowed that "if the Democrats incorporate a plank in the platform recognizing us as citizens by virtue of the fourteenth amendment, our energies will all be turned towards electing the Democratic nominees." After the Philadelphia convention, Anthony actively lobbied the Democrats to adopt "a woman suffrage plank –not a Philadelphia splinter." Elizabeth Cady Stanton echoed Anthony's sentiments when she wrote to Isabella Beecher Hooker on June 14, "I rejoice with you in the Phila plank or rather *splinter* & if Baltimore [the site of the Democratic convention on July 9] does no better we must hold a grand ratification meeting for the Republican platform." She pushed Hooker to "write a letter to Greeley & tell him that a stronger plank in Baltimore, would enable us to shut our eyes on his iniquities a[nd] swallow even him if nominated." Stanton, herself, wrote to Greeley "telling him what he must do if he desired woman's help in the coming campaign." Greeley curtly responded that he "did not desire our help, and he doubted our capacity to give any if desired." It is ironic that at least within the Stanton family itself Greeley was correct about the women's ability to influence voters. Stanton confided to Lucy Stone and Henry B. Blackwell that her "husband and four sons will go for Greeley."

Anthony attended the Democratic convention in Baltimore, just as she had the Republican the previous month. Though disappointed with the Democrats, she could not have been surprised with their rebuff of the women's demand. She bitterly wrote Stanton on July 10, the day after the Democrats adopted their platform, that "the mountain has brought forth its mole, and we are left to comfort ourselves with the Philadelphia splinter as best we may."

Anthony and Stanton were left with only one option after the party conventions of the late spring and early summer of 1872. They would simply have to make the best of the situation and support the Republicans. Anthony told Stanton that they would try to make the Republican "splinter . . . as large as possible" by "issuing an appeal to the women of the U.S. to take hold of the *promise* of the Republicans and hold them to it, and demand more and more." Indeed, Anthony and Matilda Joslyn Gage promptly issued on behalf of NWSA an appeal to the "women of the United States." They asked "women and women speakers . . . to co-operate . . . with the Republican Party" because "for the first time in the history of the country woman is recognized in the platform of a large and dominant party."

The campaign season was approaching and this preliminary appeal was intended to draft women to work for the Republicans. A month before the election was to take place Anthony and her colleagues in the movement organized a rally in New York City. According to the *New York Times*, "the large hall of the Cooper Institute was crowded to its utmost capacity." The women were fulfilling their pledge to rally support for the party that delivered its support for woman's rights, even if a specific suffrage plank hadn't been adopted. Though the meeting was sponsored by NWSA, "The audience was about equally composed of ladies and gentlemen, and, in point of numbers, enthusiasm and intelligence was almost equal to those grand Republican political gatherings which have lately been held in the same building."

It was a marvelous display, in other words, of the breadth of support women could muster for friends of their cause. Very cleverly, though the women had organized the rally, they allowed a man, the prominent lawyer, reformer, and, according to his *New York Times* obituary, one of the most eloquent orators of the age, Luther R. Marsh, to preside as chairman of the event. They also invited several other prominent progressive Republican men to adorn the dais, including Peter Cooper, Hugh Gardner, and novelist Edward Yates. In his remarks welcoming the enthusiastic crowd to the woman-sponsored rally, Marsh proclaimed that "for the first time in the history of the country, women were taking active part in the political questions of the day, and were received with enthusiasm wherever they appeared." Marsh exaggerated the point since women had been actively participating in lobbying and campaigning for decades, but his message was that this election season was particularly notable. He told his loyal Republican audience that "the women of this country had contributed largely to put down the rebellion." And as loyal Republicans, he explained, "the women of America now claimed that they had a right to raise their voices and tell the other sex how they would wish them to vote." Glaringly, Marsh acknowledged the women's moral right to tell men how to vote, but he, like the splinter in the Republicans' Philadelphia platform, said nothing about the women's right to vote themselves.

Isabella Beecher Hooker, who followed Marsh to the podium, made an entirely different argument for women's support of the Republican Party. Republicans were "working for them," most prominently the vice presidential candidate, Henry Wilson: "Even years past, when to sympathize with such a movement [woman suffrage] as theirs was a reproach, he had the manliness to stand forward [and argued that women] be permitted to exercise the glorious right of the ballot." Hooker also pointed to Grant and his wife's support for woman suffrage. Other prominent NWSA leaders followed Hooker with a similar message. They also invoked images of the late war and its sacrifices, and then, in order to generate fervor in their audience, they denounced the Democrats as Johnny Rebs who would canonize Jefferson Davis and eradicate the Union's victory. When the crowd was sufficiently roused, Matilda Joslyn Gage and the other suffrage speakers would link Republican support to the cause. Lillie Devereaux Blake went so far as to claim that "the women of the country are today supporting with remarkable unanimity the Republican Party, because that party has promised to give them liberty." The now fired up audience at the convention concluded the meeting with "a happy address on the rights of women" by "Miss Anthony," a "song from the Glee Club, and cheers for Grant and Wilson." The coming election and Republican victory were thus inextricably linked to the support of women and their demand for suffrage.

CHAPTER 3

"I Have Been & Gone & Done It!!"

Fall 1872–Winter 1873

Enthusiastic Republican cheers notwithstanding, the woman suffrage movement had little about which to cheer. The Democrats had openly rejected their claim to the franchise; the Republicans, in their party platform, had offered a meager sop to women to gain their aid in the 1872 campaign; and the woman suffrage movement itself lay in disarray. Susan B. Anthony's leadership in the movement had been marginalized by both Lucy Stone and Victoria Woodhull, as well as overshadowed by her good friend Elizabeth Cady Stanton. Anthony desperately needed something to refocus the attention of the public at large and the movement's grassroots supporters. For three years, ever since Francis Minor proposed the strategy, and certainly in the twenty months since Woodhull had publicized it— namely, to claim rather than petition for women's voting rights as citizens under the Fourteenth Amendment and then bring a challenge in the federal courts with a possible hearing before the Supreme Court—Anthony had planned to vote in a federal election. She had even, according to evidence that came out at her trial, consulted the distinguished attorney and former New York Court of Appeals judges Henry R. Selden and his brother Samuel about the legality and constitutionality of her voting.

Judge Selden

Henry Rogers Selden (1805–1885) was born in North Lyme, Connecticut, but moved to Rochester, New York, at the age of twenty to join his married sister and his brother who had, like so many in this era, left New England for the burgeoning commercial area of western New York. Shortly after he arrived in the city, Henry began studying law in the firm of his older brother Samuel Lee Selden (1800–1876).

Samuel paved the way for his younger sibling, and the two brothers' careers were strikingly intertwined. Not long after being admitted to the bar Henry was commissioned as a judge advocate in the New York militia. Samuel's law partner, Addison Gardiner, went on to serve as a lieutenant governor of New York and then served on the state's high court as an associate judge and chief judge. No sooner had Gardiner stepped down from the court than Samuel was appointed to replace him, again as associate judge and then chief judge.

Henry, like Gardiner, served a term as lieutenant governor. Then, when his brother Samuel retired from his chief judgeship, Henry was appointed by Governor Edwin Morgan to replace him. Interesting, Henry turned down the chief judgeship to accept an associate judgeship instead. His reason was that Judge Hiram Denio had served on the court longer and deserved the promotion to chief. Judge Denio, as it happens, was the legal mentor of Ward Hunt, who would ten years later preside over the trial of Susan B. Anthony. The legal world of upstate New York was very small indeed, almost incestuous.

Henry was an ardent abolitionist. He famously helped Frederick Douglass escape capture by federal marshals in 1859. It was probably through his abolitionist work and acquaintance with Frederick Douglass that Henry made the acquaintance of Susan B. Anthony. Selden was also very active in the Republican Party, which he helped organize in New York, again alongside his later adversary in the Anthony trial, Ward Hunt. Henry enjoyed a reputation as an extremely learned lawyer. For many years he had served as the reporter for the court of appeals and later published *Selden's Notes of Cases in the Court of Appeals*. At least one treatise writer considered Selden "one of our greatest patent lawyers," though the author was one of Selden's former students, and so his opinion may have been biased. Nevertheless, his reputation was such that Yale conferred on him an honorary LL.D. Though the Selden brothers were, arguably, past their prime in 1872 and neither had made a career of civil rights law, Henry and Samuel provided Anthony with legal counsel in November before she registered and then voted, and then when she was charged.

Registering to Vote

Quite a few women had already taken up the torch under the constitutional litigation strategy, but when they were rebuffed by state officials at registration offices and polling places, their civil suits against the officials were summarily dismissed. In the case of seventy-two women in the District of Columbia, the U.S. Supreme Court pointedly refused to hear their appeal from the District's federal court rejection of their cause. In a few notable instances, women actually succeeded in casting ballots. In 1871, for example, Nanette B. Gardner voted in Detroit, and "Mrs. L. D. Mansfield, the principal of the Rockland Female Institute, of Nyack, and several of her teachers" voted that same year and "were not molested in any way" by authorities. Thus a test case had yet to be successfully made to challenge the law.

As one of the national leaders of the movement, Susan B. Anthony's challenge could create the kind of public stir that would finally force the Supreme Court to agree to review the case. At the same time, if she succeeded where the other women's cases had failed she might wrest the spotlight and leadership of the suffrage movement from the flamboyant, controversial upstart Victoria Woodhull and her even more dangerous rival, the Lucy Stone–led AWSA.

All of this must have been fermenting in Susan B. Anthony's mind when on November 1, the Friday before the election and the last day voters could register to qualify to vote, she saw the front-page exhortation in the *Rochester Democrat and Chronicle*, urging its readers to "Register Now." Together with her three sisters, Guelma, Mary, and Lottie, as well as Sarah Truesdell, Mary Pulver, Ellen Baker, Margaret Leyden, Ann Mosher, Nancy Chapman, Susan Hough, Hannah Chatfield, Mary Hibbard, Rhoda DeGarmo, and Jane Cogsell, Anthony invaded the barbershop that had been set up as the local election registry and polling station.

In that sacred male bastion the women confronted the young men who served as "inspectors," or election officials, demanding their right to register to vote. Edwin T. Marsh, a thirty-two-year-old letter carrier, was later described to the newspaper as "the chap who brings our letters and papers to us, a little sort of a fellow" who "was not selected by the electors of the eighth ward as one of the inspectors of election for the first district, but was appointed by the board of aldermen to fill the vacancy caused by the resignation of James Niven, a very worthy and competent gentleman." Beverley Waugh Jones was the other Republican, and William B. Hall was the Democratic member of the board of election inspectors.

The three young men seem to have been flummoxed by the appearance of the women. They tried to politely explain that they couldn't register the women because, well, they were women, and the New York constitution and election law limited the vote to men. Anthony had come prepared. She indignantly and forcefully asserted, with the U.S. Constitution in hand, that as a U.S. citizen she had the right to vote, and if the gentlemen denied her the right to register, she would bring criminal charges against them and "sue each of you personally for large, exemplary damages!"

To add authority to her threat, according to Anthony's biographer Kathleen Barry, she proclaimed that "I know I can win. I have Judge Selden as a lawyer." The gentlemen serving as a "Board of Registry" for the Eighth Ward that day knew well the estimable Judge Selden and the formidable Miss Anthony. They were neighbors, after all, in an entire city that could boast fewer than 62,000 inhabitants as of the 1870 census. They were loathe to confront the women and even less eager to face civil or criminal charges in court. According to Edwin Marsh's testimony at the preliminary hearing on the case, "the ladies [were] there when I returned from breakfast; the other inspectors had settled the matter so far as they were concerned; they asked my opinion of it; I said I was satisfied to register them; met S. J. Wagoner (United States supervisor) at the door; he said, 'Ed, did you register those women!'; Daniel Warner (the other supervisor) said, 'you will have to register them'; that was after we put down the names; there had evidently been some discussion before I arrived; they were just putting the oath to Miss Anthony." They decided to consult their own counsel, John Van Voorhis.

John Van Voorhis Jr., unlike most of the other lawyers who played a role in the Anthony trial, was born and raised in upstate New York. His father was a farmer who also served as a Methodist minister. According to his descendant, Eugene Van Voorhis, John Sr. "believed that his son was headed for eternal damnation [be-

cause] By his reckoning not only was farming the only virtuous occupation, but the practice of law was immoral."

John Jr.'s formal schooling never went beyond eighth grade, yet
"he taught himself Latin and French." After teaching school for a
short time he commenced the study of law and was admitted to the
bar in 1851. There is some dispute among his biographers as to how
long he remained in Elmira, New York, and whether he served as
city attorney (and several other local political appointments) in that
city or in Rochester, New York. In the mid-1850s John Jr. moved to
Rochester, opened a law office, and was joined in practice by one of
his brothers. He soon began to gain a reputation for representing
clients involved in progressive causes and was one of Frederick
Douglass's attorneys. He also represented the Seneca Nation of
Indians.

Van Voorhis was reputed to be outspoken and forthright. His
great-grandson recounted one incident from his career that evokes
the man's no-nonsense and anti-authoritarian attitude: "as a lawyer,
after winning several large awards in negligence cases against the
Buffalo, Rochester, and Pittsburgh Railway, he received . . . an offer
to be its general counsel. In his response he politely declined, stating that he could make more money suing than representing them."
Like so many involved with the abolitionists, he turned to the Republican Party, and in 1872 his loyalty to the party was rewarded
with a job, counsel to the Monroe County election commissioners.
This political appointment led directly to his involvement in the Susan B. Anthony case when the three Eighth Ward inspectors turned
to him for advice about Anthony's attempt to register to vote.

Van Voorhis, a supporter of women's rights himself, advised the
inspectors to register the women. The basis for his opinion was
somewhat novel. He told them that the word "man" included in the
Fourteenth Amendment was simply a generic term intended to include both men and women. He also advised them that they could
avoid any culpability in allowing the women to register if they followed state law requiring Anthony and the other women to take the
oath for registry; the women would swear or affirm that they were
qualified to vote in the district. Following Van Voorhis's advice, the
inspectors conferred, and all three decided to accept the registration
of Anthony, her sisters, and the other women.

The afternoon papers reacted acerbically to the news that Anthony and the other women had been registered as voters calling "for the arrest of the inspectors." Hurriedly, Anthony returned to the barbershop to convince the inspectors not to renege on their actions that morning. "She also assured them that she would be personally responsible for any costs resulting from legal action against them"—a somewhat empty promise since Anthony was still deeply in debt from the loan she had taken out while trying to keep *Revolution* in print. The Saturday edition of the *Rochester Democrat and Chronicle*'s report of the previous day's events in the Eighth Ward was more circumspect. It simply reported that "the question whether women shall be allowed to vote is not, it appears, to be discussed hereafter, but put to a practical test." The newspaper also reported that "Miss Anthony, elated by her success in getting her name on the books, notified all of her friends to go and do likewise."

Anthony Votes

Early in the morning of November 5, just as the polls opened, Susan B. Anthony and her allies presented themselves at the barbershop polling place to vote in the 1872 election. They filled out four of the six "tickets" for the various local, state, and federal offices in contention that day, but did not vote on a state constitutional amendment also up for a vote. Mr. Jones stood at the window to accept the tickets Anthony had filled out; but before he could place them in the ballot boxes, a Democratic poll watcher named Sylvester Lewis, "a salt manufacturer who resided in the Eighth Ward," objected to the proceedings and "said [her] vote should *not* go in the box."

According to the letter Anthony wrote later that morning to Elizabeth Cady Stanton, the inspectors, themselves elected to their office as Republicans, responded to this challenge: "one repub [probably Beverley Jones] said to the other—'What do you say Marsh?'" Marsh responded, "I say put it in!" Jones agreed, telling Marsh "so do I" and "We'll *fight* it out on this line if it takes all winter." Nevertheless, Jones followed procedure and informed Anthony that her vote had been challenged and that "she would have to swear her ballot in if she insisted upon voting." Unsurprisingly, Anthony told Jones that she did insist upon depositing her ballot. He then "presented her the Bible and administered to her the preliminary oath, which she took." Following election procedures, Jones then turned to Lewis to ask him "if he still insisted on his challenge; he said he did." Then, as required, Jones turned to Anthony and "told her she would have to take the general oath." Jones "administered the general oath, and she took it."

As Lewis later recounted the events in a letter to the editor of the *Rochester Democrat and Chronicle*, defending his actions:

> I did require them to take all of the oaths which the constitution and laws required, and if there was anything ungentlemanly in all this I fail to see it . . . and I have yet to learn that there are two sets, one applicable to males and another applicable to females, and I am inclined to think that if B. Waugh Jones after the administering the necessary oaths had asked Miss Susan B. Anthony the proper questions you would not have brought the blush to her face more than you did by the first question you asked which was, Miss Anthony how old are you, to which she replied she was fifty, and after a moment's pause she said she was fifty-three, thus causing the poor lady to divulge the last secret, which the most of ladies are willing to impart.

This procedure was then repeated with each of the eight other women who voted that day, though some of the women took umbrage at having to take the oath. "Rhoda De Garmo [a seventy-five-year-old friend of Anthony's parents] told them she wouldn't swear nor affirm 'but would tell them the truth'—& they accepted that." Outrage again erupted in the later editions of the Rochester papers supporting the Democrats, once more calling for the immediate arrest of any inspectors who allowed the women to vote. The women who presented themselves at the polls later in the day were turned away. The local newspaper may have had some role in dissuading the inspectors from accepting any further votes from women. In an article entitled "Election Laws" published on the page with other election reporting on Election Day, it reprinted sections of the federal voting Enforcement Act of 1870.

An elated Anthony was all but bursting with the news of the morning's events as she sat down to write to her partner in arms, Stanton: "Well I have been & gone & done it!!" She explained to Stanton that the women whose registration had been denied "will immediately . . . bring action against the registrars [and] another woman who was registered but vote refused will bring action for that." Anthony clearly expected that civil suits against the election authorities would follow. Nevertheless, she was buoyed by the response the women received: "Not a jeer not a word—not a look—disrespectful has met a single woman." The new departure strategy, she assumed, was working. "If only now *all the Woman* Suffrage *Women* would work to *this* end, of *enforcing the existing constitution*—supremacy of *national law* over state law—what strides we might make this very winter." She concluded her missive to Stanton: "I hope you voted too."

The very next day the *New York Times* heralded the news that "Miss Susan B. Anthony has had the honor of leading to the polls the advanced guard of the coming squadrons of female voters." The author of the "Minor Topics" column seems to have applauded the event, declaring that "the little band of nine ladies whose ballots were received by the election inspectors at Rochester deserve a permanent place in history." The *Times* notice acknowledged that some other women had voted or tried to vote in previous elections, "but this picket guard of nine is a tangible enough force to make people reflect on the future possibilities which it involves." In other words, Anthony and her Rochester friends had succeeded in directing public attention to the cause of woman suffrage. The fact that the newspaper was a Republican organ and that Anthony and the women had undoubtedly voted the Republican ticket may have influenced the paper's coverage of the event.

Two days after the election, the Rochester paper published a letter to the editor that presented "A Woman's Opinion of the Rights of her Sex," signed "ELG," probably Elizabeth Gay, a longtime women's rights supporter who had, as early as 1860, been active in the movement. Gay applauded the Republican victory and then proclaimed that "I, as a woman and a citizen of the United States, rejoice that some of my sisters have participated in the ballot. . . . We have one ward of which Rochester ought to be proud. The eighth ward by their action of Tuesday acknowledged woman as a citizen and a 'person.'" But all was not well in Rochester. Gay recounted how "Wards one, three, six, seven and ten refused to permit women to register at all. The arguments advanced to prove that we are not citizens are ludicrous in the extreme. . . . When the lady in the fourteenth ward offered her vote, a man called out, 'I challenge that vote.' The challenger, elated at her defeat, stretched himself up and puffed himself out to his utmost capacity, resembling very much a diminutive little toad, trying to swallow something larger than himself, and exclaimed, 'A woman has no right to vote; she ain't a citizen. I can prove it by the Bible.' 'Ah, how so?' asked a bystander. 'Because,' blubbered the challenger, 'she is made out of the rib of a man.' Well, indeed, if man is minus a rib, surely he can be only a part of a citizen, and woman is the whole citizen after all. Silly argument, that." Gay was not discouraged by such boorish male opposition. She concluded her epistle with an optimistic prediction: "Our opponents may triumph for a while, but we will only say, 'Let them boast their vain glory, and we shall soon see them looking as crestfallen and deplorable as a rooster drenched by a powerful storm."

Gay's letter to the editor did not go unanswered. On the following day, a letter from a male reader responded to Gay's prosuffrage missive. The author argued that the election inspectors who had refused to register and accept the women's ballots "did a much more gallant act . . . than did the eight ward which allowed them (what shall I call them? Women, persons of what?)." Then in a clear reference to Susan B. Anthony, the letter's author disparagingly referred to "the first of three had her (I suppose I can call her *her*; they call horses her and him sometimes) vote challenged by a man."

Nearly a week after the election the Rochester newspaper grudgingly praised Anthony and acknowledged that her vote, if nothing else, had succeeded in capturing public attention and reviving the woman suffrage debate. The editorial seems almost to applaud Rochester's own: "Let nobody deny the influence of Susan B. Anthony. She has kept the United States agitated a good many years back, and the fact that she cast her first ballot a week ago will provoke discussion in the courts and outside of them, which will last— shall we say, to use an original expression, until victory perches upon her standard?" The Rochester paper then quoted an article about Anthony's feat from the downstate afternoon Democratic tabloid, the *Brooklyn Eagle*. The *Eagle*'s piece was either antagonistic editorial or sarcastic reportage. While it acknowledged that Anthony's vote had galvanized woman suffrage supporters and generated newspaper attention to the issue, whoever wrote the piece did not disguise his contempt for Anthony and her cause.

The bold enterprise of Anthony—of blessed suffrage memory—in casting a ballot at Rochester in the face of the world, last Tuesday, seems to have given a new impulse to the discussion of woman's rights. In the future feminine calendar, if there be a place reserved for the patroness of "social equality" by all means let St. Susan fill it. She has led the movement for woman's "emancipation" for years. Now she unconsciously leads the movement in Eagle columns looking to a lively debate of the question. Several essays have been contributed the last few days by lady correspondents. Some of them have assumed an aggressive attitude, but others have been thoroughly conservative in their views. A fresher stimulus to the discussion has been supplied by the publication in yesterday's Eagle of a historical sketch of the masculine work done by women.

The Enforcement Act of 1870

No official response came for over a week. Then on November 14 a complaint was filed by Sylvester Lewis with U.S. Commissioner William C. Storrs. Storrs promptly issued a warrant for Anthony's and the other women's arrest under a provision of the Federal Enforcement Act of 1870.

The Enforcement Act, under whose authority Susan B. Anthony and the other women (and the three inspectors who accepted their ballots) were charged, was the first of three Enforcement Acts passed by Congress in an attempt to ensure the right of franchise to black men, particularly in the former Confederate states, after the passage of the Fifteenth Amendment. In sum, it made provision for criminal charges in federal courts against anyone who blocked a black man from casting his ballot, any man from voting illegally, or any official who allowed a man to vote illegally. This last part was intended to prevent white men, particularly former Confederates who had been barred from voting, from voting more than once, which would have the effect of diluting the votes of black men. The specific provision under which the women were charged was Section 19, which read in part:

> *And be it further enacted,* That if at any election for representative or delegate in the Congress of the United States any person shall knowingly personate and vote, or attempt to vote, in the name of any other person, whether living, dead, or fictitious; or vote more than once at the same election for any candidate for the same office; or vote at a place where he may not be lawfully entitled to vote; or vote without having a lawful right to vote, or do any unlawful act to secure a right or an opportunity to vote for himself or any other person or by force, threat, menace, intimidation, bribery, reward, or offer, or promise thereof.

Why did Congress federalize the offense of illegal voting when state law already disqualified it? The provision under which Susan B. Anthony was prosecuted is only a small section at the end of the act, the purpose of which was to guarantee that states could not deny the vote to freedmen. It allowed the states under Reconstruction to deny the vote to former Confederates who had staged "rebellion" against the Union and to employ the force of federal law to ensure that these treasonous individuals would not vote illegally.

If unreconstructed Confederates could vote, they might very well reimpose legal restrictions and discriminatory practices against black men, their former slaves—as, in fact, they did following the end of Reconstruction and the lifting of civil disabilities by Congress at the end of Reconstruction. Thus Anthony's and the Rochester election inspectors' prosecutions were brought under federal provisions originally enacted for the purpose of protecting freedmen in the former Confederate states against disenfranchised former Confederates.

Arrest

Though the warrant had been issued earlier, the actual arrests were delayed for several more days so that the commissioners could consult with the U.S. attorney. According to an account Susan B. Anthony later gave to a meeting of NWSA, Storrs had

> sent word for me to call at his office. I sent word to him that I had no social acquaintance with him and didn't wish to call on him. . . . Then a young man [U.S. marshal Elisha J. Keeney] in beaver hat and kid gloves (paid for by taxes gathered from women), came to see me. He sat down. He said it was pleasant weather. He hemmed and hawed and finally said Mr. Storrs wanted to see me. . . . "What for?" I asked. "To arrest you," said he. "Is that the way you arrest men?" "No." Then I demanded that I should be arrested properly. My sister desiring to go with me he proposed that he should go ahead and I follow with her. This I refused, and he had to go with me. In the [horse-drawn streetcar] he took out his pocketbook to pay fare. I asked him if he did that in his official capacity. He said yes; he was obliged to pay the fare of any criminal he arrested. Well, that was the first cents worth I ever had from Uncle Sam.

A subsequent version of the arrest claims that deputy marshal Keeney was not pleased with his assignment. Supposedly, Anthony asked the marshal whether she could change her dress for the trip downtown. According to this version, Keeney replied, "Of course, just come down to the Commissioner's office whenever you're ready." Anthony only wanted equal treatment to men and told the marshal, "I'll do no such thing. . . . You were sent here to arrest me and take me to court. It's your duty to do so." When they were ready to leave, Anthony "thrust out her wrists and said, 'Don't you want to handcuff me, too?' 'I assure you, madam,' Marshal Keeney muttered, 'it isn't at all necessary.'" While the account may take some liberties with the recounting of these events, the tenor of the give-and-take between Anthony and the marshal is consistent with her own recorded account and her later conduct at the trial. Keeney was not a "young man" in 1873; rather, he was a sixty-three-year-old "former builder and twice chief of police in Rochester before the [Civil War]." Some versions of the arrest, even Anthony's own retelling, took some liberties.

Anthony wasn't the only person Keeney arrested that day for violating the voting Enforcement Act. Just like Anthony, Hugh Kelly, William Falconer, and another man were rounded up pursuant to a warrant issued by Commissioner Storrs. In their case, evidence showed that they had presented forged naturalization papers when they registered to vote in the Fifth Ward. Storrs held them over for trial in the district court. The basis of the charge was the same: they had violated the federal Enforcement Act by voting illegally. Even though they were men, they were not citizens and thus had no legal right to vote. If the government was cracking down on immigrant men who voted illegally, likely for the Democrats, then prosecuting the women who voted the Republican ticket may have seemed a political necessity if they weren't to be vulnerable to accusations of prejudicial prosecution. This may be one explanation for why the Republican federal prosecutors pursued a case against Anthony and her cohorts who they knew had cast their ballots for the Republicans. The Irish immigrants usually voted Democratic.

But the case against the immigrant men did not capture the attention of the press the way the prosecution of Anthony had. The *Rochester Democrat and Chronicle* editorial on the case published two days after Anthony was arrested evidenced a clear bias in favor of woman suffrage, telling their readers that "those who are in favor of female suffrage have always the strongest side in the argument." At the same time, however, the editors seemed to be wary of "radical ladies." The editorial on "The Voting Ladies" looked forward to the time "when the question does arise, if it ever will," but hoped that "there be no extreme measures resorted to Heaven stand between us and a war with the women. Let the men give up their own treasured right of suffrage sooner."

The Saturday after her arrest, the Rochester paper published a provocative letter to the editor, signed by "L.H.," a woman calling for the complainant in the Anthony case to go public with his charges. The Democratic poll watcher who had filed the complaint, Sylvester Lewis, had laid low since Election Day, and his name was kept off of the warrant issued for Anthony's arrest by Commissioner Storrs. According to L.H.'s letter, the warrant identified the complainant as "_____. Sylvester, Come Forth." The letter writer continued. A brief but public colloquy thus began between Sylvester Lewis and L.H. (L.H. was never identified by name but was a resident of the Eighth Ward, which is somewhat ironic since she wanted the complainant in the Anthony case to come out from behind the anonymous blank on the warrant.) Publicly exposed, Sylvester Lewis boldly responded in the Monday paper: "Now, I don't propose to enter late any lengthy controversy with L.H. or with any of those ladies who cast their ballots at the late election." Nevertheless, Lewis defended his actions, telling the public:

> I did nothing more at the registry or at the ballot box than I had a right to do . . . and in fact I did nothing more than I conceived my duty to do in guarding well the ballot box. . . . I was asked to withdraw my challenge, but declined so to do. . . . I see by the New York World of Saturday that warrants have been issued by United States Commissioner Storrs for the arrest of Susan B. Anthony. . . . So L.H. and her coadjutors will see that Sylvester will not be required to come forth with his stamps, as Uncle Sam and one of his daughters (the state of New York) step in.

Lewis pressed on to defend his attitude toward women: "Now, Mr. Editor. I disclaim any idea or wish to have any female or any number of females stand in fear of men. I am the last man that would abridge any of the rights and privileges of women; on the contrary [I will do anything] in my power to render their condition better." If Lewis had ended his response at this point, he might have avoided becoming the poster child for nineteenth-century anti–woman suffrage male chauvinism. But, of course, he had center stage and wanted to air his grievances and philosophy about the proper role of women.

> I would like to see them love their God and follow his teachings in all things, and especially not to bear false witness. There are other ways in which women can better their condi-

tion and the condition of mankind generally than by going to the ballot-box. Let them choose for themselves a legal representative, whose duty it shall be to assist in making the laws and grappling with the stern realities of life, while she contents herself to attend to the domestic affairs of her household, for when does woman appear more lovely than when ministering to the wants and requirements of her household? Let her teach her children the love of God and the precepts of the bible—teach her daughters how to manage the affairs of the house, so that they may become good wives and mothers—teach her sons the like precepts and in addition teach them, if she chooses, the science of government, political economy, the arts and sciences, and thereby prepare them to become useful members of society. . . . Let me say to you, gentlewomen, that there is no place on the face of God's footstool where women are held in greater esteem, where they are honored, caressed and loved than America.

L.H. would not let Lewis's diatribe go unanswered. As the editor announced to his readers the next day, he had received a "Second Communication from L.H.—She is Calm but Indignant— 'Sylvester' Again Challenged." Indeed, L.H.'s letter was polite but vociferous. She dismissed Lewis's letter, saying that he "has advanced no argument, therefore there is none to answer." Like Lewis, she didn't wish to get into some kind of media shouting match with him. L.H. did not "propose to step down from the high estate of true humanity to indulge in any personal or scurrilous remarks." Nevertheless, she wasn't about to let Lewis's remarks on woman suffrage and woman's true place in society, which she characterized as "the promptings of hate and malevolence mingled with the last spasmodic gushings of political despair," go unanswered. L.H. reiterated her call that "woman have full and free exercise of all her rights and then hold her fully responsible before the law for all her actions." Anticipating the trial to come she expressed her "hope . . . that those who have this decision at their disposal will give the subject . . . careful consideration."

U.S. Commissioner William C. Storrs thus had a series of decisions to make. There is little biographical information available about Storrs, the man who presided at Susan B. Anthony's preliminary hearing. A local history by William Farley Peck published in 1908 lists him as one of the lawyers admitted to the bar in Rochester, New York, in 1844. It is highly probable that he was the son of Henry Randolph Storrs, who served as a member of Congress from Oneida County. There is a notation that William C. Storrs, Esq., donated an "Autograph Journal kept by the Hon. Henry R. Storrs, while Member of Congress from Oneida County, containing [an] account of political occurrences from December 22, 1825 to May 16, 1830. In six manuscript bound volumes" in the "Full text of Certificate of Incorporation" of the Buffalo Historical Society from the time it was founded in 1862. It is a curious coincidence—though considering the small circle of the legal and political elite in western New York state in the mid-nineteenth century it might not be all that curious—that on that same document the founders of the society included the names Millard Fillmore as its first president and Nathan K. Hall as one of the organization's original "Councillors."

Henry R. Storrs was the older brother of William Lucius Storrs, also a member of Congress, though William Lucius returned to Connecticut, where the brothers had been born, to seek political and legal success. His father graduated from Yale College in 1804. Henry studied law, was admitted to the bar in 1807, and opened his practice in Champion, New York. William Lucius followed his brother to Yale, graduated exactly seven years after Henry, and then moved to New York to join his brother, who was now practicing law in Whitesboro, New York, on the Erie Canal in Oneida County. William Lucius was admitted to the bar in the nearby village of Whitestown in 1817 but returned to Connecticut shortly thereafter, when Henry was elected as a Federalist to the fifteenth and sixteenth Congresses (March 4, 1817–March 3, 1821).

Henry failed to secure renomination in 1820 but succeeded in his bid for a seat in the eighteenth Congress as an Adams-Clay Federalist. He was reelected as an Adams candidate to the nineteenth and twentieth Congresses and then successfully ran as an Anti-Jacksonian candidate to the twenty-first Congress. Concurrent with his congressional career, Henry also served as the presiding judge of the court of common pleas of Oneida County from 1825 to 1829. It was probably sometime during this period of time that William C. Storrs was born. William C. Storrs's family was a distinguished one. Nevertheless, the son and nephew of U.S. congressmen, William C. never achieved any significant political success. The highest office he attained was U.S. commissioner for the Northern District of New York, a position he held for fifteen years. Probably the most noteworthy aspect of Storrs's career was his role in *Anthony*.

Storrs's role in the *Anthony* case was limited. U.S. commissioners were only authorized to handle preliminary legal issues, such as issuing warrants, handling the preliminary examination, and determining bail. When Anthony arrived at Storrs's office, she was met by her sister and her attorney, Judge Henry Selden, whom Susan's sister must have quickly summoned. According to the *New York Times* report the next day, "Miss Anthony [was] pleased that her case is to come properly before the courts." It may be that the delay was due to the fact that Anthony's attorney refused to allow her to plead to the charges. The *Rochester Democrat and Chronicle* told its readers that "the commissioner knowing that United States District Attorney [Richard] Crowley would pass through this city on his way to Auburn where the United States court will be in session this week . . . [Storrs] apprised the law officer of the fact and received information to the effect that an interview could be had with him on the arrival of the afternoon train from Lockport." In the meantime, Crowley's assistant, John E. Pound, arrived to stand in for Crowley.

The short late winter afternoon (by this time it was 5:30) proceedings began with a formal reading of the warrant by the commissioner. Anthony's counsel, Judge Selden, then "took it and scanned it carefully and closely." Pound then addressed Selden: "I suppose you plead not guilty to the charge." But Selden refused to enter a plea. He wanted a formal trial and did not want some kind of summary proceeding before a commissioner. He told Pound, "We do not plead guilty to anything, we say just now we are not guilty. When an indictment is found we will plead." Pound did not engage Selden on his maneuver but pressed that "we want to fix a time for the examination." The lawyers consulted and agreed to continue the proceedings at 10 a.m. eleven days later.

After the hearing was adjourned, the media savvy Anthony held an impromptu press conference, or as the Rochester paper termed it, she "indulged in some pleasantries respecting the question." She provided a zesty sound bite for the journalists: "She said if it so happened that she should be compelled to eat Uncle Sam's bread for a few months, it would be for the first time in her life that such a luxury was offered her." But more seriously, she told the newsmen that she "desires her case to be made the test case. She has full confidence in the justice of her cause and that she will ultimately triumph." Indeed, she told the *Democrat and Chronicle*'s reporter that "it is just the situation she has long been wishing for." She told the reporter that "Hitherto men heard all that was said upon female suffrage with an open ear, but beyond that they did not give it any time or attention. Now when the matter is going to come before the courts it must necessarily be settled."

A Preliminary Hearing

On Friday, November 29, Anthony reappeared at Storrs's chambers for the preliminary hearing on the charges. Once again, the prosecutor on this occasion was John E. Pound, a young assistant U.S. attorney from Lockport, New York, who had graduated from Brown University. In 1871 he had been elected to the state assembly as a Republican. An ambitious man, it is interesting to note that he later served as a U.S. commissioner, was twice elected mayor of Lockport, and in 1888 became a rival Republican candidate for the U.S. Congress to his boss in 1873, the U.S. attorney for the eastern district of New York, Richard Crowley.

At Anthony's hearing, Pound called Sylvester Lewis and the three inspectors as prosecution witnesses to establish that Anthony had voted in the congressional election on November 5. "Judge Selden was in court a few minutes, but other engagements prevented him from giving his personal attention to the case." Instead, Anthony was represented by John Van Voorhis.

The hearing commenced with Pound calling one of the election inspectors, Edwin T. Marsh, to testify. Marsh testified that he knew "defendant Miss Anthony; saw her Election Day at the polls; saw her vote there; don't know what part of the ticket she voted; Mr. Jones took the tickets; the name of the voter was called and I ran my eye over the list and checked the names as they voted." Pound then asked Marsh: "Was Miss Anthony dressed as a woman and did she have on the apparel of a woman?" Van Voorhis immediately objected to the question as "irrelevant and impertinent."

The latter was not really a legal ground for objecting to the question, but it shows how even Anthony's counsel while defending equal suffrage could not repress so-called gentlemanly impulses. Storrs summarily overruled the objection. Marsh's reply, however, didn't actually answer Pound's "impertinent" question; he only recounted the fact that she had voted over Lewis's objection.

When Van Voorhis took his turn with the witness he tried to establish that Anthony's name appeared on the registry of voters, and that at the time of her voting the U.S. supervisors of elections had not protested. Now it was Pound's turn to object. In essence, Pound tried to counter that Anthony was tried for illegal voting, not for illegal registration. Thus whether her name appeared on the registry was irrelevant. Van Voorhis countered that the U.S. election supervisors had attended the registration and were required to "see that it was properly conducted." After all, "the registry was a preliminary to voting under the law," and if she had properly registered to vote then she was entitled to do so.

Selden was still in the courtroom at this point and spoke up to make the point that "it must be shown that Miss A. had voted knowing that she had no right." Selden's implication was that if Anthony had voted when her name appeared on the registry, then she was well within her rights to believe she was voting legally. This time Storrs ruled for the defendant and allowed Van Voorhis's question. Marsh admitted that Anthony had been registered with the acquiescence of the U.S. election supervisors.

Beverly Jones, another of the Rochester election inspectors, was then called to give testimony. His account was similar to Marsh's. Van Voorhis addressed the commissioner: "Miss Anthony did not deny her identity. She did not pretend to be anybody else. We admit that Miss Anthony is a woman. This was accepted by the prosecution." He was probably trying to make the point that Anthony hadn't misrepresented herself when she proffered her ballot and thus didn't violate the federal law. Nevertheless, Pound put the same question to Mr. Jones that he had used with Mr. Marsh: "How was she dressed?" Again Van Voorhis objected that the question was "immaterial and impertinent—assuming that Miss Anthony intended to commit some fraud." Storrs allowed the question, and Jones, unsurprisingly, testified that "she was dressed as a woman." Van Voorhis called Anthony to testify before Storrs in an attempt to show that she had voted in good faith believing that she did so legally. Her lawyers' position was that she couldn't be charged if she hadn't intended to vote "illegally." Her testimony centered on her visit to Judge Selden's office when she had consulted him about whether she had the right to vote.

VAN VOORHIS: Are you the person spoken of as defendant?

ANTHONY: Yes, sir.

VAN VOORHIS: Previous to voting at the 1st District poll in the 8th Ward, did you take the advice of counsel upon voting?

ANTHONY: Yes, sir.

VAN VOORHIS: Who was it you talked with?

ANTHONY: Judge Henry R. Selden.

VAN VOORHIS: What did he advise you with reference to your legal right to vote?

ANTHONY: He said it was the only way to find out what the law was upon the subject—to bring it to a test.

VAN VOORHIS: Did he advise you to go and offer your vote?

ANTHONY: Yes. Sir.

VAN VOORHIS: State whether or not prior to such advice you had retained Mr. Selden to defend in this action?

ANTHONY: No, sir; I first went to Judge Selden to sound him if we should want him.

VAN VOORHIS: Have you anything further to say upon Judge Selden's advice?

ANTHONY: I think it was sound.

VAN VOORHIS: Did he give you an opinion upon the subject?

ANTHONY: He was like all the rest of you lawyers—he had not studied the question.

VAN VOORHIS: What did he advise you?

ANTHONY: He left me with this opinion—that he was an honest man; that he would study it up thoroughly & decide according to the law.

VAN VOORHIS: Did you have any doubt yourself of your right to vote?

ANTHONY: Not a particle.

If the questioning had ended here and Storrs had accepted the defense theory that Anthony lacked the requisite intent to violate the law, the case might have ended. Through Van Voorhis's questioning and Anthony's unusually (for her) terse responses, the defense had established that she clearly believed, reasonably so, since she had consulted an esteemed lawyer on the subject, that she was legally justified in depositing her ballots on Election Day.

But John Pound had an opportunity to cross-examine Anthony and she was less circumspect in her replies to his questions.

POUND: Would you not have made the same efforts to vote that you did do if you had not consulted with Judge Selden?

ANTHONY: Yes, sir. (I hope the court understands that I did not consult anyone until after I had voted).

This parenthetical comment seems to be contradicted by her previous testimony and would later be contradicted by Judge Selden's testimony at trial. It is very possible that the record of the testimony may have contained some errors. But the remainder of her testimony makes the inclusion or exclusion of this parenthetical irrelevant. Pound continued to get Anthony to admit that Judge Selden's advice was immaterial to her decision to vote.

POUND: Was [sic] you not influenced by his advice in the matter at all?

ANTHONY: No, sir.

POUND: You went into this matter for the purpose of testing the question?

ANTHONY: Yes, sir, I had been resolved to vote at the first election that I had been home for 30 days for three years.

New York law required voters to be in residence for thirty days prior to any election in which they participated. In sum, Anthony had, by her admissions under oath, confessed to her intention to vote and that Selden's legal advice had had no effect on her decision. But did this necessarily mean that she had the intention to vote illegally? While the advice of a respected attorney helped support the contention that she believed she was doing no illegal act and perhaps indicated that she was perfectly reasonable in believing she had a legal right to vote. Nevertheless, her belief that she violated no law was still sincere. Though whether that sincere belief was sufficient under the law to acquit her of the charge would have to be determined at trial.

After Anthony testified, the complainant, Sylvester Lewis, was recalled. Van Voorhis asked him if he had told a Democratic acquaintance "that if these ladies [Anthony and her friends] voted you would get as many Greeley women to vote?" Lewis tried to protest his innocence by claiming that "it would be a good joke if we should get twelve or fourteen Irish women to offset their votes." What could Van Voorhis have been trying to do with this testimony? Probably he either wanted to show that the complainant was biased and untrustworthy or that Lewis had no objection to women voting, only Republican women. He may have thought that if he could show this he could get the original complaint thrown out and thus the charges would have to be dismissed.

To nail this point home, Van Voorhis next called a Mrs. Leyden to testify. "I reside in the eighth ward, have lived there fifteen years; am acquainted with Sylvester Lewis," she told the commissioner. Van Voorhis then asked her if Lewis had "advise[d] you to register to test the matter?" Pound objected that the question wasn't material to the current case against Anthony. Storrs allowed Van Voorhis to respond to Pound's objection. Van Voorhis "wanted to show that Mr. Lewis took the poll list for the Democratic party and when he found ladies whom he thought would vote his way, advised them to register; that he called at Mrs. Leyden's residence and said the question of her right to vote might as well be tested in the eighth ward as anywhere." Storrs ruled out this line of testimony.

Van Voorhis was not deterred. He then called the Lewis's Democratic friend, Mr. Garrigan, who admitted to a conversation with the complainant "just before election in reference to women voting." But when Garrigan was about to tell the hearing what Lewis had said, Pound objected. Van Voorhis explained that Garrigan would testify that Lewis had "declared he was going to get twenty Greeley women to register late on Saturday evening as an offset to the votes of Miss Anthony and her associates." Storrs would have no more of this and ruled the line of questioning "immaterial to the case."

Van Voorhis started to show his impatience with Storrs's rulings in favor of the prosecution. He complained that "truth crushed to earth will rise again." Storrs was clearly offended. He told the defense that "I decide honestly, as near right as I can and there is no occasion for these continued comments." Van Voorhis asked Storrs: "You don't propose to gag us[?]" But Storrs complained that "I can scarcely make a decision without hearing uncalled for remarks" and then told "counsel [to] proceed with his witnesses." The testimony was just about finished at this point, but Pound decided to put one more question to Susan B. Anthony: "Did you consult other counsel besides Judge Selden?" Now it was Van Voorhis's turn to object to a question as immaterial. Pound responded that "if the fact that Judge Selden had been consulted [and] was admitted in evidence, there could be no objection to showing that other advice had been taken. However, if counsel for defense didn't wish it known that other counsel had been consulted, he would not press the matter." Having made his point to the commissioner, Pound appears to have let the matter drop, and Storrs declared that the examination was "closed at this point."

Now that testimony had concluded, the attorneys started to make their arguments to Storrs about whether or not he should dismiss the charges. Selden spoke first: "Are these ladies to be held criminally when they imagined they had a right to vote? The offense must be committed *knowingly*, according to the statute." Pound countered: "It is their business to know the law. Ignorance of the law is no excuse. A man voted once, got drunk and voted again, and he was held guilty, although he did not remember voting the second time." Judge Selden knew that the cause of woman suffrage required a test case but put what he thought was his client's welfare first: "If there was any way to get this case before the supreme court of the United States," he told the court, "I should not desire it to end here, as I now do. But there are too many contingencies against such a result. . . . However, it don't seem to me there is any possibility of conviction. These ladies did not vote *knowingly* in contravention of the law." Pound insisted that "They ought to know the law and are clearly guilty."

Van Voorhis stepped in at this point. He knew Selden was getting nowhere by insisting on this one line of defense and arguing back and forth with Pound. He may have also worried that Selden was abandoning the strategy that Anthony had embraced of voting then litigating if necessary. He spoke to Storrs directly: "Are you prepared to dismiss this defendant, or do you wish to hear an argument on the case?" Storrs seemed to be prepared to finish up the hearing that very day, telling counsel, "I am ready to hear all that may be offered on both sides." Van Voorhis probably wanted to ensure that he and Selden were on the same page with regard to Anthony's defense. In particular, Van Voorhis wanted them to prepare an argument that would turn on the constitutional rather than simply the criminal statutory grounds Selden had argued thus far. He told Storrs, "Then you must set a time for the hearing as we are not ready for an argument." According to the newspaper account of the hearing that appeared the next day, the lawyers conferred to decide on a date when they might continue the proceeding, at which point Susan B. Anthony interrupted to tell them that she would be "engaged in Central Ohio until December 10th." Pound seemed rather startled by this and told Anthony, "You are supposed to be in custody all this time." Anthony replied, "Oh, is that so? I wasn't aware of it." Storrs agreed to postpone the remainder of the hearing until December 18 (the postponement was later extended to December 23). The case against the other women who had voted with Anthony and who were included in the complaint was not taken up, since "it being agreed that a decision in [the Anthony case] should determine the rest." The newspaper concluded its coverage by noting that "the commissioner's room was crowded during the afternoon showing the interest which the case has excited."

————

Another Hearing

Between the first hearing on November 29 and the resumption of the proceedings on December 23, Anthony busied herself with appeals to friends in Congress and making arrangements for the

NWSA national convention in January. She also consulted John Van Voorhis about what she might expect to happen in Storrs's court. It was highly likely, he advised her, that she would be bound over for the grand jury, which would then return an indictment against her.

Van Voorhis thought there was a way to take a shortcut around the proceedings to get her case heard expeditiously before the U.S. Supreme Court. On December 18, Anthony met with Van Voorhis and he outlined his strategy. If Storrs bound her over for the grand jury, Anthony could refuse to post bail and would then be imprisoned. Once in jail, her attorneys could file a writ of habeas corpus in the federal district court and when (as they expected the district judge would rule) her petition was denied, she could then appeal to the Supreme Court.

Habeas corpus, or "the great writ," allowed a prisoner to challenge the lawfulness of that imprisonment and its jurisprudential basis. Writs of habeas corpus received expedited review. If the court agreed that the imprisonment was against the law, in effect agreeing with the jailed individual that whoever had thrown them into jail had no legal basis to do so, then that ruling would in essence uphold the prisoner's interpretation of the law. In effect, had the Supreme Court heard the appeal in Anthony's case and found that it had merit, Anthony would have won and established woman suffrage throughout the nation with the stroke of the Court's pen. But another event took place between the time of Anthony's arrest and the hearing before Commissioner Storrs that, while Anthony and her counsel might not yet realize it, would throw a monkey wrench in their trial strategy. On December 11 the U.S. Senate confirmed a new Supreme Court associate justice: Ward Hunt.

First Selden and Van Voorhis would present their arguments to Commissioner Storrs, their objective to either derail the prosecution of Anthony and the other women and thereby succeeding in thwarting the U.S. government's prosecution of the women under federal law or establishing a record they could use as the basis for an appeal to the U.S. Supreme Court. On December 23, the parties gathered in the city of Rochester common council chambers.

Because this was an informal hearing rather than a trial, Judge Henry Selden, Anthony's counsel, spoke first. Selden's argument equivocated. He asserted Anthony's right to vote but at the same time told Storrs that there was no general agreement about the right of women to vote, nor were there any real legal precedents upon which he could rely, and he admitted that "no authentic adjudication had been made upon which the public mind is content to rest as conclusive."

Selden first relied upon the minority report authored by Benjamin Butler and William Loughridge to argue that since voting was "a leading feature of citizenship" it necessarily followed that the Fourteenth Amendment, which guaranteed a citizen's rights against state infringement, guaranteed women citizens the right to vote. States could regulate elections but could not deprive an entire class of citizens, women, of their right to vote. The second point Selden argued was that under the federal statute the prosecution bore the burden of proving that Anthony had the requisite intent to violate the law. According to his interpretation, "the fact must be established that the party who has not the right to vote, and knows that he has not that right, attempted to vote."

According to the report of the hearing, which appeared in the late edition of the *Rochester Evening Express*, Pound "said he should not attempt to follow the learned counsel in his extended argument, as he did not regard this as the place where the questions discussed should be traversed." He claimed that "there is no dispute as to the facts" only "the question of intent." Pound, for the prosecution, then declaimed at length, not on the question of intent required in the statute, but on whether the Fourteenth Amendment's provision on the privileges or immunities of U.S. citizens included a guarantee for all citizens to vote.

First, Pound addressed the question of whether suffrage was a fundamental right. He cited both Daniel Webster and Justice Joseph Story to support the proposition that it was not. Then, to further buttress his argument, he pointed out that "in most countries females are excluded as interfering with sound policy, and in the few cases in which it has been allowed, experience has not justified the permission." This last comment did little to advance his position but clearly exposed his masculine prejudice against granting women the vote. He was on firmer legal ground when he told Commissioner Storrs that "in construing the fourteenth amendment, we must not consider one section by itself, but take it as a whole."

Pound made the point that the first section of the amendment, which guaranteed the rights of citizens, should be read together with the second section, which explicitly outlined the penalties states would face if they interfered with voting by "male" citizens. Pound rhetorically asked, "What was the object of the second section?" Selden piped up in answer: "To settle a new principle of representation." But Pound retorted, "There we disagree." And to buttress his interpretation, he continued: "The 15th Amendment follows, and the court makes a very fine distinction . . . The prohibition relates to color, race or previous servitude, and not at all to sex." The intent of the Framers, Pound averred, was quite clear on this point and nailed it down by reminding Selden (and the commissioner) that "the defendant in this case has been before a committee of Congress upon the questions of the right of women to vote, and reports were made upon her petition." And the very fact that the congressional committee in response to Anthony's testimony had denied that Congress had intended that women had the right to vote under the Fourteenth Amendment showed that Anthony had the requisite intent to violate the law under the Enforcement Act. After all, the Congress's reports "must have come to her knowledge." It would seem obvious, therefore, that "she at least knew that there was very grave doubt of her right; and notwithstanding she declared her intention to exercise it whenever she got a chance, and actually did have her name registered and voted." The newspaper summed up Pound's position: "It seemed to him there could be no doubt as to the intent, or as respects the law, and he therefore asked that the defendant be held to bail."

Van Voorhis rose to take exception to some of Pound's statements about the history of the states with regard to allowing women to vote. More important, perhaps, he rebutted Pound's argument based on interpreting the Fourteenth Amendment strictly by looking at the intent of the Framers. He argued that "whatever may have been the views of those who wrote the sections, we have nothing to do with them. But must construe it in its evident purport and meaning." This was the "plain text" doctrine of constitutional interpretation in its earliest incarnation. As to Anthony's intent or state of mind when she cast her ballot, Van Voorhis insisted that "this defendant believed she had a right to vote, and exercised it. She had no intent to break the law and is no criminal." He appealed to Storrs: "You must find that they committed an immoral act and intended to violate the law, or you cannot hold them."

Before Storrs could decide whether to hold Anthony for the grand jury, "some further discussion ensued between [Pound and Selden] respecting the right of States to regulate the right of voting." According to the Rochester newspaper, Pound argued "that Judge Selden's views would prevent any regulation," but Selden responded "that he distinctly admitted that the exercise of the right may be regulated, but it must be upon a basis of *equality*." For example, "It may be provided that no citizen shall vote till he is 21, or 25 years of age, but it cannot be denied to one person to vote at all, and the right be granted to another to vote when he becomes twenty-one years of age." Storrs had apparently heard enough, though he decided he could not deliver his decision. He "adjourned the case until Thursday at 2 p.m."

The next day the election inspectors who had registered the women and allowed them to vote appeared before a different commissioner, A. P. Ely. John Pound presented the case against Beverly W. Jones, Edwin T. Marsh, and William B. Hall, but according to the *New York Times*, the men did not have legal counsel. Instead, "Miss Susan B. Anthony appeared as counsel for the inspectors, and made an able argument in their behalf." The decision about whether to hold them for the grand jury was postponed until after the commissioner in the Anthony case delivered his decision. This made sense since the inspectors' case was tied to Anthony's; if Commissioner Storrs did not find probable cause that Anthony had violated the law, then there would be no reason to prosecute the inspectors.

At two o'clock on December 26, Anthony's hearing before Commissioner Storrs reconvened in his "office in the arcade." The newspaper account provides a vivid picture of the gathering:

The ladies on trial were pretty well represented and a number of their male relatives and friends were also at hand to lend them what aid and comfort they might stand in need of. The office presented rather the appearance of a social gathering than the arraignment of criminals. . . . The whole affair was conducted in an easy good natured style and the transgressors, for such the law now considers them, seemed to have little of the terror of their evil deeds before their eyes.

The commissioner was finally ready to announce his decision: there was sufficient evidence to find probable cause that Anthony and the other women had violated the law. He issued the order that "he would hold each of the accused to bail in the sum of $500," but since most of the other defendants were not present, Storrs decided "to adjourn the case until [the following] Monday when all the ladies accused would be present and then if bail is not put in he will commit them to Albany jail to await trial." At this point, "Deputy Marshal Keeney took a sort of informal charge of the prisoners but they remain in reality at liberty until Monday."

Though the newspaper tried to reassure the public that the women would not be jailed, since "bail will be forthcoming if desired," Anthony told everyone assembled in Storrs's office that she intended to "'fight it out on this line if it takes all summer' and will rather choose to be committed." The reporter for the Rochester paper told readers that though he was "not authorised to give any official statement of her plans and those of her counsel, yet our own conjecture is that she has no intention of spending any of the winter at Albany jail." Van Voorhis's strategy to challenge Anthony's imprisonment was no secret. The newspaper foresaw that "a writ of habeas corpus with the proceedings appropriate to testing its validity, would probably be the most direct method of procedure."

The *Democrat and Chronicle* clearly evinced a bias for the accused women in the case. "We looked more carefully at the ladies present than perhaps the rules of strict politeness would justify," the reporter admitted. He reassured his readers that "the majority of them were elderly and matronly looking women with thoughtful faces." Indeed, "the idea suggested itself that many of them were just the kind of persons one would like to see in charge of a sick room—considerate, patient and kindly. . . . They were all dressed plainly and in the style of garments adapted by their less strong minded sisters. . . . There was no indication in their appearance that any very rich or fashionable ladies belonged to the sacred band. . . . They seemed neither to belong to the poor nor the rich but to that middle class which is often more intelligent and always more independent than either." Obviously, such women were no threat to the community. All of the women, the reporter noted, "were distinctively American, there not being so far as we could judge a single foreigner among them," perhaps an inadvertent echo of the anti-immigration stance of the old American Party (Know-Nothing) members who had joined the Republicans in 1856.

At the reconvened hearing on the next to the last day of the year, Storrs allowed each of the women to post $500 bail. Though Anthony refused to post bail, the authorities released her when she filed her petition for a writ of habeas corpus. Anthony somewhat erroneously summed up the outcome of the hearing to Sarah Tucker Huntington in a letter later that evening: "The verdict of guilty was pronounced against the *Inspectors* & *Women* voters this A.M. & all refused to give bail." She also expressed confidence in Van Voorhis's strategy, telling "Mrs. H" that "we shall be rescued from the Marshall's hands on Writ of Habeus Corpus—& case carried hence to Supreme Court of the U.S.—the speediest process of getting there." That was the plan, perhaps, but as the ancient Greek proverb goes: "There's many a slip 'twixt the cup and the lip." Susan B. Anthony would learn the lesson of that saying for herself.

CHAPTER 4

"There Is No Time Now to Indulge in Personal Enmity"

January 1873–May 1873

While she waited for the district court to rule on her habeas corpus petition, Susan B. Anthony kept busy with her correspondence. She mailed off copies of the news reports of her arrest to contacts throughout the country and solicited contributions for a defense fund. Letters of support arrived daily. One of these came from her nemesis at the NWSA convention earlier in the year, Victoria Woodhull. Woodhull tried to mend fences. "There is no time, now," Woodhull wrote Anthony, "to indulge in personal enmity." She told Anthony that she had "not given serious attention to your case" because she had thought Anthony and the government had essentially concocted the case together, "to test the question of the right of citizens to the ballot."

But her own trouble with federal authorities—she had run afoul of the recently passed Comstock Act (which prohibited using the U.S. mail to disseminate lewd materials) when she had included reports of the Beecher-Tilton adultery scandal in her *Journal*—combined with the reports she had read of the December proceedings before Commissioner Storrs had changed Woodhull's mind. She told Anthony, "I think I have been in error as to the animus; and I fear they intend to crush out, in your person, the Constitutional Question of Woman's right to suffrage, as they are attempting, in my person, to establish a precedent for the suppression of recalcitrant Journals." Anthony was neither impressed by nor inclined to accept Woodhull's proffer of an olive branch. She simply ignored the missive, never bothering to reply to her flamboyant adversary.

Waiting idly did not suit Anthony. She planned for the national NWSA convention scheduled to be held in Washington, D.C., in mid-January 1873. "My time is full," she told her Wisconsin friend and ally Mathilde Franziska Anneke. "Washington *stares* me in the face for the 16th—hearing before Judge Hall the 10th & between times, working hard to get *my argument* proving our *women's votes not illegal* perfected & strong as possible." Nevertheless, she was extremely enthusiastic about the convention because she felt "that it is the most important hour—inasmuch as we are *nearing the final battle*." Her upcoming trial or the appeal of a denial of her writ would be the showdown that she expected would secure the movement's goal. She wrote to suffrage ally Martha Coffin Wright just the day before John Van Voorhis was to appear before the district judge to argue for the writ that while she worried about "the contingencies of getting our question to the Supreme Court," she nevertheless continued to "hope & trust that some of the chances will turn in that direction." She told Wright that she "never dreamed of the U.S. officers prosecuting *me* for voting—thought only that if I was refused—I should bring action against inspectors—But 'Uncle Sam' waxes wroth with *holy indignation* at such violation of his laws!!"

———

Speaking Out

Anthony appeared for the hearing on her petition for a writ of habeas corpus before federal district court judge Nathan K. Hall on January 10, 1873, in Buffalo, New York, where Hall was holding court that week. She "entered the United States court room at half past 10 o'clock . . . and took her seat, with raised veil, within the bar beside" her counsel, the honorable Henry R. Selden. The newspaper report of the hearing went to some trouble to describe her appearance: "The lady was dressed in a dark purple frock, dark cloth cloak, red scarf, black bonnet, plaid comforter and gold spectacles. Some slight streaks of gray appeared in her dark brown hair, but her face showed no wrinkles." As in the proceedings held the previous month in Rochester a little over seventy miles east of Buffalo, Anthony's appearance attracted spectators, "and all were curious to get a peep at one of whom they had heard so much." When she arrived in court a bankruptcy case was in process, "and Miss Anthony sat and listened in an apathetic manner, evidently impatient for the lawyers to leave off their other 'devilish work' and begin with her case."

It must have been a letdown for Anthony when her case was finally called. After the judge and the lawyers consulted, Hall took the matter under advisement and "decided to adjourn the case until the 21st," when Hall would be holding court in Albany. The delay was primarily due to the fact that the U.S. attorney for the northern district of New York, Richard Crowley, was "not prepared to make arg't for Gov't."

Whatever disappointment she might have felt at the delay in the progress of her case, the change of schedule and venue provided two advantages for her cause. First, although Albany, New York, was considerably farther from her home in Rochester, a little over 200 miles east and slightly south of the latter, Albany was the capital of the state and considerably closer to New York City; thus, public attention and press coverage of the hearing would be considerably greater. Second, the postponement gave Anthony the opportunity to preside at the NWSA meeting in Washington on the sixteenth. Ostensibly, Anthony continued in the custody of U.S. Deputy Marshal Elisha J. Keeney, but when she boarded the train to New York City on January 11, the first leg of her trip to D.C., "Marshall Keeney [was] at [the] Depot" and "quite protested against my going," but he did not detain her.

While U.S. Attorney Crowley was getting up to speed on the issues and arguments in the *Anthony* case, and the evidence and testimony that had been presented in Storrs's preliminary hearing, Anthony presided at the convention of the National Women's Suffrage Association. As the *New York Times* reported the event, the meeting "commenced its session . . . at Lincoln Hall," and "the audience was composed largely of ladies." Anthony made hay of her arrest in her opening remarks when she told the assembled women that "she stood here today by the kindness of the Marshal of the Auburn Prison." She was surrounded by stalwart supporters of woman suffrage, including her closest allies, Elizabeth Cady Stanton, Matilda Joslyn Gage, Lillie Devereaux Blake, and Belva Lockwood (who would complete her law school studies five months later and become the first woman lawyer admitted to practice before the U.S. Supreme Court in 1879).

Victoria Woodhull did not attend, and the proceedings went smoothly with no interruptions or dramatic confrontations. What a difference a year, and an arrest, had made. Discussion of Anthony's arrest and prospective trial dominated the proceedings. Stanton's "long speech" alluded "to what she considered the outrage perpetrated on Miss Anthony by imprisoning her, thus depriving the friends of women's rights of the services of a powerful advocate." Stanton also presented to the assemblage a "series of resolutions . . . declaring among other things that so long as women were denied the right of suffrage they were politically, civilly, socially enslaved, and that it is the duty of Congress, by appropriate legislation to protect women in the exercise of the right of suffrage under the Fifteenth [sic] Amendment to the Constitution of the United States."

Anthony's arrest had imbued the NWSA women with just the sense of unity and renewed purpose she had hoped for when she had marched down to the Rochester barbershop to register to vote less than three months before. The electrifying highlight of the convention came when Anthony herself took to the podium. When she submitted her manuscript to the printers, her lengthy speech, variations of which she would repeat to audiences numerous times before her trial, was entitled "Is It a Crime for a U.S. Citizen to Vote?" The title summed up her subject: a personal version of her legal brief in her defense.

The first part of her talk focused on a Natural Law argument for the right of all citizens to suffrage. Pointing to "the grand documents left to us by the fathers" of the country, she argued that they are "all alike, propose to *protect* the people in the exercise of their God-given rights: not one of them pretends to *bestow* rights." Though most of those documents espoused those rights on behalf of "men," Anthony made the case numerous times during the course of her speech to extending those rights to women. After invoking the *Declaration of Independence* on how government derives its power from the governed, she called upon an unnamed "Quaker preacher" for the proposition that God had conferred "the right *of all men*, and, '*consequently*' . . . '*of all women*,' to a voice in the government." This was a rare explicit reference to her background and experience in the Society of Friends. The Quakers, particularly the Hicksite Progressive branch in which Anthony had been raised, had a remarkably egalitarian view of gender participation in services and public life.

Somewhat later in her speech she took an even more direct approach to support her claim that the pronoun "male," when used in the law, was only shorthand for all persons, whether male or female. For, indeed, if you followed the interpretation that "the use of the masculine pronouns, he, his, and him in all the constitutions is proof that *only men were meant* to be included in their provisions . . . we shall insist that you be consistent and accept the other horn of the dilemma, and exempt women from taxation for the support of the government and from the penalties for the violation of laws."

A little later in her speech, she provided further authority for why the law's use of masculine pronouns should be interpreted to encompass women as well as men. In a U.S. Supreme Court case, *Silver v. Ladd* (74 U.S. 219 [1868]), handed down after the adoption of the Fourteenth Amendment, Anthony told the assemblage, the high court reversed all the lower state courts' interpretation of the use of the term "single man" in an Oregon homesteading statute to include women as well. Anthony quoted from the "Syllabus" of the case (a summary or headnote extrapolated from language sprinkled throughout the opinion and prepared by the reporter of the decision when it was published), though Anthony seemed to think she was quoting from Justice Miller's actual opinion. She told her audience that "the court said: 'In construing a benevolent statute of the government, made for the benefit of its own citizens . . . the words "single man" and "married man" may . . . be taken in a *generic sense*.'"

Misquotation, quoting headnotes or other sources' versions of a document rather than the body of the original, or taking a quotation out of context seems to have been a systematic problem with Anthony's rhetoric. Only a short time after her quotation from the *Silver v. Ladd* case, Anthony quoted another Supreme Court justice from an 1823 case that would be frequently and prominently quoted in both Anthony's trial and the civil suit brought by Virginia Minor to test the refusal of Missouri election officials to register her as a voter. The opinion in *Corfield v. Coryell* ostensibly supported the litigation strategy contention that voting was a fundamental right of citizens. Justice Bushrod Washington, a justice who few remember today and was a relatively obscure member of the Court even in the late nineteenth century, but who Anthony described as "one of the most distinguished judges of the Supreme Court," delivered the opinion while he was presiding as a circuit court judge for the Eastern District of Pennsylvania. In what was dicta, essentially a nonbinding aside, Washington had outlined some of the "fundamental" rights necessarily included in the "privileges and immunities" clause in Article IV, Section 2, of the Constitution (and by extension could be applied to the Fourteenth Amendment). Anthony cited Washington's opinion, though again she quoted not from the justice's actual opinion but rather from a speech to the House Judiciary Committee by former Ohio congressman and Washington, D.C., lawyer, Albert Gallatin Riddle.

The version Anthony quoted seemed to unequivocally support the interpretation that voting was a fundamental privilege of citizenship, but Washington's actual words were of a different order: "some of the particular privileges and immunities of citizens, which are clearly embraced by the general description of privileges deemed to be fundamental: to which may be added, the elective franchise, *as regulated and established by the laws or constitution of the state in which it is to be exercised*" (emphasis added). In other words, Washington recognized how essential the right to vote was to citizenship, but at the same time acknowledged that states could regulate the franchise. That last clause would seem to undercut the suffragists' claim to Washington's opinion as authority for their argument that voting was a fundamental right, one that the Fourteenth Amendment barred states limiting to men.

Indeed, Anthony's stirring rhetoric, time and again masked inherent weaknesses in her underlying arguments. In 1871 she told the women at an NWSA meeting that she had written to Senator Sumner, and his response, Anthony implied, provided unequivocal support to their cause. A careful reading of the quoted passage from Sumner's letter to Anthony suggests a more ambiguous stance. Sumner told her, "there is not a doubt but women have the constitutional right to vote," but asserted, "I will never vote for a 16th amendment [a proposed woman suffrage amendment] to guarantee it to them." Sumner's principled stance, he told Anthony, was that "the *original* Constitution" protected "*all citizens* in the equal enjoyment of their rights." In his own fashion, thus, Sumner had endorsed the New Departure or litigation strategy Francis and Virginia Minor had proposed and the woman suffrage movement had adopted. "I insist that they shall appeal to the courts, and through them establish the *powers* of our American Magna Charta to protect every citizen of the Republic," he said. Anthony did not dwell on the other message in Sumner's letter, that he would make no personal effort to guarantee women's right to vote.

In a similar fashion, Anthony selectively quoted from a letter Massachusetts congressman Benjamin F. Butler wrote her. Like Sumner, Butler agreed with the principle of woman suffrage but did not think congressional action to ensure the issue was warranted. "I do not believe anybody in Congress doubts that the Constitution authorizes the right of women to vote," he wrote Anthony, but "it is not *laws* we want; there are plenty of laws, good enough too." In other words, don't look to Congress for legislative redress. Rather, the problem for women's rights was that "*Administrative ability to enforce law* is the great want of the age. . . . If everybody would insist on the *enforcement* of law, the government would stand on a firmer basis; and questions would settle themselves." Butler and Sumner, ardent abolitionists before the war, focused their energies on ensuring the rights of freedmen against the encroachments of racist Southern resistance to Reconstruction—Butler authoring the original version of the 1871 Civil Rights Act (the Ku Klux Klan Act) and he and Sumner later writing the doomed Civil Rights Act of 1875—both of which were legislative attempts to fight racial discrimination. They saw legislative action as the answer to state-sponsored or condoned racial discrimination, but neither of them promised substantive legislative support to redress the grievances of women, certainly not in their correspondence with Anthony.

Anthony's first objective in her January 16, 1873, speech to the NWSA women was to exploit the federal prosecution against her to rally the faithful. Her second objective was to rehearse her rhetorical arguments for the campaign she would launch in New York to sway public opinion generally and the potential jury pool in particular. The most stirring passages echoed the women's rights arguments she and Stanton had been making for decades.

The first of these was to insist that without the vote, with no say in government or the laws that governed them, women were reduced to mere subjects, and "the blessings of liberty are *forever withheld* from *women* and their *posterity.*" This was not the principle on which the republic had been founded and "against which our Revolutionary *mothers* as well as fathers rebelled." The founding generation's eighteenth-century Enlightenment rhetoric resounded with equality and liberty language upon which the women's rights movement had relied since the Seneca Falls Declaration of Sentiments over twenty years earlier. Anthony employed it again to condemn a government restricted to men. "To women this government is not a democracy; it is not a republic," she forcefully proclaimed to the assemblage. "It is an odious aristocracy—a hateful oligarchy of *sex!*" One can almost imagine the fervent applause that must have erupted as Anthony uttered that last sentence with its published (and undoubtedly oral) exclamation point.

Anthony was not finished with this point. After further textual analysis of case and statute, she exhorted her audience: "Then, to be a citizen of this republic is no more than to be a *subject of an empire!* You and I, and all true and patriotic citizens, must *repudiate* this *base* conclusion. We all *know* that *American citizenship,* without addition or qualification, means the possession of equal rights, civil and political. We all know that the crowning glory of every citizen of the United States is that he can either give or withhold his vote from every law and every legislator under the government."

The second theme she borrowed from antebellum women's movement rhetoric was to analogize the plight of women, particularly married women, to that of slaves. "I will prove to you that the class of citizens for which I now plead, and to which I belong," Anthony instructed her audience, "may be and are, by all the principles of our government, and many of the laws of the states, *included* under the term of 'previous condition of servitude.'" After all, she argued, "What is servitude?" Her answer: "The condition of a slave." The next obvious question was "What is a slave?" Then, answering her own question, she promulgated that a slave is "a person who is robbed of the proceeds of his labor," or "a person who is subject to the will of another." She pointed to the abhorrent laws of the late Confederate states that had so defined "the negro." It was not a stretch, given those propositions, she argued, that "by the *law* of every state in this Union to-day, North as well as South, the *married woman* has no right to the custody and control of her person. The wife belongs to her husband; and if she refuses obedience to his will, he may use *moderate* correction." The analogy to slavery was a pointed one—its tip aimed at the male abolitionists who had failed to support woman suffrage.

She went on to point to the various oppressions under which married women functioned in most states. Anthony concluded her comparison of antebellum negro slavery to woman's condition by calling on a bit of the Bard (though she simply attributed her quotation to "an old saying"): "A rose by any other name would smell as sweet." Or, she implied in this case, slavery by another name would be just as odious.

The convention responded enthusiastically. Rededicated to the cause and galvanized by Anthony's words and her imminent federal criminal prosecution, the organization agreed to pursue a project to raise $100,000 through shares of stock in a company to publish a new "Woman's National Paper." Anthony could finally put to rest her disappointment in the failure of her and Stanton's *Revolution*. It is an ironic postscript that though Anthony's upcoming trial inspired the convention to pass the plan for the new women's newspaper, it ultimately failed because Anthony's attention and efforts went into preparing for her defense rather than fund-raising for the newspaper project. Still, on Monday, January 20, when Anthony boarded the train to Albany, she must have been rejuvenated by the convention and quite optimistic about the next day's proceedings in the district court. She would at last get her case argued in a federal courtroom, and Judge Hall would finally rule on her habeas corpus petition.

———

Back to the Courtroom

Anthony seemed comfortable with the district judge who would hear her petition; she had been told that district court Judge Nathan K. Hall was "considered an honest judge." Hall, described in his *New York Times* obituary as "a man of much ability" and "a genial though retiring disposition," was born in the small town (population of approximately 4,750 at the time of Hall's birth) of Marcellus, southwest of Syracuse, in Onondaga County. After working as a cobbler and farmer in the rural town that averaged over one hundred inches of snow per year, he decided to study law. He was lucky to be taken on to study law in the offices of future president Millard Fillmore, who made him his law partner after Hall passed the bar in 1832.

Like his mentor, Hall assayed a career in politics. He served as deputy clerk of Erie County, was then elected clerk of the Board of Supervisors, and, finally, he served as a member of the Board of Aldermen of Buffalo. In 1839, then governor of New York, William Henry Seward appointed Hall a "master of chancery," which in New York at that time was essentially a judge of equity cases. Seward was a reformer, a Whig who became a leader of the new Republican Party, an ardent abolitionist, and secretary of state under Lincoln. Hall served for two years before being elected a judge of Erie County. Four years later, in 1846, Hall was elected as a Whig to both the New York State legislature and to the U.S. House of Representatives but served only one term in Congress. When Fillmore acceded to the presidency upon the death of President Zachary Taylor, he appointed his old friend and law partner postmaster general and then two years later, when a federal district judgeship opened up in the northern circuit in New York, Fillmore appointed Hall to it.

On Tuesday afternoon in the Albany City Hall courtroom, Judge Hall convened the hearing on Anthony's petition for a writ of habeas corpus. According to the *Rochester Democrat and Chronicle*, which dispatched a special correspondent to the capital to report on the proceedings, "Rochester overflowed into Albany to-day." A surfeit of Rochester's ruling elite made the trek, leaving one to wonder who was left behind to run and protect the city. "Wherever you turn," the hometown reporter told his readers, "you notice familiar faces." Among the onlookers, he listed "chief Sherman and several of the best known members of our police force, Marshal Quinby and his associates, Colonel Brinker and his military associates, and . . . Mabbitt, [the] county clerk, and Morrison city clerk."

All listened to Henry Selden's lengthy two-hour argument on behalf of Anthony "for her discharge from custody." Later in her diary, Anthony confided that she thought "Judge Selden's ag't vastly improved." Richard Crowley, the U.S. attorney, probably confident of what Hall would decide, "made no reply." When the lawyers finished making their cases, Judge Hall announced his decision. Later newspaper accounts disagreed as to whether Hall commented on the right of women to vote. According to the *Rochester Union and Advertiser*, Hall's opinion told the court that "I think the petitioner has no right to vote." According to the Republican *Rochester Democrat and Chronicle*, Hall never expressed "any opinion on the merits of the question whether women have a right to vote or not."

But neither paper claimed Hall was unaware of why Anthony's counsel had filed for the writ and what she really hoped to do. Hall told the court that he knew that the petitioners had filed "this order for the purpose of allowing the case to be moved to a higher tribunal." Hall would oblige them, ruling that "I discharge the writ of habeas corpus and allow the defendant to go to the Supreme Court of the United States." Though before the high court heard the appeal all expected that "the appeal from [Hall's] decision will be taken to the circuit court, and Judge Woodruff and Mr. Crowley will decide in the morning what time it may be heard." Anthony was then "remanded . . . back to Marshall Keeney," though "custody" was still virtual since she was not yet placed under lock and key.

From her diary we know that she stayed at the Albany home of friend and suffrage ally Lydia Mott after the hearing. She even appeared before and spoke to the suffrage committee of the state's constitutional commission. Anthony also began her public relations campaign to convince potential male jurors in her case to the rightness of her cause. In her account of the trial, Ann Gordon found that Anthony "arranged for 3,000 copies of [Selden's] argument to be published as a pamphlet . . . [and] While awaiting the printer, she carried page proofs to the offices of New York City's principal newspapers and mailed them to editors as far away as St. Louis." But before she departed the state capital she contacted a friendly publisher of a western New York newspaper. Indeed, he was guaranteed a scoop, according to Anthony. She urged him to publish Judge Selden's courtroom argument from two days previously: "now don't delay a minute—& you can have this argument of Mr Selden's same date with the Albany City Journal." She admitted that she had also "sent copies to Democrat & Union [the two papers in her home

{ *Chapter Four* }

town of Rochester] & urged both to publish it—If you will only *all* do so—all *Western New York* will be convinced that my *vote* was *legal* & *not a crime.*" Thinking that her trial would take place in the city where she had voted, Anthony told this publisher, Mr. Rew, that "we must get the *men* of Rochester so *enlightened* that no *jury* of *twelve* can be found to convict us."

Anthony had either lost sight of the U.S. Supreme Court appeal strategy and instead had started to hope for vindication of woman suffrage by an acquittal by the jury or was playing the acquittal card for the benefit of the media. Or she was hedging her bets.

The *New York Times* editorialized about the outcome in Hall's court. "In the circuit Court at Albany, yesterday," the *Times* editors wrote, "Miss Susan B. Anthony made one more step toward the consummation of her hopes—a final decision on the right to vote under the recent amendments to the Constitution." The paper was by no means applauding Anthony's stand. They argued that "Miss Anthony is not in the remotest degree likely to gain her case, nor if it were ever so desirable that women should vote, would hers be a good case." The editors condemned Anthony's attempt to win woman suffrage through what they clearly thought was a judicial end run around the legislative process. "When so important a change in our Constitution as she proposes is made, it will be done openly and unmistakably, and not be left to the subtle interpretation of a clause adopted for a wholly different purpose."

Stanton did not let the editorial go unanswered. She methodically challenged each of the assertions in the piece. In answer to the claim that Anthony was unlikely to win her case, Stanton recounted how her friend won over Judge Selden when she had gone to him for advice in advance of casting her ballot. "When she first applied to Henry R. Selden, one of the ablest lawyers in the State of New-York, to defend her in the Courts, he said, 'You have no law to stand upon, and I do not like to go into Court with any client whose case is not backed by law.'" According to Stanton, Anthony replied: "You are mistaken, Sir . . . I have law, Constitution, and the opinions of able Judges and lawyers on my side, and here are the documents for your thoughtful consideration, and $100 fee for your trouble. I will call again in a few days, after you have had time to read" the materials.

Indictment

Immediately after Hall denied Anthony's habeas corpus petition, the federal grand jury was impaneled to determine whether Anthony should be indicted. After the prosecuting attorney presented his case, the grand jury deliberated whether to issue the indictment. Neither the defendant nor her counsel got to present their case or dispute the prosecutor's evidence.

At trial in a criminal case, the prosecution bears the initial burden of proof and must make their case by the familiar and highest standard of proof: beyond a reasonable doubt. For an indictment the prosecutor need only convince the grand jury that he has met the "preponderance of the evidence" standard, essentially that the scales of justice tip just a little in favor of the prosecution over the defense. In the *Anthony* case, the U.S. attorney for the Northern District of New York, Richard Crowley, easily met that standard.

Richard Crowley was born in rural Pendleton, New York, a town on the southern edge of Niagara County east of the city of Niagara Falls. When he was only twenty-nine years old he was elected to the New York senate but served only four years. He had made some powerful friends, however, including New York political boss Senator Roscoe Conkling and his protégé, future president Chester Arthur. Crowley, a devotee of the spoils system, ran afoul of Arthur when as president Arthur decided to become a champion of civil service reform. This undercut almost all of Crowley's political clout in western New York. According to an 1895 *New York Times* political portrait of Crowley, when he tried one more time for election to the state senate, he was "only a power for evil in Niagara County . . . unable to get anything for himself or very much for his friends, but he has kept his enemies out of a good many things." Crowley was indifferent to the value of money, having spent several fortunes, and as of 1895 he was reported to be poor, "although he has always had a lucrative law practice." It was political power that Crowley held dear. He was described as "a man of reticence," who "invariably wears a slouch hat . . . but in adversity holds his friends better than any other man in Western New-York." At the time of the *Anthony* trial, Crowley was serving as U.S. attorney for the Northern District of New York. President

Grant had appointed him to the post in March 1871, and he served for eight years until he "resigned this office to go to Congress."

There is little left in the record of the twenty "good and lawful men" who voted to indict Susan B. Anthony. There are only a few about whom one can derive additional information. In 1846 Brace Millerd, who lived near section 11 of the Erie Canal (Amsterdam, New York), gave a deposition to a Select Committee of the Assembly of the State of New York "investigating frauds in the expenditures of public moneys upon canals." He testified that from what he had observed, the quality of work the Petrie and Harrington Company had done in the construction of the canal had been necessary, and "it was well-done, and the wall well laid." He admitted that he was a close acquaintance of both Petrie and Harrington for fifteen or twenty years. James D. Wasson was a prosperous New Yorker also connected to the canal trade. He was a founder and partner in the Butterfield and Wasson Company, which specialized in "the express transport of goods, valuables, and specie between New York City and Buffalo, New York, and points in the Midwest" and which, in 1850, had consolidated with two other companies to form what would eventually become the American Express Company. The New York State "Red Book" (a register of the state government and its officials) recorded that Wasson served as "Doorkeeper" in the 1835–39 sessions of the New York State legislature. Peter H. Bradt, a resident of Albany, served as a justice of the peace in the 1830s, while Loring W. Osborn did the same in 1867. James Goold was the Democratic nominee for mayor of Albany in 1847 but lost to the incumbent, William Parmelee.

The remaining fifteen grand jurors are lost to history other than as names recorded on the Anthony indictment, though many carried surnames with long and distinguished genealogical histories in New York: Whitbeck, Van Schoonhoven, Van Natten, and Winne. Even from this meager biographical information it is clear that the grand jury convened to indict Anthony was hardly a jury of her peers. These jurors were all men of substance and property, members of the social and political elite of the state brought together to uphold the status quo. The indictment came down, as expected, by the end of the week.

The indictment itself followed a standard format. It named Anthony and asserted that she had "with force and arms, etc." and "knowingly, wrongfully and unlawfully" voted in the 1872 election "against the peace of the United States of America and their dignity." The only variation from the usual form of such indictments was the inclusion of the parenthetical phrase "the said Susan B. Anthony being then and there a person of the female sex," a fact which "the said Susan B. Anthony then and there well knew." This, of course, was the basis for the indictment's claim that Anthony had voted "without having a lawful right" to do so.

The indictment actually articulated two counts upon which she was being charged, though close reading of the second count shows a mere repetition of the first. The only reason for the two identical counts was that she had cast two federal ballots (any ballots she might have cast for state or municipal offices was not the province of federal law or courts). The two federal votes were for "a Representative in the Congress of the United States for the State of New York at large, and for a Representative in the Congress of the United States for said twenty-ninth Congressional District." The at-large representative was actually the delegate pledged to vote for Grant in the electoral college; the other vote was for the representative that the district would send to the House of Representatives in the forty-third Congress. The indictment concludes with the endorsement of U.S. Attorney Richard Crowley, the date of January 24, 1873, and a notation that Anthony "pleads not guilty."

As soon as the indictment was delivered, bail of $1,000 was set and Anthony's trial was scheduled for May, four months later, at the district court for the Northern District of New York, in her hometown of Rochester. Judge Selden promptly put up Anthony's bail, and she was released. There was some dispute as to whether Selden's paying Anthony's bail was responsible for Anthony's appeal of Hall's denial of her writ of habeas corpus case not reaching the Supreme Court on the fast track. Evidence that Anthony later blamed Selden's chivalry in posting her bond for derailing her appeal is controversial. Since she was not in jail she couldn't claim unlawful detention. But Ann Gordon argues that whatever Anthony believed, "the legal situation is not clear; the Court considered other cases in which defendants were on bail."

Taking the Case to the People

In the meantime, the indefatigable Anthony was off on her travels once again to fight for the cause, though winter weather, a "terrible snow storm—trains delayed west & south," succeeded in slowing her progress. While awaiting the resumption of train service she collected the page "proofs of Judge Seldens arg't at 9—& [then] took [the] *ten* [o'clock] train for N.Y." She visited friends and supporters at every stop, as well as making a point to drop off copies of Selden's argument at the offices of various New York City newspapers. She recorded in her diary that on Saturday she "breakfasted at cousin E. Caldwells—all well—called on Mrs Phelps, Wilbour & Murray—then Tribune Times, Sun, Herald, World, with proof of Judge Seldens argument." Though the *New York Times* did not publish Selden's arguments, it did report on the indictment: "Miss Anthony and Other Lady Voters Indicted."

Then it was back on the train for Anthony's next stop in Philadelphia, finally reaching Washington, D.C., on Sunday. In the capital, Anthony met with Helen M. Barnard, a member of NWSA with a background in journalism, who Anthony planned to have edit the new journal the convention had agreed to launch. She remained in D.C. for several more days, and despite another "terrible snow storm" she "still made [the] round" to look after business. The peripatetic Anthony proceeded to ride to Baltimore, Philadelphia, Toledo, Ohio, Chicago, Fort Wayne and Marion, Indiana, and Buffalo, New York, before finally returning home to Rochester on March 3.

The very next day, Tuesday, March 4, Anthony and two of her friends and supporters defied election officials by voting in the city election. On this occasion, she was not arrested, probably because officials believed that with a case already pending there was no need to charge her again. But the prosecution against Anthony did suppress some of her fellow Rochester suffragists. As she recorded in her diary, there were "only three of us . . . the rest of women all frightened lest fine & imprisonment come."

Anthony returned to Philadelphia for the Pennsylvania Citizens Suffrage Association meeting. There she addressed the gathering, and donations for the cause (and probably for her defense fund) were collected at the door. As the *Philadelphia Inquirer* reported on March 19 under the heading "More Male Oppression," "The woman's suffrage convention was brought to an abrupt termination last night." The reason for the disruption was that "an officer appeared on the scene, and, after observing several parties pay for admission, demanded to be shown the license for the *entertainment*"(emphasis added). Apparently, Anthony took umbrage and "Susan B. Anthony, in characteristic words," whatever the newspaper thought those might be, "adjourned the convention." Not satisfied with merely disrupting the meeting, the following morning the Philadelphia authorities served a warrant "on Miss Anthony and her associates for violation of the license ordinance."

It was now time for Anthony to turn her energies to Monroe County, where her trial was scheduled to be held in May, "to prove to the *men* of Monroe—who may possibly—12 of whom must—*be* my *jurors* at the May term—that it is *not a crime* for a U.S. citizen to offer a vote." Winter in upstate New York can be bitterly cold and severe snowstorms frequent. Despite a third "terrific snowstorm" and illnesses among her family and close-knit circle of friends, Anthony trudged on through her speaking tour of Monroe County. Even when on March 22 she came down with a severe cold or flu, "myself feeling unable to stir," she boarded the train to West Henrietta, New York, for her next speech. She treated herself with "gruel & wet compress" on her arrival. Three days later, after three more talks before audiences in Henrietta and then Fairport, she recorded that despite the "fine audience" she suffered the "hardest hotel bed—added to cold . . . just about all I can do to keep going." The next day she confronted that "terrific snowstorm" and complained that "my cold most dreadful," but found "there were a 100 people" waiting to hear her speak, which served as "proof that one must never fail to be on hand." She traveled between March 27 and April 20, visiting fifteen more towns, including Rochester. On April 3, in Corinthian Hall, one thousand people paid admission to hear her, she boasted.

Late spring, exhausted and still feeling the aftereffects of her illness, Anthony remained at home "trying to rest." She did visit with her sister Guelma, "Sister Gula seemed very much brighter than for a long time—Oh if it would only *last*." Guelma had loyally joined

Anthony in voting the previous November, but she suffered from tuberculosis and died on November 9, 1873.

The rest, if not the visit, must have benefitted Anthony, because on Saturday she recorded in her diary that she treated herself to a new ten dollar bonnet—"enormous just for the ribbon & jet ornament & inside lining & face blue silk—but very tasteful—yes & half yard of spotted lace for veil." The staid Quaker schoolteacher had a taste for fashion, within moderation, and undoubtedly planned to wear the new bonnet with veil at her trial.

The next day she met with her attorneys, Judge Selden and John Van Voorhis, even though it was a Sunday. The time set for her trial was rapidly approaching, and now that she had returned to Rochester, Anthony and her attorneys needed to clarify their defense strategy. The meeting may have also been prompted by news from only a little over a week earlier about the Supreme Court decision in the Myra Bradwell case, an ill omen. Bradwell had sued the State of Illinois for refusing to grant her a license to practice law. Her case was relevant to Anthony's own because Bradwell, too, had relied on the privileges or immunities clause of the Fourteenth Amendment.

After discussing with Selden and Van Voorhis the discouraging news about the Supreme Court's rejection of Bradwell's suit and the justices' narrow reading of the privileges or immunities clause to allow Illinois the right to discriminate against women, Anthony contacted Republican congressman Benjamin F. Butler, the same correspondent she had quoted in her January convention address. NWSA had a meeting scheduled in New York in the beginning of May, and Anthony had to have something to present to the assemblage to counteract the blow the *Bradwell* decision had dealt against the cause. She begged him, "please—help our Cause just now—by giving me your opinion of the decision—whatever it is." No doubt she thought Butler, with his Washington contacts, may have seen Justice Miller's opinion.

In fact, few had access to the full opinion. Publication of Supreme Court opinions in the nineteenth century took weeks. Anthony had written to another contact, Washington attorney Francis Miller, about *Bradwell* and the *Slaughter-House Cases*, which had been handed down on consecutive days in mid-April, but he informed her that he "had not then seen those decisions, indeed they were not ready for distribution until today [May 5]." Without access to the Court's opinion and reasoning, Anthony had only partisan and unreliable newspaper reports—and she was thoroughly disgusted with press coverage of the case and worried about its effect on the feminist faithful.

Even though Butler had probably seen the coverage for himself, Anthony complained in her letter to him that "the whole Democratic Press is Jubilant over this infamous interpretation of the amendments." The partisan reports in the Democratic papers could not have surprised Anthony, but she was furious that "not a Republican paper that I have seen has dared to declare the amendments mean *just what they—say all persons* &c." She angrily denounced the decision and its reception by the press in no uncertain terms: "It is a virtual concession of all we fought for in the late War" which she asserted was "the supremacy of the *National Gov't* to *protect* the rights of *all persons—all citizens—against the state's attempts* to *deny* or *abridge*."

Anthony connected the *Bradwell* decision to her own upcoming trial in her plea to Butler: "The right word spoken at our Convention—will greatly help my *trial the* week following." A letter from Butler, she hoped, would not only excite the convention audience but also assist in her own case. "I find *Judges* & Courts are influenced by *popular opinion*—not a little," she told the Massachusetts congressman. She had certainly been trying to do that with her speaking tour of the county. "I have just closed a canvass of this county—from which my jurors are to be drawn." And she was confident that she had, indeed, had an impact on the jury pool. She told Butler, "I rather guess the U.S. District Attorney who is very bitter—will hardly find *twelve men* so *ignorant* on the *citizen's rights*—as to *agree* on a *verdict* of *Guilty*." Anthony appeared unconcerned with the notion of an impartial jury or one that had no preconceived sense of the matter before it.

The annual NWSA meeting, to which Anthony referred in her letter to Senator Butler, was a relatively low key affair—"[it was as] good as could be with *no* newspaper advertising," she recorded in her diary. But it was an important anniversary for woman suffrage and women's rights. As every speaker applauded and the newspaper coverage prominently reported, 1873 marked "the twenty-fifth anniversary of the movement for woman's enfranchisement." Indeed, it was "twenty-five years ago, in the little village of Seneca Falls, N.Y. [that] Mrs. E. C. Stanton and Lucretia Mott issued a call for a meeting advocating woman's right to suffrage." Despite the slight revisionism of the history of the Seneca Falls conference they heard, the congregation in Apollo Hall in New York City that day could justifiably celebrate. Anthony told the audience of "the progress that had been made . . . and spoke in glowing terms of the success that had attended [their] efforts since that time."

The convention adopted several resolutions, some of which looked toward the past and recognized Stanton and Mott's role "as the pioneers in this grandest reform of the age." But the three central resolutions focused on the present: Anthony's upcoming trial. The first asserted the general proposition "that in the prosecution and trial of Susan B. Anthony, a citizen of the United States for having cast a ballot at the last election, the Government of the United States declares it is a crime to vote, thus attempting to undermine the very foundation of the Republic." The second connected Anthony's trial to the woman's movement generally because, "in this trial, Susan B. Anthony represents one-half of the people; that on this trial the whole power of the United States is arrayed against the women of the nation—against law-abiding, tax-paying women citizens." Thus, the prosecution of Anthony became a prosecution against all American women.

A third resolution turned this grievance into a rallying cry that warned that the citizenship rights of every American were at stake if Anthony and the women could be denied their rights: "*Resolved*, That this trial of Susan B. Anthony, though ostensibly involving the political status of women alone, in reality questions the right of every man to share in the Government, that it is not Susan B. Anthony or the women of the Republic who alone are on trial to-day, but is the Government of the United States which is on trial; it is republican institutions which are on test, and that as decision is rendered for or against the political rights of citizenship, so will the men of America find themselves free or slaves."

Several additional resolutions adopted at the convention, while not specifically mentioning the case against Anthony, indicated how far the arrest had riven the fabric of the alliance between the women's movement and the Republican Party. After citing all the contributions women had made during the Civil War and afterward to the Republican cause, they resolved that "the Republican Party, since its last election, has broken faith with woman."

It was now time for Anthony to turn her attention to the trial, which was scheduled to begin in less than a week. As soon as she stepped off the train back in Rochester on Friday, May 9, she met with Judge Selden, John Van Voorhis, the other indicted voters, and the indicted inspectors at the home of her cousin Asa's son Daniel, the husband of Lottie Anthony, one of the women who had voted with Susan. At this meeting the group undoubtedly discussed what impact the recent *Slaughter-House* and *Bradwell* Supreme Court cases might have upon their trials.

Anthony had gotten a reply from Francis Miller, the Washington attorney she had beseeched for information about the cases, and he had enclosed with his letter copies of the opinions. On the day before the scheduled trial, Anthony studied Justice Miller's analysis of the issues. She told Isabella Beecher Hooker in a letter dated March 12 that "this last eve before the Court convenes—I have given to Mr. Justice Fields dissenting opinion—As Mr Francis Miller says—on any other class of persons, save women—this opinion would settle *our* question." Miller's analysis of *Bradwell* and the *Slaughter-House Cases* was not as sanguine as Anthony portrayed it in her letter to Hooker. He quoted language from both Justice Field and Justice Bradley in the *Slaughter-House Cases* that, if "applied to any other subject than the rights of women, would indicate that the minority were fully prepared to admit, that recent amendments to the constitution—the new *magna charta* as one of the Justices styles them, recognised the rights of suffrage in women. . . . Such language on any other subject would be conclusive, but the crust of custom and prejudice is hard and strong, and the heat of the lava of regeneration may not yet have weakened it sufficiently to allow of its destruction and removal."

Anthony put the best face on what would turn out to be precedent against the woman suffrage question at her trial and later in the Virginia Minor case in the Supreme Court. She also remarked to Isabella Hooker on other dramatic news from the Court that she worried might have an even greater impact on the cause: "So the Chief Justice is gone over the river," by which she referred to the death of Salmon P. Chase. Chase had dissented without opinion in the *Bradwell* case. President Grant's choice for his successor could have an enormous impact on the Anthony case if it reached the Court, as she told Hooker, "who shall fill his seat—is now the question that will determine much for or against us." Indeed, the next chief justice would author the opinion in the woman suffrage case that would make it to the Court, but that case would not be Susan B. Anthony's.

The Trial that Wasn't

On Tuesday, May 13, Anthony and her fellow defendants—the women who had voted with her and the inspectors who allowed them—dutifully showed up in the U.S. District Court and waited for their case to be called, but there was "no call of either case." The next day everyone returned, "hanging round the U.S. District Court but no hope of a call of our case." For the next several days, Anthony attended to other matters; on Thursday she joined a group of disaffected Rochester women to found the Women Taxpayers' Association of Monroe County, a "large group," according to Ann Gordon, "that supported SBA during her trial." She also spent time "devot[ing] [her]self to [her] sister Gula," who was "very feeble" and "too ill."

Finally, on Thursday, May 22, the cases of Anthony, the other women voters, and the election inspectors were called in Judge Nathan K. Hall's district courtroom. After nearly ten days of delay, the public had wondered "if any action was to be taken in the case," but some leak from the courthouse must have alerted the press and court watchers that a hearing was imminent. "In the afternoon there was a large attendance of spectators who watched the proceedings with much interest. . . . About 3 o'clock an end was put to the suspense of both the principal actors themselves and the lookers on [when] Mr. Pound, the assistant district attorney, who with a formidable bale of legal documents in his hand arose" and began to call on each of the women defendants to stand for the "formal recital of the charges" against them. He then called upon each of them to plead guilty or not guilty. As each woman's name was called, she responded "with a clear and firm voice that she was not guilty." One of Anthony's codefendants, "Mrs. De Garno, a venerable looking lady, adding with much emphasis that she had 'done only what she had a perfect right to do.'"

Some of the indicted women had not shown up for the arraignment, "which Judge Selden explained by stating that some of the 'criminals' were at that time engaged in teaching the men of the future in our public schools but after school hours they would not be missing." Selden was chiding the Court for both the sudden notice for calling the case and pressing the point that while society entrusted future voting men's education to women but at the same time refused to entrust their teachers with the vote.

At this point U.S. Attorney Richard Crowley made a motion to the court to have "the indictments against these persons be sent to the Circuit Court for trial, at Canandaigua, on the third Monday in June." According to the *Rochester Democrat and Chronicle*, "Crowley said that after due consideration he had determined . . . [because Supreme Court justice Ward] Hunt was to hold and preside at that term." Was this the reason Anthony had sat waiting in vain to have her case called for over a week? It is highly probable that, in fact, Crowley had been working behind the scenes with Judge Hall to arrange this very maneuver. Crowley even mentioned in court when he made his change in venue motion that "Judge Hall might be associated with [Hunt] and thus the question involved be decided with an added weight of authority."

Reading between the lines, Crowley's suggestion that Hall would sit with Hunt in judging the case could be read as a concession to the district judge that the high profile case was not being taken away from him so as to gain Hall's assent to the motion. Judge Selden vigorously opposed the motion, undoubtedly because Rochester was Anthony's home and she had spent the last three months giving talks to audiences throughout Monroe County. Any jury drawn from Rochester and its environs was very likely to be friendly to Anthony and her cause.

Selden told the court "that his clients had been indicted in Albany but resided in this city. They had always been ready and even anxious for trial—in fact it was against the wishes of both the accused and their counsel that their cases were not now moved." Of course, this was probably the very reason Crowley wanted the trial venue changed. One newspaper editorial writer, in the *Worcester (Massachusetts) Daily Spy* came out and said as much: "The district attorney is afraid to trust the case to a jury from [Monroe] county." Crowley had also asked Judge Hall that "all [the defendants] be continued under bail," despite the delay in the trial and the fact that "it had been agreed that the case of Miss Anthony, who had been indicted and arraigned at Albany, would be made a test case. [And] It would not be necessary for the other accused ladies to be present."

Selden must have sensed that the postponement and change of venue were a done deal even before the Judge Hall ruled on Crowley's motion. He conceded that "if they were not to be tried here, he had no disposition to oppose the motion of the district attorney to send them to Canandaigua; but he protested earnestly, against keeping them under bonds, other than their own recognizance." Crowley protested this last point, as he "saw no reason why the usual forms of law should not be gone through in this case, or why any indulgence should be shown to the accused." Crowley might refer to them as "accused ladies," but "he did not feel justified in conceding anything to them which he would not to other violators of law."

Selden responded by pointing Crowley to the law of the state, which stated that "when a prisoner stands ready for trial and the prosecution does not proceed with it, he is entitled to be discharged on his own recognizance." In other words, Selden was not requesting special treatment for the defendants because they were women; he only asked that they be treated equally as men under the law.

"Against the strenuous opposition of counsel for the defendants, the Court ordered all the indictments to be tried at the June Circuit Court," the *New York Times* recorded the next day. But Judge Hall seemingly gave one concession to the defense, claiming he "had a discretion which he might exercise in this case." He explained that "the use of bail was to prevent escape; but no disposition appeared in any of the defendants to shirk any responsibility that might be cast upon them." Thus he ruled that, "in view of all the circumstances, he would order no more than that each of the accused be allowed to depart upon her own recognizance in the sum of $400 to appear at Canandaigua in June."

In fact, Hall had not granted the defendants anything. When the accused is released on his own recognizance, that means no money bail is required—that his word that he will appear is all that is necessary. By requiring $400 bail, though that was a reduction over the $1,000 previously required, Hall had actually conceded, in principle, the bail issue to Crowley. By phrasing the ruling so contradictorily, the judge, knowing he was sitting court in Anthony's home town, was probably playing to the public and to the press, who he hoped would not realize what he had actually done.

No further objections were raised and "the required bonds were promptly made out and executed, and the strong-minded asserters of their right to the ballot once more inhaled the air of freedom." Free or not, this was not the time for Anthony to rest. With the case moved to Canandaigua on June 17, she had less than a month to prepare. As she noted in her diary the day after the hearing in Judge Hall's court, she "made out [a] programme to canvass [the] County of Ontario & ordered bills printed" to be distributed announcing her speaking tour.

At least one supportive editorial writer at the *Worcester Daily Spy* alerted to Anthony's plans to campaign throughout Ontario County supported her right to blanket the county by speaking to crowds that might include potential jurors. "Some foolish and bigoted people who edit newspapers in that part of the world, are complaining that Miss Anthony's proceedings are highly improper, inasmuch as they are intended to influence the decision of a cause pending in the courts. They even talk about contempt of court, and declare that Miss Anthony should be compelled to desist from making these insidious harangues." But the editorial writer believed "that she has the same right which people, male or female, have to explain her political views and make converts to them if she can. We have never known it claimed before that a person accused of an offence was thereby deprived of the common right of free speech." Though the prosecution and their supporters were right to fear Anthony's ability to sway public opinion, that same newspaper went so far as to predict that "by the time the case comes on an Ontario jury will be as little likely to convict as a Monroe jury is now supposed to be."

Anthony was not alone in carrying her message to potential jurors. Her NWSA colleague Matilda Joslyn Gage spoke to audiences in Canandaigua "and 16 other towns of Ontario county previous to Miss Anthony's Trial." Matilda Joslyn Gage was a longtime supporter of women's rights and suffrage and an ally of Anthony and Stanton. Gage, like Stanton, was married and the mother of four children. She was reputed to have been quite feminine and dressed quite stylishly. One contemporary reporter, according to Elizabeth B. Warbasse, her biographer, described Gage in 1852 "as a 'medium-sized, and lady-like looking woman, dressed in tasty plaid silk, with two flounces.'" Her contemporaries all commented on her weak constitution, poor health, and invalidism, despite which she traveled; attended nearly every NWSA meeting, serving as president of the group from May 1875 to May 1876 and testifying before House and Senate committees; published numerous articles and tracts; and in 1880 attended all the national political conventions to lobby for woman's suffrage. She titled her speech to audiences in Ontario County "The United States on Trial; *not* Susan B. Anthony." However, Gage "never developed an outstanding platform personality."

NWSA's secretary, Lillie Devereaux Blake, agreed. In an eloquent and lengthy letter to the editor of the *New York Times*, she declared that if "the District Attorney thinks of these means to bring [the Anthony case] among people who had not heard Miss Anthony, he was entirely mistaken, for that dauntless woman has already started on the canvass of Ontario County." Blake concluded her missive with an appeal to the *Times*'s readers: "Such courage and energy as [Anthony's] deserve admiration, and what is more, support. The expenses which she has assumed are very heavy and she has no resources to depend upon but what she can earn for herself from day to day. . . . Contributions to the Anthony defense fund are to be sent to Mrs. C. S. Lozier, Chairman of the Committee, No. 361 West Thirty-fourth-street."

CHAPTER 5

"On the Part of the Government, There Is No Question"

June 17–18, 1873

When Susan B. Anthony's trial finally took place June 17–19, 1873, it turned into a formidable confrontation between America's foremost woman suffragist and a newly minted justice of the U.S. Supreme Court. While much has been written about Anthony and the woman suffrage movement she championed for most of her life, little is known about her nemesis, Associate Justice Ward Hunt. The two clashed philosophically and, according to the trial transcript that Anthony herself had printed and distributed, verbally. No one could, however, have foreseen the dramatic and unprecedented twist that would come at the end of the trial.

Ward Hunt

Hunt has been portrayed in the literature as an unreasonable, misogynistic troglodyte who abused his discretion as a judge. Anthony and Elizabeth Cady Stanton certainly promoted this view of Justice Hunt. There is no biography of Hunt, and brief discussions of his career on the Court focus primarily on his ignominious later years, when after a debilitating stroke he was eventually forced to resign from the Court by a special law passed by Congress to award him a pension, but only if he accepted it within thirty days of the bill's passage. The anonymous Wikipedia entry erroneously claimed that while serving on the Supreme Court, Hunt "wrote only four dissenting opinions and none for the majority."

In fact, Hunt was responsible for 153 majority opinions during his tenure, five dissents, and three concurrences. He had written

150 opinions and ten dissents as a justice, commissioner, and later chief justice of the New York high court. Who was this man who so famously clashed with the formidable Susan B. Anthony in June of 1873?

Ward Hunt was a longtime New York politician born in Utica whose father was a cashier at the Bank of Utica. A graduate of Union College in Schenectady he studied law first in Litchfield Connecticut and then in the Utica law offices of Hiram Denio, who later served on the New York Court of Appeals. (In New York, the trial courts were termed "supreme court," and the highest court of the state was called the "court of appeals.") After he was admitted to the bar in 1831 he joined his old mentor's law practice. Though successful as a corporate and railroad lawyer, Hunt had political aspirations. He was elected to the state assembly as a Jacksonian Democrat in 1838. He then looked higher, according to his *New York Times* obituary, for "his preference was for the Bench, for which he was eminently fitted by what is generally called a 'judicial mind.'" His judicial connections were ideal. Not only was he the partner and protégé of Denio, his first wife was the daughter of John Savage, who served as chief justice of the state's high court 1823–1836.

Hunt twice ran for a supreme court judgeship but was defeated at the polls. Again, according to the *New York Times*, his first defeat came as the result of his successful representation of a policeman "charged with the murder of an Irishman." Along with his fellow Martin Van Buren allies, the so-called Barnburners in the Democratic Party, he abandoned the Democrats for the Free Soil Party, an alliance that doomed his second run for an elective judgeship in 1853. Hunt's political peregrinations suggest a social and economic conservative who ardently opposed the extension of slavery to the western territories and states, though it is not clear that he supported abolition.

On July 1, 1856, Hunt joined seventy-five like-minded Free-Soil New York Democrat Republicans in an attempt to reform the party. Unhappy with the Democrats' recent conventions that had nominated candidates favoring slavery, the Free-Soilers called for a convention on July 24. Its purpose was "in favor of maintaining the political principles and practice of Jefferson, Jackson, and Tompkins (probably Daniel D. Tompkins, former New York governor and

James Monroe's vice president during his first term) and Silas Wright (a Van Buren stalwart who served as governor of New York in 1846–47)." The proposed rump convention was to "meet in Syracuse . . . for the purpose of consultation, and if deemed proper, for political organization and action." The Republican Party, which had its origins in the Midwest, had held its first national convention in Pittsburgh earlier that year, and Ward Hunt and his fellow disaffected New York Democrat Republicans eventually founded the Republican Party in New York State. Hunt then gave that party "his zealous support."

In 1865 Hunt finally achieved his judicial ambition with his election, as a Republican, to the New York Court of Appeals. In 1872, as an ally of New York Senator Roscoe Conkling's "Stalwart" Republicans, who supported Grant's reelection, he became a natural choice to fill the Supreme Court seat vacated by fellow New Yorker Justice Samuel Nelson upon his retirement. Thus it was the very election in which Susan B. Anthony cast her vote for Grant that resulted in Ward Hunt's elevation to the Supreme Court.

Hunt was a meticulous and knowledgeable judge. If one selects a few of those over 300 opinions he wrote during his judicial career in New York and on the high court having to do with women, one can detect some clues to his attitudes toward law and women. In 1867, for example, Hunt heard a case involving the validity of a promissory note issued by a man named Austin to a married woman named Polly Plucker. Plucker had brought a charge of rape against Austin, and the question was whether the promissory note for $100 had been given to her as a settlement for civil damages, which would have been acceptable, or whether Austin had attempted to pay her off to rid himself of a criminal rape charge, which would have been invalid as against public policy. In cross-examining Plucker, the defendant's counsel attempted to impeach her character, and therefore her credibility, by questioning her about messages she had sent to Austin inviting him to a clandestine meeting.

Hunt held the questions to be "competent for the purpose of impeaching the witness." He reasoned that "if a female witness admits herself to have broken down those barriers which the virtue and religion of every civilized country have reared for her improvement and protection, her oath would be of little value before a jury of intelligent men . . . the point was made, that, being a married woman, making a charge against Austin of having ravished her person, she could not deny that she had made him these clandestine communications. I think it was a depreciation of her character, that might justly have been considered by the jury." In these comments Hunt revealed something of his views of women, particularly married women, their place in society, and their morality. Women were an object of the law's protection and a married woman who departed from the narrow path of propriety and virtue lost her claim to the law's protection and society's trust in her character and credibility. He also demonstrated a willingness to allow judges some latitude in their instructions to juries.

In an opinion Hunt wrote only three months later, he expressed another important aspect of his judicial philosophy. One of the children of a deceased gentleman named Laban Russell challenged the transfer of some real estate in Rye, New York, by their mother, as executrix of her husband's estate, to his brother, supposedly in settlement of a $3,000 debt owed by his late father to the brother. In finding that the deed was invalid and that the mother had lacked the power to legitimately convey the property, Hunt was unmoved by arguments that her estate upon her death could reimburse the other children who had been entitled to the property as the result of a trust created by their father. The current owners of the land tried to claim that "no injustice would be committed by allowing the deed to stand," since the children would receive the cash equivalent of the purchase price. Hunt summed up his position: "This is a short cut toward justice, which tramples upon the principles of law." And Hunt seemed to find the woman's actions incompetent. Apparently ignorant of proper procedure, she exceeded her powers as executrix.

Even though these cases suggest that Hunt held a very proscriptive view of women's role in society and was a stickler for applying the law, Hunt was no misogynist. He was sympathetic to the plight of "good" women, particularly widows. In two cases, one before the New York Court of Appeals in 1868 and a second after he became an associate justice of the U.S. Supreme Court in 1872, Hunt found reasons to uphold two widows' claims against insurance companies that had tried to refuse payment of their deceased husbands' life insurance policies. In the first case, the company tried to prove that the husband's death had not been accidental, but rather he had committed suicide in violation of the terms of the policy. In their attempt to prove this version of events, they asked a witness about the deceased's religious beliefs. They "proposed to show that [the dead husband] was an infidel," or at the very least "an atheist." The suggestion was that if he had been anything other than a good Christian he would have had little compunction about taking his own life. Or, just as likely, they were trying to prejudice the jury against the husband.

When the trial judge disallowed the questions on the grounds that they were irrelevant and prejudicial, the insurance company appealed the judge's decision. Hunt, now chief justice of New York, upheld the trial judge's ruling. The presumption of the insurance company that a man's religious persuasion was relevant to whether he could violate the Christian tenet against "self-slaughter" was unreasonable. Hunt's reasoning illustrates his deeply held and conventional social and religious views. "It is not necessary to say how far, or how precisely, the presumption of personal Christianity exists. That we live in a Christian country is certainly true. It is acknowledged by the laws of the land, which prohibit blasphemy and profanity, and enjoin the observance of Sunday. That we believe in a governing Providence, by whom crime will be punished and virtue rewarded, is assumed in every oath that is administered." But he was not so naive as to believe "that every man is presumed to be a personal Christian, upon whose mind and upon whose actions the precepts of the Gospel exercise an influence, is so much against our common experience, that it cannot be assumed as a legal principle." Thus a man did not have to be an "infidel" or an "atheist" to commit a crime or act in an un-Christian manner; therefore, to question a man's Christianity wasn't relevant to suggest that, without other evidence, he had committed suicide. Note also that Hunt was validating the trial judge's ruling on whether a particular line of argument might go forward.

The other case involved a widow who challenged the denial of her life insurance claim. It turned on the definition of insanity. Hunt supplied a landmark opinion that anticipated modern standards for the insanity defense, such as the Model Penal Code formulation put forth in the latter half of the twentieth century. In this case, the life insurance company again argued that the deceased husband committed suicide, thus voiding the widow's claim. There was no doubt that George Terry had taken the poison that ended his life. The insurance company's proposed charge (the judge's instructions to the jury at the close of the trial) would have limited the widow's argument that her husband was insane when he ingested the poison to a narrow definition of insanity. If Mr. Terry "had sufficient capacity to understand the nature and consequences of his act, that is, that he was about to take poison, and that his death would be the result, he was responsible for his conduct, and the defendant is not liable; and the fact that his sense of moral responsibility was impaired by insanity, docs not affect the case."

As in the previous case, Victorian religious and moral standards insinuated themselves into the legal question of when someone was likely or not to commit suicide. A good Christian who retained enough of his mental faculties would understand that his immortal soul would be forever condemned if he terminated his life. Thus the insurance company in the New York case wished to prove Gibson was not a Christian. Mrs. Terry's counsel in the second case insisted that the jury should also consider "that a higher degree of mental and moral power must exist; that although the deceased had the capacity to know that he was about to take poison, and that his death would be the result, yet, if his reasoning powers so far gone that he could not exercise them on the act he was about to commit, its nature and effect, or if he was impelled by an insane impulse which his impaired capacity did not enable him to resist, he was not responsible for his conduct, and the defendant is liable."

In an era when mental illness was little understood and the legal system struggled to determine the liability and culpability of those suffering from it, Justice Hunt's opinion in *Life Insurance Co. v. Terry* (1873) is a remarkably enlightened piece of jurisprudence. Hunt painstakingly reviewed the limited American and English case law and found the cases divided on whether to accept the second definition of legal insanity that allowed for an overwhelming impulse resulting from the mental illness (and despite the fact that the individual may have understood the rightness or wrongness of his or her act) to negate their liability or culpability for the act. He also cited medical treatises. "The causes of insanity," he concluded from examining these experts, "are as varied as the varying circumstances of man. . . . When we speak of the 'mental' condition of a person, we refer to his senses, his perceptions, his consciousness, his ideas." How did he translate this into the legal question of liability or culpability?

> If his mental condition is perfect, his will, his memory, his understanding are perfect, and connected with a healthy bodily organization. If these do not concur, his mental condition is diseased or defective. . . . The intellect and intelligence of man are manifested through the organs of the brain, and from these, consciousness, will, memory, judgment, thought, volition, and passion, the functions of the mind, do proceed. Without the brain these cannot exist. With an injured or diseased brain, their powers are impaired or diminished.

Hunt concluded that "the act was not the voluntary intelligent act of the deceased." Though "the physical act of self-destruction was that of George Terry," whether you looked at "the moral and intellectual incapacity of the deceased . . . In neither was it truly his act. In the one supposition he did it when his reasoning powers were overthrown and he had not power or capacity to exercise them upon the act he was about to do. It was in effect as if his intellect and reason were blotted out or had never existed. In the other, if he understood and appreciated the effect of his act, an uncontrollable impulse cased by insanity compelled its commission. He had not the power to refrain from its commission, or to resist the impulse. Each of the principles put forth by the judge rests upon the same basis,— that the act was not the voluntary intelligent act of the deceased." In accepting the uncontrollable impulse alternative definition of legal insanity, Hunt was at the forefront of American medical jurisprudence. Once again, Hunt stood up for a virtuous widow against a life insurance company that would have deprived her of desperately needed funds in her hour of loss and need.

What was Hunt's attitude toward women as independent actors in law? In another case from his years as chief justice of the New York Court of Appeals, *James Cassin v. Lawrence Delany and Ann A. Delany* (1868), Hunt had to rule on whether a married woman was independently liable in a civil action against her and her husband for the tort of malicious prosecution. At the time the case arose, in 1856, New York law held that "where a tort or felony of any inferior degree is committed by the wife in the presence, and by the direction, of her husband, she is not personally, liable." In this instance, Hunt merely had to determine whether the trial court incorrectly excluded Ann Delany's husband's testimony as to whether she had committed the act in his presence and at his direction. Such testimony might have added weight to her defense against the charge, and the damages awarded to the plaintiff would have been reduced.

Hunt sustained Ann Delany's claim that the amount of damages were excessive because she hadn't been able to show through her husband's testimony that under coverture principles she was not an independent actor in the incident; she was controlled by her husband. Hunt pointed out that "the authorities are clear." If Ann Delany had committed the offense at his direction but not in his presence, she would have been independently liable. If Delany had committed the offense in his presence but not at his direction she would have also been independently liable. Both elements were necessary to insulate her from liability. The lower court erred in not admitting Lawrence Delany's testimony and was therefore reversed. It is interesting to note that Hunt assumed that if the wrongful act had been committed by a married woman in her husband's presence it "affords a presumption of his direction," though that presumption wasn't conclusive and further evidence would be necessary to prove she had acted at his direction. A married woman could act independently, though he assumed, to an extent, that she probably did not.

Two other cases Hunt ruled on involved the role of married women in nineteenth-century society. Both came before the high court in New York shortly before Hunt heard *Anthony*. The first, *The Corn Exchange Insurance Co. v. Armina Babcock* (1870), involved Armina Babcock's "special indorsement" of three promissory notes issued by her husband. She had endorsed the notes as a guarantor, or "surety," for the debts, though she personally stood to gain nothing from any of the three transactions. On each of them she had written "For value received I hereby charge my individual property with the payment of this note," followed by her signature. The question before the court was whether, as a married woman,

Babcock in fact had property of her own against which the note holders could seek repayment, and, if so, could such property be used to pay a debt incurred by her husband.

Hunt cited the New York statutes of 1860 and 1862 (statutes Stanton and Anthony had actively supported) that granted married women a right to their own property and the right to do business in their own name. He pointed out that under that statute "when a married woman assumes to act in reference to her separate estate, the question is not whether her action is really for her own benefit. The right to act, and to bind her estate, carries with it the right to act unwisely, and to her own injury, if she so wills." Hunt concluded that "this case comes within those statutes," and though the debt was incurred on her husband's behalf Hunt allowed the endorsement to stand against her separate property because she was entitled to encumber it any way she pleased. Faithful to the law, Hunt bowed to the changes in its treatment of married women.

A second case involving a married woman conducting business, *Caroline Abbey v. Abraham Deyo, Jr. Sheriff of Ulster County*, came before the New York court in 1871. It concerned an action by a wholesaler of grain who wished to collect for a bill incurred, again, by the defendant's husband, who had apparently been working as her agent. Once again Hunt sided with the plaintiff, who wished to collect the debt on the basis of the 1860 statute, which placed the burdens as well as the benefits on a married woman who asserted her autonomy as a business woman.

In sum, these cases paint a portrait of a sound jurist who took the law seriously and applied it conscientiously. But the Victorian gentlemen's conventional views of women peek out from behind this sober visage. Women, one can reasonably infer from Hunt's opinions, were entitled to the law's protection, but only if they remained within fairly circumspect roles. A poor widow would prevail against a life insurance company denying her claim; but a married woman who invited another gentleman to an assignation, a woman who presumed to act as executrix of her husband's estate, a woman who carried on commercial business affairs, all would lose this judge's sympathy, and the law would no longer protect her and her property. How would such a judge view an independent single woman who wished to assert her political rights as a citizen of the United States?

The Opening Rounds of the Trial

The case of *The United States of America v. Susan B. Anthony* commenced at 2:30 p.m. on June 17, 1873, in the Ontario County courthouse in the city of Canandaigua, New York. After all the machinations to bring the trial to this venue, it seems appropriate that Canandaigua in the Iroquois language means "chosen spot." The jury had been impaneled in the morning and Justice Hunt sat in position on the bench. U.S. Attorney Richard Crowley opened for the government. Judge Hall was not present.

Though he spoke to the jury, Crowley's remarks were plainly addressed to Justice Hunt, for he argued that "the question in this case, if there be a question of fact about it at all, will, in my judgment, be rather a question of law than one of fact." Crowley implied that if there was no question of fact, then the jury had no real role in the case. This might be colorable in a civil case, but it was not correct in a criminal one. He went even further to claim that "on the part of the Government, that there is no question about it either one way or the other, neither a question of fact, nor a question of law."

Crowley was clever. He knew he would be fighting an uphill battle before this jury. Though the jury was comprised entirely of men, the district had been saturated by Anthony's propaganda campaign the previous month, and this area of New York, not far from Anthony's home ground of Rochester was, as we have seen, relatively supportive of women's rights. Crowley dared not let a jury nullify the law by a free vote on guilt or innocence. In his opening remarks he was appealing to the judge to remove the case from the jury on the principle that there was no question of fact or law for them to decide in disregard of the Sixth Amendment right to trial by jury ("in all criminal prosecutions, the accused shall enjoy the right to a speedy and public trial, before an impartial jury"). Yet, for now, he was before a jury, and so he contented himself with telling the jury that if "she did vote without having a lawful right to vote, then there is no question but what she is guilty of violating a law of the United States."

The law was one of the enforcement acts to prevent voter fraud in federal elections, but the jury might have believed that simply voting didn't appear to be a fraud. Crowley anticipated such a misunderstanding. "We don't claim in this case, gentlemen, that Miss Anthony is of that class of people who go about 'repeating.'" In other words, she was not the usual fraudulent voter who cast a ballot more than once at various polling places. "But we do claim that upon the 5th of November, 1872, she voted, and whether she believed that she had a right to vote or not, it being a question of law, that she is within the Statute." It didn't matter, according to Crowley, whether she intended to break the law, whether she believed she was acting lawfully. Crowley was arguing that this was, in modern parlance, a strict liability offense. She needn't have a guilty state of mind; it only mattered that she performed the proscribed act.

Crowley "*Conceded*, that on the 5th day of November, 1872, Miss Susan B. Anthony was a woman." Unsurprisingly, there was no objection from Anthony's counsel. He proceeded to call his one and only witness, Beverly W. Jones, one of the inspectors of elections who had accepted Anthony's vote and was indicted along with her for violating the Enforcement Act. In his examination of Jones, Crowley established the facts that supported the charge against Anthony.

CROWLEY: Q. Do you know the defendant, Miss Susan B. Anthony?

JONES: A. Yes, sir.

[. . . .]

Q. Upon the 5th day of November, did the defendant, Susan B. Anthony, vote in the first election district of the 8th ward of the city of Rochester?

A. Yes, sir.

Q. Did you see her vote?

A. Yes, sir.

Q. Will you state to the jury what tickets she voted, whether State, Assembly, Congress and Electoral?

At this point, Anthony's counsel objected to the question because it called for a conclusion by the witness. Crowley wanted to establish that Anthony had voted in the federal election, thus violating federal law. If she had only voted in state or local elections, she would only be subject to state prosecution, and this federal charge would have to be dismissed. Crowley regrouped to establish that Anthony had voted in the federal election by posing questions to Jones to show that Jones had direct knowledge of the fact that Anthony had voted in the federal elections.

> CROWLEY: Q. State what tickets [ballots] she voted, if you know, Mr. Jones.
> JONES: A. If I recollect right she voted the Electoral ticket, Congressional ticket, State ticket, and Assembly ticket.
> [....]
> Q. Did you receive the tickets from Miss Anthony?
> A. Yes, sir.
> Q. What did you do with them when you received them?
> A. Put them in the separate boxes where they belonged.
> [....]
> Q. Was Miss Anthony challenged upon that occasion?
> A. Yes, sir—no; not on that day she wasn't.
> Q. She was not challenged on the day she voted?
> A. No, sir.

That was all Crowley needed from the witness. He had shown by eyewitness testimony that Anthony, a woman, had filled out ballots, or tickets, for candidates running for federal office and submitted them to the official to be deposited in the collection box. It was now Judge Selden's opportunity to cross-examine Mr. Jones. Rather than focusing on Anthony's ballot on the day of the election, Selden asked Jones about the registry of eligible voters.

> SELDEN: Q. Prior to the election, was there a registry of voters in that district made?
> JONES: A. Yes, sir.
> Q. Was [sic] you one of the officers engaged in making that registry?
> A. Yes, sir.
> Q. When the registry was being made did Miss Anthony appear before the Board of Registry and claim to be registered as a voter?
> A. She did.

Q. Was there any objection made, or any doubt raised as to her right to vote?

A. There was.

Q. On what ground?

A. On the ground that the Constitution of the State of New York did not allow women to vote.

Q. What was the defect in her right to vote as a citizen?

A. She was not a male citizen.

Q. That she was a woman?

A. Yes, sir.

Q. Did the Board consider that and decide that she was entitled to register?

At this point Crowley leveled an objection against Selden's line of questioning. He could see where Selden was going: if Susan B. Anthony was duly registered to vote by the Board of Registry, then her voter registration was facially legal, and she then had the legal right to cast her vote. Crowley wanted Justice Hunt to cut off any more questions about the apparent legitimacy of Anthony's registration. Whatever the board had done, Anthony had no right under the letter of New York law to vote in the election. But, for the time being, Justice Hunt was willing to allow Selden to continue with this line of questions and overruled Crowley's objection. Selden returned to Jones.

SELDEN: Q. Did the Board consider the question of her right to registry, and decide that she was entitled to register as a voter?

JONES: A. Yes sir.

Q. And she was registered accordingly?

A. Yes, sir.

Q. When she offered her vote, was the same objection brought up in the Board of Inspectors, or question made of her right to vote as a woman?

A. She was challenged previous to election day.

Q. It was canvassed previous to election day between them?

A. Yes, sir; she was challenged on the second day of registering names.

Q. At the time of the registry, when her name was registered, was the Supervisor of Election present at the Board?
A. He was.

Q. Was he consulted upon the question of whether she was entitled to registry, or did he express an opinion on the subject to the inspectors?

Crowley was becoming desperate to cut off this line of questioning because Selden was about to prove that Anthony had been, to all intents and purposes, lawfully registered and thus entitled to vote. Did he see his case slipping away from him? He almost certainly believed Selden was making points with the jurors. He may have seen some of the gentlemen in the jury box nodding or giving other visual clues that they were finding this line of questioning and the witness' answers very interesting.

MR. CROWLEY: I submit that it is of no consequence whether he did [express an opinion on Anthony's registration] or not.

JUDGE SELDEN: He was the Government Supervisor under this act of Congress.

MR. CROWLEY: The Board of Inspectors, under the State law, constitute the Board of Registry, and they are the only persons to pass upon that question.

THE COURT [Justice Hunt]: You may take it.

Again, Hunt allowed Selden to proceed with trying to establish that the actions of the local county board and the federal supervisor had legally entitled Susan B. Anthony to vote, and thus she couldn't be guilty of illegally voting. Jones finally replied to Selden's question:

JONES: A. Yes sir; there was a United States Supervisor of Elections, two of them.

SELDEN: Q. Did they advise the registry, or did they not?
A. One of them did.

Q. And on that advice the registry was made with the judgment of the inspectors.
A. It had a great deal of weight with the inspectors, I have no doubt.

Selden was finished with Mr. Beverly Jones; he had made a strong point about the facial legality of Anthony's November 1872 vote, whatever the New York constitution or electoral laws might say about the limitation of suffrage to "male citizens." If the Eighth Ward inspectors and at least one of the U.S. supervisors on site had agreed to allow her to register to vote, she would appear to have had the right to cast her ballot come Election Day. Crowley couldn't let Selden's cross-examination of his own witness undermine his case. He rose to ask additional questions under "Re-direct Examination."

> CROWLEY: Q. Was Miss Anthony challenged before the Board of Registry?
> JONES: A. Not at the time she offered her name.
> Q. Was she challenged at any time?
> A. Yes sir; the second day of the meeting of the Board.
> [....]
> Q. Won't you state what Miss Anthony said, if she said anything, when she came there and offered her name for registration?
> A. She stated that she did not claim any rights under the constitution of the State of New York; she claimed her right under the constitution of the United States.
> Q. Did she name any particular amendment?
> A. Yes, sir; she cited the 14th amendment.
> Q. Under that she claimed her right to vote?
> A. Yes, sir.

Crowley appeared to be laying the groundwork for his next question; at least that is a generous interpretation of what Crowley was doing. Up to this point his questions about the inquiry held the day after the inspectors had initially accepted Anthony's registration simply established Anthony's constitutional argument through Crowley's witness. Could he yet salvage something through his redirect questioning? Crowley focused on the response by the federal supervisors, but it is clear that Crowley was about to violate the cardinal rule for the examination of witnesses: never ask a question for which you do not already know the answer the witness will provide.

CROWLEY: Q. Did the other Federal Supervisor who was present, state it as his opinion that she was entitled to vote under that amendment, or did he protest, claiming that she did not have the right to vote?

JONES: A. One of them said that there was no way for the inspectors to get around placing the name upon the register; the other one, when she came in, left the room.

Q. Did this one who said that there was no way to get around placing the name upon the register, state that she had her right to register but did not have the right to vote?

A. I did'nt [*sic*] hear him make any such statement.

Q. You didn't hear any such statement as that?

A. No, sir.

Obviously, Crowley did not get the answer he had hoped for or expected. Jones had confirmed what Selden had been trying to do in his cross-examination: that the board and the federal supervisors had not challenged Miss Anthony's right to vote under her constitutional claim but had allowed her to register without protest. One can almost hear the gears grinding in the U.S. attorney's mind. He had to do something to redirect the jury's attention away from the blunder he had made in his redirect. For this purpose props are always useful. Crowley handed two books to Jones and asked him to identify them for the court. Jones said that they were the poll list and register books for the Eighth Ward.

CROWLEY: Q. Turn to the name of Susan B. Anthony, if it is upon that poll list?

JONES: A. I have it.

Q. What number is it?

A. Number 22.

Q. From that poll list what tickets does it purport to show that she voted upon that occasion?

A. Electoral, State, Congress and Assembly.

Having brought the testimony back to the simple fact that Crowley had tried to make in his direct examination of Jones that Anthony had voted in the federal election, the U.S. attorney finally announced that the "United States rests."

He had established the only two things he thought he needed to show: Susan B. Anthony was a woman and she had voted in a federal election against the constitution and law of New York State. End of story. Or was it? Anthony's attorney, Judge Selden, had scored some points in his cross-examination of Crowley's witness, and now it was time for Selden's opening address to the jury.

Selden Argues the Law

In 1873 Selden was not in the best of health. He had resigned from the New York Court of Appeals nine years before because of ill health. Apparently, he suffered from a "paralysis of the muscles of his larynx," a terrible affliction for a lawyer or judge who had to orate in a courtroom. After traveling to London to consult a specialist, he was ultimately treated by having "a tube with a valve controlled by a hollow aluminum ball that closed automatically on speaking." Yet despite his disability, Henry Selden performed his role as Susan B. Anthony's advocate valiantly. In his opening statement, he tried to emphasize the momentousness of this trial and its importance in constitutional jurisprudence. He apparently wanted the jury to know that they had an opportunity to play a role in making history. And he wasn't above some rhetorical flourishes to gain the jury's sympathy for his client.

> *If the Court please, Gentlemen of the Jury:*
> This is a case of no ordinary magnitude, although many might regard it as one of very little importance. The question whether my client here has done anything to justify her being consigned to a felon's prison or not, is one that interests her very essentially, and that interests the people also essentially.

He then laid out two theories in her defense. He was allowed by New York law to argue "in the alternative." The first was that she hadn't violated the law because what she had done was legal: "when she offered to have her name registered as a voter, and when she offered her vote for Member of Congress, she was as much entitled to vote as any man that voted at that election, according to the Constitution and laws of the Government under which she lives." Obviously, "if I maintain that proposition, as a matter of course she has committed no offence, and is entitled to be discharged at your hands." But Selden had an alternative theory he put to the jury in Anthony's defense. Even if the jury could not find that she had the right to vote (which he much preferred they conclude), nevertheless they should acquit her because "if she sincerely believed that she had a right to vote, and offered her ballot in good faith under that belief, whether right or wrong, by the laws of this country she is guilty of no crime."

In other words, under ordinary principles of criminal law that required the accused to have a "guilty mind," the mens rea of knowing that they were performing a wrongful act, Anthony was not guilty because she believed herself to be voting legally, "whether she was entitled to vote or not." He challenged the jury to reject Crowley's theory that voting without the legal authority to do so was a kind of "strict liability" offense, that Anthony's state of mind, her sincere belief that what she was doing was legal, was irrelevant; that she merely had to commit the act to be guilty of the criminal offense. This "proposition to me [is] most abhorrent, as I believe it will be equally abhorrent to your judgment."

To support his contention that Anthony had sincerely believed that what she had done was within the law, Selden told the jury that "before the registration, and before this election, Miss Anthony called upon me for advice upon the question whether, under the 14th Amendment of the Constitution of the United States, she had a right to vote." He then sheepishly admitted that until she had come to his office to consult him, "I had not examined the question. . . . She went away and came again after I had [researched] the question." His conclusion, he told her, was that "she was as lawful a voter as I am, or as any other man is," and he then "advised her to go and offer her vote."

Selden was a gentleman and did not want "Miss Anthony" convicted of a crime. He thus tried to deflect any guilt that might be attributed to Anthony for illegal voting to himself and the possibly incorrect advice he had offered her. He told the jury that "I may have been mistaken in that [advice to offer her vote], and if I was mistaken, I believe she acted in good faith." While his comments to the jury were offered in an honest attempt to serve what he saw as his client's best interest, he nevertheless undermined her real objective to bring a test case under the Fourteenth Amendment. He was less interested in promoting the cause of woman suffrage and the litigation strategy to challenge the current restrictive male-only voting laws in the courts with any eye to an appeal to the U.S. Supreme Court. He concluded, again sending mixed signals: "I believe she acted according to her right as the law and Constitution gave it to her. But whether she did or not, she acted in the most perfect good faith, and if she made a mistake, or if I made one, that is not a reason for committing her to a felon's cell." It was this last nightmare image that probably propelled Selden's weak two-pronged strategy. He couldn't bear to see a proper lady, as he undoubtedly saw Susan B. Anthony, go to jail even though that outcome would have served her cause.

Selden then opened the defense case with a particularly unusual maneuver: he called himself as his first witness. In his brief testimony, he essentially reiterated what he had told the jury in his opening argument about how Miss Anthony came to him for advice and what he had told her. He had to repeat this information under oath as a witness because opening arguments by counsel are not "evidence" that can be properly considered by the jury when they deliberated their verdict in the case. Crowley did not cross-examine Selden after he gave his testimony. After all, under his theory of the case Anthony's "intent" was irrelevant.

Selden then attempted to call his second witness. He told the court: "I propose to call Miss Anthony as to the fact of her voting— on the question of the intention or belief under which she voted." Crowley immediately rose to object to Anthony's testimony on the basis that "she is not competent as a witness in her own behalf." Crowley did not elaborate on how she was "not competent," but Justice Hunt, without explanation, sustained his objection.

This was a particularly strange ruling, a harbinger of stranger rulings to come. Under the federal Judiciary Act of 1789, federal courts were supposed to follow the procedural rules of the jurisdiction in which the federal court was sitting. Hunt himself had heard a case when he was a justice on the New York Court of Appeals in which a woman charged with grand larceny had testified on her own behalf. Hunt's opinion in *Sarah Brandon v. The People of the State of New York* held her testimony perfectly acceptable, since she "chose to avail herself of the statute of 1869 [Laws of 1869, chap. 678 (Act of May 7, 1869)], which permitted her to make herself a 'competent witness' in the case. She was not compelled to take this position, the statute declaring that the failure to testify should not create any presumption against her. She elected, however, to make herself a witness. She became and was a competent witness." Unfortunately, for Miss Brandon, once she placed herself on the stand as a witness to deny her culpability in the larceny, she could be challenged on cross-examination by counsel bringing up the fact that she had a record of having been arrested for a prior theft, a fact that called her character and thus her credibility into question.

Whatever the outcome of that case or the benefits to the defendant of her own testimony, New York law clearly allowed that a woman charged with a crime could take the stand in her own defense as a competent witness, and Hunt was well aware of the fact. It is astonishing and confounding that Justice Hunt would sustain Crowley's objection to Selden calling Anthony to take the stand to give testimony in her own behalf. Were Hunt's patriarchal and protective instincts toward women, as exhibited in his earlier judicial record, involved? Perhaps. But it is more likely that Hunt, the professional judge, had no patience for political theater. He could not have been unaware of the numerous speeches Anthony had given throughout the county in the months prior to her trial; one had been published in the local newspaper just that morning. He could be reasonably sure that, if she had taken the stand, Selden's examination would simply give her an opportunity to orate in his courtroom to the jury, spectators, and journalists. Hunt might tolerate a test case on woman suffrage, but he had no patience for testimony as performance art. Nevertheless, he should have been more confident in his ability to preserve order in his court without his ruling, which defied law, justice, and precedent. And Selden should have filed an exception—that is, formal grounds for appeal based on Hunt's ruling on the law.

Rebuttals

Having been thwarted in calling his client and star witness to testify, Selden rested his case. Crowley responded to Selden's case by calling a rebuttal witness, John E. Pound, the assistant U.S. attorney for the Northern District of New York, who had attended the hearing before Commissioner Storrs the previous December and had recorded the proceedings in his notes. Crowley entered Pound's notes into evidence and began to question him about Anthony's testimony on that occasion: "Did she, upon that occasion, state that she consulted or talked with Judge Henry R. Selden, of Rochester, in relation to her right to vote?" Judge Selden immediately jumped up to object. He rightly observed that the prosecution was using Anthony's prior testimony against her without letting her testify in the current proceedings in her own behalf. Selden argued that "if they refuse to allow her to be sworn here, they should be excluded from producing any evidence that she gave elsewhere, especially when they want to give the version which the United States officer took of her evidence."

This last comment questioned the veracity and credibility of the minutes recorded by Pound that Crowley wished to use as a record of Anthony's testimony. Hunt ignored Selden's objection and instructed Crowley to "go on." There is nothing in the record we have that indicates that Selden filed an exception against Hunt's overruling of his objection; it was an obvious point at which Selden could have claimed that Hunt had made an error.

Crowley continued his examination of Pound to refute Selden's contention that Anthony sincerely believed she was within the law when she cast her vote.

CROWLEY: Q. State whether she stated on that examination, under oath, that she had talked or consulted with Judge Henry R. Selden in relation to her right to vote?
POUND: A. She did.
Q. State whether she was asked, upon that examination, if the advice given her by Judge Henry R. Selden would or did make any difference in her action in voting, or in substance that?

A. I should have made the same endeavor to vote that I did had I not consulted Judge Selden. I didn't consult anyone before I registered. I was not influenced by his advice in the matter at all; have been resolved to vote, the first time I was at home 30 days, for a number of years.

Pound's testimony, actually Anthony's testimony as recorded and read by Pound, clearly undercut Selden's contention that Anthony had consulted him and followed his legal counsel. At this point John Van Voorhis, the lawyer representing the electors who had been indicted along with Anthony and who had been coordinating the defense with the Selden brothers, rose to cross-examine Pound.

VAN VOORHIS: Q. Pound, was she asked there if she had any doubt about her right to vote, and did she answer "Not a particle?"

POUND: A. She stated "Had no doubt as to my right to vote," on the direct examination.

Q. There was a stenographic reporter there, was there not?

A. A reporter was there taking notes.

Q. Was not this question put to her "Did you have any doubt yourself of your right to vote?" and did she not answer "Not a particle"?

Van Voorhis's questions were intended to make two points to the jury. The first was that Pound's notes weren't reliable. The second was to show Anthony's state of mind at the time she registered and voted: she was absolutely convinced of the lawfulness of her right to vote. Justice Hunt interjected to allow that Pound conceded that Anthony "had no doubt of her right to vote" and so Van Voorhis should be content with that and not belabor the issue of whether there were any discrepancies between Pound's notes of the hearing versus the stenographic record. Van Voorhis, nevertheless, had scored some points in his cross-examination of Crowley's rebuttal witness.

Hunt's rulings on motions up to this point were odd at best, and clearly wrong at worst, but his interjection at this point was something else indeed, an act much controverted in American criminal trial procedure. Many states had statutes or rules of procedure that barred sitting judges from commenting on evidence. It was common practice in England for judges to tell juries what to think about evidence at the time it was offered, but it was decidedly not common practice in state or federal courts.

If the case for the defense had closed at this point, the issues for the jury would have been clear, but Judge Selden undercut his side by requesting an opportunity to correct his own testimony. Selden stood up to ask: "I beg leave to state, in regard to my own testimony, Miss Anthony informs me that I was mistaken in the fact that my advice was before her registry. It was my recollection that it was on her way to the registry, but she states to me now that she was registered and came immediately to my office. In that respect I was under a mistake." Thus, at the close of evidence the jury was left with an impression that Anthony had either no reason to think she had a right to vote or that Judge Selden's advice was irrelevant, though that was the only evidence Anthony and her counsel had been permitted to present for their side.

Selden's Oration

Selden had one last chance to redeem himself and plead for Anthony and the right of women to vote in his closing argument before the jury. And he did a creditable job of making his case. He began by quoting the words of the statute under which Anthony had been indicted. She could be convicted if, and only if, she had violated the letter of that law, if she had "knowingly . . . vote[d] without having a lawful right to vote." He then appealed to the jurors' sense of justice, since "the only alleged ground of illegality of the defendant's vote is that she is a woman. If the same act had been done by her brother under the same circumstances, the act would have been not only innocent, but honorable and laudable; but having been done by a woman it is said to be a crime." Thus, he extrapolated that "the crime therefore consists not in the act done, but in the simple fact that the person doing it was a woman and not a man." It was simply contrary to an American sense of justice, because, he continued, "I believe this is the first instance in which a woman has been arraigned in a criminal court, merely on account of her sex." Selden, having made a plea to fairness and reason, was just getting started, though his next comment might have been less than helpful to his cause. He needlessly pointed out to the all-male jury that "if the advocates of female suffrage had been allowed to choose the point of attack to be made upon their position, they could not have chosen it more favorably for themselves; and I am disposed to thank those who have been instrumental in this proceeding, for presenting it in the form of a criminal prosecution." Here he was probably alluding to the fact that Anthony and her allies had expected to be turned away from the polls and would then bring a civil suit against the authorities, who had denied them their right to vote. But he was also thumbing his nose at the state for bringing a criminal charge against her and thus reinforcing the perception of injustice in the case. His casual sarcasm may have boomeranged against him, for rather than inciting the antiauthoritarian prejudices of the jury he probably exacerbated Justice Hunt's antipathy for Anthony's cause.

Selden next tried to make the case for woman suffrage. After all, "Women have the same interest that men have in the establishment and maintenance of good government; they are to the same extent as men bound to obey the laws . . . and upon principles of equal justice, as it would seem, should be allowed equally with men, to express their preference in the choice of law-makers and rulers." And since women were equally subject to the laws, Selden passionately explained, "no greater *absurdity*, to use no harsher term," though he was obviously tempted to, "could be presented, than that of rewarding men and punishing women, for the same act, *without giving to women any voice in the question which should be rewarded, and which punished.*"

Selden tried to sum up the legal questions as he saw them:

1. Was the defendant legally entitled to vote at the election in question?
2. If she was not entitled to vote, but believed that she was, and voted in good faith in that belief, did such voting constitute a crime under the statute before referred to?
3. Did the defendant vote in good faith in that belief?

Selden then explained, according to his interpretation of law, that "if the first question be decided in accordance with my views, the other questions become immaterial; if the second be decided adversely to my views the first and third become immaterial. The two first are questions of law to be decided by the court, the other is a question for the jury." At this point, one can wonder at Selden's competency as a lawyer. By agreeing that the legality question and whether her mental state was material to her culpability were matters for the Court—that is to say, the judge—to decide and thus not questions for the jury, Selden was all but handing over his case to Justice Hunt. Or was this a deliberate strategy by Selden, since if Anthony was acquitted by the jury she would have no case to appeal for a ruling by the Supreme Court. It is hard to say which interpretation is correct. In any event, Justice Hunt interrupted Selden here to suggest "that the argument should be confined to the legal questions," thus apparently telling Selden that his case was now being pled to the bench on the legal issues. Any appeal to the jury on the fact of whether Anthony truly believed she had the right to vote when she cast her ballot should be "suspended" until Hunt's "opinion on those questions should be made known." For whatever reason, probably because he had little choice in the matter, Selden consented to this "suggestion" by Hunt, and he proceeded with his argument. But now he was arguing the law to Justice Hunt.

Before arguing the constitutional principle and "purely legal question" that Anthony "had the same right to vote as any other citizen who voted at that election," Selden decided to present an extended disquisition on the "propriety and justice of the rule which I claim to have been established by the Constitution." In other words, he would rehearse for Justice Hunt all the arguments the suffrage movement claimed supported a woman's right to vote. "Miss Anthony, and those united with her in demanding the right of suffrage, claim, and with a strong appearance of justice, that upon the principles upon which our government is founded, and which lie at the basis of all just government, every citizen has a right to take part, upon equal terms with every other citizen in the formation and administration of government." This principle had not, of course, been established in the U.S. or most other countries even up to that time. But he could quote the hallowed Declaration of Independence to support this point (even though the founders had granted the franchise to few men, let alone women): "governments derive their just powers from the consent of the governed." He also quoted William Blackstone, though that eminent jurist had never supported universal suffrage, and then apologized that "quotations, to an unlimited extent, containing similar doctrines from eminent writers, both English and American . . . from the time of John Locke to the present day, might be made." He then proceeded to quote them.

The necessity for a woman's vote was Selden's next point. He claimed that he could "discover no ground consistent with the principle on which the franchise has been given to all men, upon which it can be denied to women." The only rationale for denying women the vote "is based upon the position that women are represented in the government by men, and that their rights and interests are better protected through that indirect representation than they would be by giving them a direct voice in the government." But history and experience, Selden argued, proved this concept wrong, and "even at the risk of being tedious, I will give some examples from my own professional experience." Though he may have been trying to be self-deprecating, he was all but warning the court (and the jurors who, though supposedly exempted from a role in these arguments, were nevertheless still seated in the courtroom) that they could take a short nap for the next few minutes while Selden related anecdotes from his legal practice. He rationalized that "I do this [providing these stories from his own law practice] because nothing adds more to the efficacy of truth than the translation of the abstract into the concrete." Before launching into these reminiscences, he cautioned that though he was "withholding names [so as to not breach client confidentiality], I will state the facts with fullness and accuracy."

He then told the court, with heart-rending eloquence, of the plight of a good and honest woman and her two daughters who had been unjustly slandered as "harlots" by the "wealthy but miserly" uncle of a young man who had been "specially attentive" to her eldest daughter. Since the honest woman "had been many years before deserted by her drunken husband," she could bring no action for slander against the uncle, because under the law at that time "the wife's rights were merged in those of the husband. She had in law no individual existence, and consequently no action could be brought by her to redress the grievous wrong." He then told another sad tale of a woman wronged by laws she had no role in making. It was a case of a mother, again abandoned by her no-good husband, who returned from an extensive sojourn in the "western states" and demanded custody of their very young child. The judge who heard the custody case "remanded the infant to the custody of the father. He thought the law required it, and perhaps it did," though Selden ardently claimed that "if mothers had had a voice, either in making or in administering the law, I think the result would have been different."

It was a good point—that women were subject to laws they had no political voice in creating—but Selden's argument was undercut by the fact that both cases he related to the court took place in New York before 1860. Even Selden had to admit that "in most of these respects the state of the law has undergone great changes within the last 25 years." He conceded that now, in 1873, "if a married woman is slandered she can prosecute in her own name the slanderer, and recover to her own use damages for the injury." Likewise, "the mother now has an equal claim with the father to the custody of their minor children." Moreover, all of these changes to the law to correct injustices toward women had been accomplished without New York women having the vote.

Selden must have realized the inconsistency in his argument and tried to explain. "These are certainly great ameliorations of the law; but how have they been produced? Mainly as the result of the exertions of a few heroic women, one of the foremost of whom is her who stands arraigned as a criminal before this Court to-day." That didn't quite reconcile the contradiction Selden had introduced into his argument, so he went on: "Much has been done, but much more remains to be done by women. If they had possessed the elective franchise, the reforms which have cost them a quarter of a century of labor would have been accomplished in a year."

Selden, like the women suffragists he represented, was somewhat optimistic about the power the ballot would afford them, though he seemed to realize it when he continued by exhorting the court (and the jury and the spectators), "Give them the ballot, and, although I do not suppose that any great revolution will be produced, or that all political evils will be removed, (I am not a believer in political panaceas,) but if I mistake not, valuable reforms will be introduced which are not now thought of. . . . At all events women will not be taxed without an opportunity to be heard, and will not be subject to fine and imprisonment by laws made exclusively by men for doing what it is lawful and honorable for men to do."

But before turning to the constitutional arguments, Selden tried once more to invoke the specter of the injustices women had traditionally been subjected to because they had lacked the political wherewithal to protect themselves. Realizing the anecdotes from his own decades-old legal practice might not have made the strongest practical and moral case for woman suffrage, Selden turned to graphic examples from international experience. "If Chinese women were allowed an equal share with men in shaping the laws of that great empire, would they subject their female children to torture with bandaged feet . . . that they might be cripples for the residue of their lives? If Hindoo women could have shaped the laws of India, would widows for ages have been burned on the funeral pyres of their deceased husbands? If Jewish women had had a voice in framing Jewish laws, would the husband, at his own pleasure, have been allowed to 'write a bill of divorcement . . . and send her out of his house'? Would women in Turkey or Persia have made it a heinous, if not capital, offence for a wife to be seen abroad with her face not covered by an impenetrable veil? Would women in England, however learned, have been for ages subjected to execution for offences for which men, who could read, were only subjected to burning in the hand and a few months imprisonment?" Selden's citation of these (somewhat exaggerated) examples from world societies had little to do with American law and precedent. His point was to illustrate that "the condition of subjection in which women have been held is the result of this principle; the result of superior strength, not of superior right, on the part of men."

Selden's next argument on this point may have had more resonance for Hunt, the former antebellum Free-Soiler. He linked that the denial of the right to vote meant that those persons "are essentially slaves, because they hold their rights, if they can be said to have any, subject to the will of those who hold the political power." Drawing upon the atrocities against freedmen during Reconstruction, Selden reminded the stalwart Republican Hunt that it was "for this reason it has been found necessary to give the ballot to the emancipated slaves. Until this was done their emancipation was far from complete." The security of women within society was equally endangered without the vote because "without a share in the political powers of the state, no class of citizens has any security for its rights." This was the very reason Republicans had crafted the Fifteenth Amendment.

Selden closed this section of his argument by addressing critics of suffrage who feared that "the character of women would be radically changed—that they would be unsexed, as it were, by clothing them with political rights, and that instead of modest amiable and graceful beings, we should have bold, noisy and disgusting political demagogues, or something worse, if anything worse can be imagined." In other words, women's "delicate nature" and femininity would be endangered should they be drawn into the political sphere. Another concern was that women voters would inevitably elect women to public office, an apparently frightening prospect for some nineteenth-century men.

Selden attempted to allay both of these concerns by employing all the Victorian notions of "true womanhood." First, the women's natures would not be transformed, since "the innate character of women is the result of God's laws, not of man's, nor can the laws of man affect that character beyond a very slight degree. . . . Their modesty, their delicacy, and intuitive sense of propriety, will never desert them." And, second, as to their potential role as political leaders and office holders, men need not worry because "nature has put barriers in the way of any excessive devotion of women to public affairs. . . . Such offices as women are qualified to fill will be sought by those who do not find other employment, and others they will not seek, or if they do, will seek in vain." Selden was reassuring men that they need not fear that women would take over government or seek to rule men if they were given the ballot.

Selden finally turned to examine the legal and constitutional grounds for woman suffrage and the innocence of his client. He admitted that there was no legal basis for Anthony's vote under the New York constitution or state laws. "Consequently, the right of Miss Anthony to vote at the election in question, can only be established by reference to an authority superior to and sufficient to overcome the provisions of our State constitution." The obvious source of this "superior authority" was the U.S. Constitution. He then provided a list of sections that would provide the authority required. The first four sections came from Articles I and II relating to the election of members of the House and the Senate and the electors who would vote for the president. The next section was Article IV, Section 2, which established that "the citizens of each State shall be entitled to all the privileges and immunities in the several States." This meant that no state could impose restrictions on citizens of another state different from the restrictions it imposed on its own citizens. He also cited Section 4 from the same article that "the United States shall guarantee to every State in the union a republican form of government." This has been traditionally interpreted to mean that if a state experienced an insurrection or some kind of coup d'état upending legitimate government, the federal government would intervene on behalf of the state's citizens. Though a great deal of constitutional debate and interpretation has been expended on exactly what this section means. In *Luther v. Borden* (1849) (a dispute growing out of the Dorr Rebellion in Rhode Island) the high court backed away from an expansive interpretation of the Guarantee Clause, introducing the "political question" doctrine to explain that reticence. A more expansive view could have applied it to instances when state government either denied the civil rights of some group of citizens or failed to intervene when some of its citizens' civil rights were being infringed.

Finally, Selden read the texts of the three Reconstruction amendments, the Thirteenth, Fourteenth, and Fifteenth. He argued that while the original Constitution may or may not have protected a woman's right to vote, after the passage of, in particular, the Fourteenth Amendment, prosecuting a woman for voting was clearly unconstitutional. The explicit wording in the latter amendment that "absolutely prohibited the States from making or enforcing *any law which shall abridge the privileges or immunities of citizens of the United States*" clearly protected women citizens in the assertion of their "privilege" to vote without state interference.

Thus Selden got to the crux of the litigation strategy argument. Women clearly were citizens just as much as men. "If there is any privilege of the citizen which is paramount to all others, it is the right of suffrage." Selden quoted dictionaries, books of usage, and "lexicographers" for definitions of the word "citizen." Many of the standard published American word books of the day include the right to vote as one of the attributes that defined the concept of "citizen." For example, Selden quoted *Webster's Dictionary*: "In the United States, [a citizen is] a person, native or naturalized, who has the privilege of exercising the elective franchise, or the qualifications which enable him to vote for rulers, and to purchase and hold real estate."

If common usage was not sufficient to satisfy legal standards, Selden next cited legal authorities as to the centrality of suffrage to the concept of citizenship. First of these was the dicta Justice Bushrod Washington issued in *Corfield v. Coryell* (1823). According to legal historian William E. Nelson, it is the "most frequently quoted [case] . . . both in the period 1830–1860 and in the debates on the adoption of the Fourteenth Amendment." Anthony had already cited it and may have called it to Selden's attention. Justice Washington, riding circuit in western Pennsylvania, tried to define what the founders understood by "privileges and immunities" in the Comity Clause of the Constitution. Selden, like the attorneys who would argue the woman's voting case *Minor v. Happersett* before the Supreme Court two years later, invoked Washington's inclusion of the "elective franchise" in the list of essential "privileges and immunities" of citizenship.

Selden pointed out that both Chancellor James Kent of New York, author of the four-volume *Commentaries on American Law*, and Supreme Court Justice Joseph Story, author of the three-volume *Commentaries on the Constitution of the United States*, cited Washington's opinion "with approbation." Selden (somewhat ironically, given the larger context of their views on slavery) quoted the *Dred Scott v. Sanford* (1857) opinions of Chief Justice Roger Taney and Associate Justice Peter Daniel that defined citizenship, in Justice Daniel's words, as "participation in [government's] functions."

Selden's next point was one that the attorneys representing Anthony's friend and suffrage ally Virginia Minor failed to emphasize when they took her case to the Supreme Court in 1875. Anthony's attorney conceded that the states retained the power to regulate elections and the franchise. He told the court, "It is not necessary for the purposes of this argument to claim that this amendment prohibits a state from making or enforcing any law whatever, regulating the elective franchise, or prescribing the conditions upon which it may be exercised." But, he argued, this did not vitiate his primary argument that a denial of the franchise to one group of citizens was an abrogation of the Fourteenth Amendment.

Having traversed the whole of Western jurisprudence, the landscape of American federal statute and constitutional law, and the Reconstruction amendments—and even venturing into the darker regions of the human heart—Selden rested. The next day the prosecution would have its say, and, presumably, the case, with instructions from Hunt, would go to the jury. That is not, however, what happened.

CHAPTER 6

"Had the Defendant, Being a Female, the Right to Vote?"

June 18–19, 1873

Anthony's trial continued on the morning of June 18, 1873, with Richard Crowley's arguments for the prosecution. Crowley had patiently sat through Selden's sometimes eloquent, sometimes meandering closing arguments knowing that he would have the last word and could counter any claims his legal opponent had made for the defense. The first thing he did was to sum up the question, "the only question in the case," by his lights that the jury had to answer: "had the defendant, being a female, the right to vote?" Since the defense had "conceded that she is a female, and did vote at the time and place, and for members of Congress," Crowley contended she had violated the Enforcement Act under which she had been indicted because she had cast a vote in a federal election when she had no legal right to do so. Did she have a legal right to vote or not? Her guilt, therefore, turned on the answer to that one question. For him it was open and shut.

The Prosecutor's Turn

Crowley could have sat down, but lawyers are loathe to leave any thread untied. He dismissed the argument that Anthony, through her counsel Judge Selden, asserted—namely, that "she bases her right to vote on the Fourteenth Amendment to the Constitution." After quoting the precise language to the jury, Crowley rejected Selden's interpretation of the amendment. "The Framers of the amendment did not mean, and we think it cannot be claimed, that this language gives the right to vote to all citizens." His laid out his reasoning: if the amendment's privileges or immunities clause did bestow suffrage on all U.S. citizens, "then there is no limitation as to sex or age or disqualification on account of conviction for crime, or unsoundness of mind." After all, "persons of unsound mind, criminals, and persons under twenty-one years of age, are citizens, if born or naturalized in the United States and subject to the jurisdiction thereof" would then be allowed to vote, a proposition Crowley found patently absurd.

It was obvious that the amendment's Framers, he argued, would want the states to be allowed to restrict the vote to prevent "impaired" individuals from participating in the body politic. While Crowley's reasoning was logical, it never occurred to him that he was including mentally competent adult women in the same category as children and the insane. The common law, Crowley undoubtedly knew, had long recognized that there were within society the weak and feeble who required the special protection of the law and who could not be trusted with the legal rights and political power of men. It was inconceivable to him, and probably to many in the courtroom that day, that adult women were not and should be distinguished from infants, the feebleminded or insane, and convicted felons. But Crowley's point was that nothing in the Fourteenth Amendment restricted the states' discretion to award or deny suffrage to anyone, including women.

Even so, Crowley conceded that the Fourteenth Amendment did place restrictions on the states, preventing them from interfering with the "privileges or immunities" of U.S. citizens. But Crowley argued "that under the Constitution of the United States, the right to vote without restriction or qualification on the part of the States, is not given, nor included in the words 'privileges or immunities.'" Countering Judge Selden's legal precedents to argue the opposite interpretation, Crowley asserted that "these words have a well defined meaning." Then he rather abstractly outlined that meaning: "Ordinarily their signification is to carry exemption or immunity from some general duty or burden, or protect a right peculiar to some individual or body."

Crowley quoted the language from the second paragraph of Section 2 of the amendment that Judge Selden had pointedly ignored— namely, the penalty states would suffer if they interfered with the right to vote in elections of federal officers, members of Congress, the president, and the vice president. That section's language (language as we have previously discussed that Anthony, Stanton, and their allies had vociferously rejected) provided that if that right was "denied to any of the *male* inhabitants of such state, being twenty-one years of age, and citizens of the United States, or in any way abridged, &c.; the basis of representation in such State shall be reduced in the proportion which the number of such *male* citizens shall bear to the whole number of male citizens twenty-one years of age in such State." Just as Anthony and her allies had feared that the inclusion, for the first time in the history of the U.S. Constitution, of the word "male" in the amendment would provide the basis for an argument to exclude women from the rights and protections of the Constitution, Crowley trumpeted it: "Here [in the quoted section of the Fourteenth Amendment] the distinction of *sex* and *age* is clearly and explicitly maintained, and precludes the theory or supposition that the right to vote, was, by that amendment conferred upon females."

After dismissing Anthony's Fourteenth Amendment argument, Crowley turned to the question of whether she had a right to vote under New York state law. His first point about the state law was that New York treated the right to vote as "conventional, not natural." In other words, people (whether male or female) had no inherent right to vote under a Natural Law jurisprudence in New York; voting rights were granted at the discretion (or whim) of the state legislature. And, according to Crowley, "Nothing in the Constitution of the United States, except the Fifteenth Amendment, takes from the respective States the right to prescribe the qualifications of its voters." Again, just as Anthony and Stanton had foreseen, the Fifteenth Amendment, while confirming the rights of freed African American male citizens to suffrage, could then be cited to exclude black and white women from the franchise.

Crowley succinctly summed this up for the court: "The Fifteenth Amendment, takes from the United States and respective States, the right to prescribe qualifications in regard to voting, only 'on account of race, color, or previous condition of servitude'—leaving them untrammeled as to sex, and other qualifications." It was thus obvious to Crowley that since the Fifteenth Amendment had been passed after the Fourteenth, "the principle applied in the construction of statutes, to ascertain the meaning of Legislatures, it must be held that the adoption of the Fourteenth Amendment did not in any respect take from the States the power to regulate the qualifications of voters, so far as sex is concerned, if at all." The later amendment would not have been required if the earlier one had already constrained the power of the states to determine who could vote in their jurisdiction.

Finally, Crowley gave short shrift to Judge Selden's interpretation of the Enforcement Act's language that the defendant had to have had the intention to vote illegally, that she must have known that her vote was illegal and intentionally voted with that guilty knowledge. Recall that Judge Selden averred that Anthony believed she had the constitutional right to vote, and thus had no intention to cast an illegal ballot. Crowley refuted Selden and argued that "the true meaning of the word 'knowingly,' as used in the statute, was only that the party charged should know that she was at the time engaged in the act of voting."

The Directed Verdict

The two sides now submitted the case to the court. Ordinarily, in a criminal trial, the judge would at this point give a set of "instructions" to the jury on points of law, usually explaining the charges and what options the jury had for returning their verdict. After the judge's instructions, the jury would be sent to a room to deliberate, discuss the case, and take one or more votes on whether to find the defendant guilty or not guilty of any of the charges laid against him or her. When they finally reached a unanimous decision they would return to the court to announce their verdict. Anyone who has watched *Law and Order* or any other popular legal television shows is quite familiar with this standard process for trying criminal cases. But that is not what happened in the Canandaigua courtroom that late spring morning. Instead, Justice Hunt stunned Anthony, her attorneys, and probably most of the spectators in what Anthony later confided to her diary was "the greatest outrage History ever witnessed."

Justice Hunt assured the jury and everyone in the courtroom that he had "given this case such consideration as I have been able to," and, perhaps because he knew that what he was about to say in court would be construed as highly controversial, he told them "that there might be no no [sic] misapprehension about my views, I have made a brief statement *in writing*" (emphasis added). Then Hunt read from his prepared opinion. Anthony, Stanton, and their allies later fulminated over the fact that Hunt had clearly prejudged the case, even before the trial had begun. It is not clear when Justice Hunt wrote his opinion. There is probably some truth to the suffragists' claim, and Hunt undoubtedly came to the case with some notion of what the case was about and how the law lay. Whether that meant he had written out his opinion before the trial commenced or whether he waited to hear if any arguments or evidence on that first day might influence his decision, one will never know.

After reciting, once again, the charge against Anthony, Hunt immediately addressed her claim that New York's constitution and statutes that limited suffrage to men violated the provisions of the Fourteenth Amendment. In his recital of the Reconstruction amendments' history and purpose, we can see glimpses of the antebellum Free-Soiler and later Republican Unionist. "The 13th, 14th and 15th Amendments," Hunt reminded his audience, "were designed mainly for the protection of the newly emancipated negroes." This was the cause Hunt had enthusiastically supported and to which he had devoted his political life. "The 13th Amendment," he continued, "provided that neither slavery nor involuntary servitude should longer exist in the United States. If honestly received and fairly applied, this provision would have been enough to guard the rights of the colored race."

Hunt expressed anger at states that had resisted Reconstruction: "In some States it was attempted to be evaded by enactments cruel and oppressive in their nature, as that colored persons were forbidden to appear in the towns except in a menial capacity; that they should reside on and cultivate the soil without being allowed to own it; that they were not permitted to give testimony in cases where a white man was a party. They were excluded from performing particular kinds of business, profitable and reputable, and they were denied the right of suffrage. To meet the difficulties arising from this state of things, the 14th and 15th Amendments were enacted."

Hunt's ire at the injustices meted out to the newly freed African Americans was not a pose adopted simply for the purpose of justifying the denial of suffrage to women. Even a short recounting of his biography indicates Hunt's longtime dedication to the end of slavery. In *U.S. v. Reese* (1875), an important Supreme Court case on African American voting rights decided less than three years after Susan B. Anthony's trial, Hunt filed one of his few dissents. At issue was the very same federal Enforcement Act of 1870 as in the *Anthony* case. In *Reese*, the Court refused to sustain indictments against two Kentucky election inspectors who refused "to receive and count . . . the vote of William Garner, a citizen of the United States of African descent." In other words, the Kentucky inspectors did the reverse of the election supervisors in Rochester who had accepted the vote of Susan B. Anthony. Both accepting an illegal vote and refusing one were violations of the Enforcement Act. Hunt vehemently disagreed with Chief Justice Waite's opinion for the Court's majority.

As Hunt emphasized by quoting the act's provisions, the act clearly required that state election officers not discriminate against "any citizen" of the United States. In accepting ballots or any prerequisite to voting, such as a poll tax, as in this case, such officials must do so "without distinction of race, color, or previous condition of servitude." The act also articulated specific penalties for violating the act: "for every such offence, [the offending official shall] forfeit and pay the sum of $500 to the person aggrieved thereby . . . and shall also, for every such offence, be deemed guilty of a misdemeanor, and shall, on conviction thereof, be fined not less than five hundred dollars, or be imprisoned not less than one month and not more than one year, or both, at the discretion of the court."

Hunt was outraged that the Court had emasculated the federal statute by finding that the statute and the indictments of two Kentucky officials were "insufficient." He chastised his fellow justices who had voted in the majority, telling them "that the intention of Congress on this subject is too plain to be discussed." He then reminded his brethren of recent history, the background for the passing of the Enforcement Act: "The Fifteenth Amendment had just been adopted, the object of which was to secure to a lately enslaved population protection against violations of their right to vote on account of their color or previous condition." One can imagine Hunt thinking out loud as he pointed out to the majority of the Court, "The act is entitled 'An Act to enforce the right of citizens of the United States to vote in the several States of the Union, and for other purposes.'"

Of course, in decrying the Court's decision Hunt was only passionate about the rights of freed African American *male* citizens. To be fair to Hunt, Congress had explicitly included only male citizens in the wording of the Fifteenth Amendment, and so he undoubtedly believed he was only following the letter of their legislative intent. Indeed, Hunt had reviewed the Senate debates of the statute "at the time of its passage" and based his dissent on well-established principles of statutory interpretation, a technique Hunt regularly relied upon in crafting his judicial opinions. But he thought that the majority had misapplied those principles in their narrow interpretation of the Enforcement Act: "I cannot but think that in some cases good sense is sacrificed to technical nicety, and a sound principle carried to an extravagant extent." After all, Hunt reasoned, "The object of an indictment is to apprise the court and the accused of what is charged against him, and the object of a statute is to declare or define the offence intended to be made punishable," which, in the case of Reese and his fellow inspector, any reasonable interpretation would lead to a finding that both were adequate or sufficient.

Hunt was adamant and eloquent in his defense of his interpretation of the intent of Congress in protecting male citizens' right to vote. Legal historian Robert Goldman's detailed and clearly admiring examination of Hunt's dissent concluded that "it was the brief that Attorney General Williams and Solicitor General Phillips should have submitted on behalf of the government, but didn't." Goldman also notes that though "Hunt's dissenting opinion does merit attention," it "was pretty much ignored at the time, and since."

When Hunt's opinion in *Anthony* is seen through the lens of his later dissent in *Reese*, an interpretation of his approach, other than simple misogyny, begins to come into focus. Like many supporters of freedmen's rights, Hunt saw the movement to include women in the Reconstruction era's civil rights revolution as a distraction, perhaps even a threat to the more important goal of securing the rights and dignity of emancipated black men. Certainly this played out in the postwar debates over the passage of the Reconstruction amendments and split the universal suffrage movement over whether pressing for woman suffrage might endanger the cause of freedmen. Even after the passage of the amendments and the enforcement acts, the threats to African Americans' civil rights, particularly in the former slave states, was far from guaranteed. The events behind *Reese* (and many others who were prosecuted but not convicted in this era) illustrate this point. Ward Hunt's opinion in the Anthony case itself described the precarious situation for blacks. Hunt undoubtedly believed, along with many in the Republican Party, that attention and legal challenges should be focused like a laser on the plight of African Americans, rather than on women whose lives and interests were less in jeopardy.

Hunt appeared to take the legal arguments Selden made seriously. After pointing out the civil rights objectives of the Fourteenth Amendment, Hunt closely examined the rights of citizenship claim the suffragists promoted. As a recently minted Supreme Court justice, Hunt was well aware "that these rights were separate and distinct, [as] was held in the Slaughter House cases recently decided by the United States Supreme Court at Washington." Selden had pointedly ignored the explicit holding of the high court on the limits of the privileges or immunities section of the Fourteenth Amendment in the *Slaughter-House Cases*, but Hunt cited his fellow Justice Samuel Miller's majority opinion that enumerated only the barest bones of privileges protected by the amendment.

Another privilege of a citizen of the United States, says Miller, Justice, in the "Slaughter House" cases, is to demand the care and protection of the Federal Government over his life, liberty and property when on the high seas or with the jurisdiction of a foreign government. The right to assemble and petition for a redress of grievances, the privilege of the writ of *habeas corpus*, he says, are rights of the citizen guaranteed by the Federal Constitution.

Not included in those rights, however, was suffrage. "The right of voting, or the privilege of voting," Justice Hunt continued, "is a right or privilege arising under the Constitution of the State, and not of the United States."

The states had wide discretion to award this privilege however they saw fit.

> If the State of New York should provide that no person should vote until he had reached the age of 31 years, or after he had reached the age of 50, or that no person having gray hair, or who had not the use of all his limbs, should be entitled to vote, I do not see how it could be held to be a violation of any right derived or held under the Constitution of the United States. We might say that such regulations were unjust, tyrannical, unfit for the regulation of an intelligent State; but if rights of a citizen are thereby violated, they are of that fundamental class derived from his position as a citizen of the State, and not those limited rights belonging to him as a citizen of the United States.

Justice Hunt recognized that there might be some limitations on the states' ability to regulate who could vote, for instance, "if the Legislature of the State of New York should require a higher qualification in a voter for a representative in Congress than is required for a voter for a Member of Assembly, this would, I conceive, be a violation of a right belonging to one as a citizen of the United States." And, of course, under the recently ratified Fifteenth Amendment, "the inability of a State to abridge the right of voting on account of race, color, or previous condition of servitude, arises from a Federal guaranty. Its violation would be the denial of a Federal right—that is a right belonging to the claimant as a citizen of the United States." But nowhere was the right to vote guaranteed to women. Indeed, Hunt pointed out that "if the 15th Amendment had contained the word 'sex,' the argument of the defendant would have been potent," but "the amendment, however, does not contain that word."

The argument that women were not protected against discrimination on the basis of their gender was reinforced, Hunt noted, by another case. "The case of Myra Bradwell, decided at a recent term of the Supreme Court of the United States, sustains both the positions above put forth, viz: First, that the rights referred to in the Fourteenth Amendment are those belonging to a person as a citizen of the United States and not as a citizen of a State, and second, that a right of the character here involved is not one connected with citizenship of the United States." After summarizing Bradwell's claim that Illinois had violated her rights by denying her a license to practice law simply because she was a woman, Hunt briefly cited the concurrence by Justice Joseph Bradley "that a woman was not entitled to a license to practice law."

In what had been up to that point a very reasoned constitutional analysis, the fact that Hunt specifically cited Bradley's rather incendiary antifeminist concurrence, rather than simply relying on Justice Miller's majority opinion, is telling. While he did not actually quote Justice Bradley's rant that "the paramount destiny and mission of woman are to fulfill the noble and benign offices of wife and mother," he seems to have approved of it by particularly citing it.

Finally, Justice Hunt addressed the question of whether Anthony was innocent of violating the law because she sincerely believed she had the right to vote when she cast her ballot and thus had no "intent" to violate the statute. Hunt had little sympathy for this argument. "Two principles apply here," he reminded the defense. "First, ignorance of the law excuses no one; second, every person is presumed to understand and to intend the necessary effects of his own acts." Applied to the present case, he pointed out, "Miss Anthony knew that she was a woman, and that the constitution of this State prohibits her from voting." He didn't accept that she might have believed the state law violated her federal rights. "She intended to violate that provision—intended to test it, perhaps, but certainly intended to violate it."

Testing a law she thought unconstitutional, therefore, was no excuse, according to Hunt. Parenthetically, Hunt's characterization of Anthony's challenge to the New York voting law as a test case was one of the first times the concept of a "test case" appeared in the legal literature. As far as he was concerned, she had tested the law and she had failed. "The necessary effect of her act was to violate it, and this she is presumed to have intended. There was no ignorance of any fact, but all the facts being known, she undertook to settle a principle in her own person. She takes the risk, and she cannot escape the consequences."

If Justice Hunt had stopped, using his comments as a summary of law and as instructions to the jury before he sent them out for their deliberations, he might have avoided the ignominy he faced in nearly every later account of the trial and public examination of the case. But Hunt did not stop here. After delivering his analysis of the law of the case, he seemed to come to a decision in his own mind that he then translated into a formal ruling: "Upon this evidence I suppose there is no question for the jury and that the jury should be directed to find a verdict of guilty."

Judge Selden jumped up to object "that it is for the jury to determine whether the defendant is guilty of a crime or not." Selden, an experienced courtroom attorney and trial judge, knew that in a criminal case the defendant had a right to a jury verdict. The Sixth Amendment clearly stated that "in all criminal prosecutions, the accused shall enjoy the right to a speedy and public trial, by an impartial jury of the state and district wherein the crime shall have been committed." Selden tried to get Hunt to submit four questions to the jury about whether Anthony had had a justifiable belief that she had the right to vote when she cast her ballot. Again, he was relying on the argument that she had relied on the advice he had given her and so thought what she was doing was legal. The questions Selden argued that Hunt should submit to the jury also worked as his own recommendation for jury instructions and a tactic to force Hunt to submit the case to the panel.

Hunt's only response to Selden's objection was "you have made a much better argument than that, sir." The justice was probably commenting on the fact that Selden was not asking for an instruction or question to the jury based on Anthony's right to vote under the Fourteenth Amendment. Selden responded to Hunt: "As long as it is an open question I submit that she has not been guilty of an offense. At all events it is for the jury." But Hunt dug in his heels. "I cannot charge these propositions of course," he told Selden. He then addressed the jury directly:

The question, gentlemen of the jury, in the form it finally takes, is wholly a question or questions of law, and I have decided as a question of law, in the first place, that under the 14th Amendment, which Miss Anthony claims protects her, she was not protected in a right to vote. And I have decided also that her belief and the advice which she took does not protect her in the act which she committed. If I am right in this, the result must be a verdict on your part of guilty, and I therefore direct that you find a verdict of guilty.

Selden rose once more to object to Hunt's actions. Selden was shocked and furious. Running the risk of a citation for contempt of court, Selden lectured Hunt: "That is a direction no Court has power to make in a criminal case." Hunt ignored him and instructed the clerk to "take the verdict." The clerk duly spoke to the jury: "Gentlemen of the jury, hearken to your verdict as the Court has recorded it. You say you find the defendant guilty of the offense whereof she stands indicted, and so say you all?" But before the jury or its foreman could answer, Selden rose again to his feet: "I don't know whether an exception is available, but I certainly must except to the refusal of the Court to submit those propositions, and especially to the direction of the Court that the jury should find a verdict of guilty. I claim that it is a power that is not given to any Court in a criminal case."

Selden then asked the court to let the clerk poll the jury and ask each member if he agreed to the guilty verdict. One could almost see the color rising in Hunt's face as he curtly responded: "No. Gentlemen of the jury, you are discharged." Court was then adjourned for the luncheon recess. But in the heat of the moment, Hunt seems to have forgotten one incredibly important detail: the jury had never responded to the clerk's question as to whether they agreed to the directed verdict of guilty. In other words, Hunt not only directed the verdict but presumptively delivered the verdict for the jury. As Susan B. Anthony later confided to her diary, the trial had descended into "farce."

Hunt was wrong in his ruling as a matter of law. He did not assay a "judgment notwithstanding the verdict" after the jury had returned. In any case, there was no precedent for overturning a not-guilty verdict in this manner. There was Supreme Court precedent for a directed verdict in civil cases when one side failed to produce any evidence that a jury might consider. In these cases, the high court, following the Rules of Decision Act, upheld lower federal courts' rulings based on state procedural law. In *U.S. v. Breitling* (1857), Chief Justice Roger Taney found a lower federal court sitting in Alabama correct in instructing a jury verdict when one party had produced "no evidence" to support its case. In *Home Improvement Company v. Munson* (1871), Justice Nathan Clifford, speaking for a unanimous High Court in another civil case, held that a lower federal court could charge or instruct a jury when a party had not offered any evidence that they might consider. Three years later, Justice Samuel Miller found sufficient case law to adjudge that "recent cases of high authority" had imposed on the trial court judge "a preliminary question, not whether there is literally no evidence, but whether there is any upon which a jury can properly proceed to find a verdict for the party producing it." None of these cases involved criminal trials, however.

Why then did Hunt so deliberately violate established constitutional law and conventional criminal procedure? It is possible that Hunt who had never served as a trial judge merely forgot himself. Something of his conduct resembled that of the appeals court judge he had been for so long. Recall that his judicial experience had been limited to his career on the appellate high court of New York and then the U.S. Supreme Court. He was used to having attorneys argue a case on appeal, where the only question was how the appellate judge would rule on questions of law. That is, essentially, what Hunt did in the *Anthony* case.

Given that precedent allowed judges to direct a verdict in a civil case where one party sues another for damages, perhaps in Justice Hunt's mind these two factors might have merged. If so, he did what he did because he was determined that Anthony would not prevail. He had worked it all out in his mind and there could be only one legal outcome. Then an instruction to the jury had become a directed verdict.

One cannot ignore another possibility. He undoubtedly knew that Anthony and Matilda Gage had been canvassing the district giving speeches to influence the pool of potential jurors on the justness of their cause. It was very possible that the men in the jury box, like the supervisors who had permitted the women to vote, might be persuaded to their cause. Despite what Hunt considered the clear law of the case, the jury might deliver a not-guilty verdict, what lawyers call "jury nullification." As the morning wore on, Hunt clearly became impatient with the defense and probably thought, "Not in my courtroom!"

The Inspectors' Trial

In the afternoon, court resumed to try the case of the inspectors of elections who were also indicted under the Enforcement Act for their role in accepting the women's ballots. The three inspectors, Beverly W. Jones, Edwin T. Marsh, and William B. Hall had been indicted for registering Susan B. Anthony and the other women as voters and accepting their ballots on Election Day, though they had known the women were ineligible under New York state law. At the preliminary hearing in January, Jones and Marsh had pled not guilty and Hall had not pleaded at all. Crowley again represented the government and John Van Voorhis represented the defendants. Justice Hunt again was on the bench and a jury had been impaneled.

Crowley presented another meticulous case to prove "just the facts" of the inspectors' actions on the day in October, when Anthony and the other women had appeared to register, and then on Election Day, when they cast their votes. He did this by calling the city clerk of Rochester, New York, William F. Morrison, and having him produce the registration and poll lists for the first election district, the Eighth Ward. The two books contained the certified lists of registered voters and those who had actually voted.

Morrison testified that Jones, serving as chairman of the board of inspectors had personally delivered the documents to him. That testimony authenticated the lists. Crowley entered them into evidence and used them to prove the inspectors had registered the women and accepted their ballots for congressional candidates. Van Voorhis did not bother to cross-examine the city clerk. Crowley then called Sylvester Lewis as a witness. Lewis was acting as an assistant (poll watcher) on Election Day. His duties were to keep track of the voters who cast a ballot and make sure they were on the registration list. Crowley established that Lewis had personally seen several of the women and had placed a check mark on the memorandum of registered voters with their names on it.

Van Voorhis tried to shake Lewis's testimony by establishing that he had no firsthand knowledge that the women had actually voted in the federal congressional races. If Lewis had only seen them vote but couldn't swear to whether they had voted in the state elections only, the United States would not have jurisdiction to charge them with violating federal law. Lewis "thought" he had been told the women had voted in the congressional election, but he couldn't "say so positively." Van Voorhis should have been satisfied with Lewis's equivocation, but then he attempted to impeach the witness's credibility and inflame the jury by asking Lewis about a comment he had supposedly made to bystanders on Election Day "that he would go and get twenty Irish women to vote, to offset these votes." Crowley objected that the question was immaterial and Hunt sustained the objection. Crowley then recalled Morrison, the Rochester city clerk, to support Lewis's testimony by attesting to the markings next to each of the women's names in the voter list book to show that each had been recorded as voting for a member of Congress.

Crowley's next witness must have been something of a surprise to the spectators in the court. Margaret Leyden, one of the fourteen women who had voted with Anthony, took the stand. Crowley would buttress the testimony of the city officials with one of Anthony's allies who could give firsthand testimony that she had voted in the federal election. Leyden forthrightly answered Crowley's question, "Did you vote for a candidate for Congress?" with a simple affirmative: "I did." Thus if the jurors had any doubts after Van Voorhis's cross-examination of Morrison and Lewis about which ballots the women had handed to the inspectors on Election Day, Leyden's admission on the stand clarified that point in Crowley's favor.

But Van Voorhis was a wily trial attorney and was able to earn back some of the points he had lost after Crowley's maneuver. Van Voorhis asked Margaret Leyden, "Was your ballot folded up?" Leyden answered, "It was." He followed up to establish that inspector Jones, who had received her ballot, had not opened or read it; in other words, Jones dropped the folded ballot into the box and did not know what it contained. Van Voorhis then asked: "Was your husband present when you voted?" At which point Crowley objected, but before Hunt could rule, the questioning continued.

VAN VOORHIS: No one had seen your ballot except for your husband before you handed it in?

LEYDEN: No, sir.

VAN VOORHIS: And when you handed it in it was folded, so that no one could see it?

LEYDEN: It was.

At this point Hunt interjected, without a motion from the prosecution (in effect commenting on the evidence): "What is the object of this?" Van Voorhis justified the relevance of his questions: "The District Attorney inquired if she voted a certain ticket, and assumes to charge these inspectors with knowing what she voted. It is to show that the ticket being folded, the inspector could not see what was in it." Of course he needn't have asked about Leyden's husband's presence and knowledge of her ballot to make that point. Van Voorhis may have been trying to send a subtle message to the men of the jury that the proper married woman had voted with the knowledge and support of her husband. The prosecution rested shortly thereafter.

Van Voorhis opened the defense case by calling Beverly W. Jones, one of the indicted inspectors. Jones had been reluctant, at first, to register Anthony, according to his testimony. He told her that she was ineligible because the New York State constitution restricted suffrage to male citizens. She then told him that she claimed the right to vote not under the New York constitution but under the U.S. Constitution, particularly under the Fourteenth Amendment. She "asked me if I was conversant with the 14th amendment; I told her I had read it and heard of it several times." Van Voorhis then interrupted Jones to ask who else was present during his exchange with Anthony. He named two federal supervisors and a U.S. marshal. Jones then continued to tell the court how Anthony had recited the Fourteenth Amendment and discoursed on several key points, one presumes on the Privileges or Immunities Clause.

Jones continued that one of the U.S. supervisors, Daniel Warner, had interjected a comment, but Crowley objected to any recounting of what the U.S. supervisors may have said as "entirely immaterial." Justice Hunt agreed with Crowley but then posed a question of his own to the witness/defendant: "Was your objection to registering Miss Anthony on the ground that she was a woman?" Again, judges were not expected to interrogate witnesses on the stand in criminal cases. Hunt ignored that custom. Jones answered in the affirmative. While it isn't totally inappropriate for a judge to ask a question of a witness in order to clarify something so that he might make a ruling on the relevance or materiality of a line of questions by the attorney, Hunt was not apparently doing that here.

Van Voorhis tried to get Jones's testimony back on track: "You may proceed and state what occurred there?" When Jones started to again recount what the U.S. supervisor had said, Crowley immediately reminded the court that he had objected to Van Voorhis's attempt to introduce testimony about the role of the federal officials present.

Again Hunt agreed with Crowley, but this time Van Voorhis tried to justify his line of questioning: "The district attorney has gone into what occurred at that time, and I ask to be permitted to show *all* that occurred at the time of the registry." Again Hunt told Van Voorhis that he thought such testimony was not "competent." After some additional give and take between Hunt and Van Voorhis, Hunt definitively announced, "I exclude it." Even then Van Voorhis continued to argue with the judge, but Hunt would have none of it and countered each of the defense counsel's arguments with a reiteration of his ruling. Van Voorhis asked Jones whether "in receiving those ballots did you act honestly in accordance with your sense of duty, and in accordance with your best judgment?" Jones answered simply: "I did."

The line of questioning next turned to Election Day and the circumstances under which Jones and the other inspectors accepted the women's ballots. The procedure under the New York voting statute was that if an objection was filed against the right of any individual to cast their ballot, the prospective voter might still vote if he must take an oath on a Bible. An objection had been filed against the women's right to vote, and Jones followed the procedure. Anthony and the other women all took the oath. Jones contended that after the procedures had been followed, he was then required to accept the proffered ballots.

Van Voorhis now called William Storrs, the U.S. commissioner who had presided over the preliminary hearing. Crowley objected to any substantive questions Van Voorhis posed, and the defense attorney conceded (for the time being) that "if the counsel objects I will not insist upon the evidence." The defense case seemed to be floundering, and so Van Voorhis decided to inject some excitement. He called Susan B. Anthony to the stand to testify for the defense.

Anthony's testimony at her own trial had been ruled incompetent. Anthony hadn't forgotten, and before she had even been sworn she addressed the court in a feisty manner: "I would like to know if the testimony of a person who has been convicted of a crime, can be taken?" Hunt stoically responded: "They call you as a witness, madam." The clerk then administered the "affirmation" (a common legal alternative for Quakers). Anthony was then questioned by Van Voorhis, though even with friendly counsel Anthony displayed some pique with the proceedings:

> VAN VOORHIS: Q. Miss Anthony, I want you to state what occurred at the Board of Registry, when your name was registered?
>
> ANTHONY: A. That would be very tedious, for it was full an hour.
>
> Q. State generally what was done, or what occupied that hour's time?

Crowley objected at this point, but it isn't clear on what basis he did so. Van Voorhis, without waiting for a ruling on the objection, tried to reform his question to jump to the issue he thought was most essential. "Well, was the question of your right to be registered a subject of discussion there?" Anthony said it was and then the defense counsel tried to elicit from Anthony what the role of the U.S. supervisors was in the decision to allow her to register, information Crowley had successfully blocked earlier witnesses from telling the court. Here again Crowley jumped up to object, and Hunt agreed that nothing Anthony could say would, within his previous rulings, add to the accounts of prior witnesses.

But Anthony decided to speak anyhow. Referring to Jones's testimony about the oath she took under the statute on the day of the election, Anthony told the court: "I would like to say, if I might be allowed by the Court, that the general impression that I swore I was a male citizen, is an erroneous one." Van Voorhis decided to follow her lead and started to ask Anthony about the oaths she took that day, but Justice Hunt interrupted to question Anthony himself: "You presented yourself as a female, claiming that you had a right to vote?" In answering Hunt's question, Anthony took issue with the way he phrased it: "I presented myself not as a female at all, sir," she reproved the justice.

She then affirmed her position under the litigation: "I presented myself as a citizen of the United States. I was called to the United States ballot box by the 14th amendment, not as a female, but as a citizen, and I went there." Van Voorhis apparently decided that Anthony had made her case, and Crowley refused to engage Anthony, so she was allowed to step down. The defense counsel then proposed to call several other witnesses, but Crowley objected, arguing that they would add nothing new to the case. Hunt agreed, telling Van Voorhis: "I think you have all the evidence that any questions could give you in the case. These men have sworn that they acted honestly, and in accordance with their best judgment. Now, if that is a defense [though obviously Hunt didn't think so], you have it, and it will not make it any stronger to multiply evidence." With that ruling Van Voorhis closed his case for the defendants.

Van Voorhis's closing arguments focused on two points:

> "May it please the Court, I submit that there is no ground whatever to charge these defendants with any criminal offense.
> 1. Because the women who voted were legal voters.
> 2. Because they were challenged and took the oaths which the statute requires of Electors, and the Inspectors had no right, after such oath, to reject their votes."

If Van Voorhis had only been interested in defending the inspectors, his second point would have been sufficient. They had done all New York law had required of them, and thus in allowing the women to vote after they had taken the oath they had committed no crime under state or federal law. But Van Voorhis included an argument that the women were legally entitled to vote under the Fourteenth Amendment and so linked the prosecution of the inspectors to the cause of woman suffrage; thus, for all intents and purposes, he was trying to give Anthony the jury verdict she had been denied at her own trial. He supported his argument with ample precedent and then concluded with an appeal that "the defendants should be discharged by the Court." Audaciously, and in contrast to the outcome in Anthony's trial, by asking the court to dismiss the charges against the defendants, Van Voorhis tried to get a kind of "directed verdict" of not guilty.

Crowley ignored the opposing counsel's ploy and started to rise to give his own closing argument, at which point Hunt interrupted:

THE COURT: I don't think it is necessary for you to spend time in argument, Mr. Crowley. I think upon the last authority cited by the counsel there is no defense in this case. . . . Now this is the point in the case, in my view of it: If there was any case in which a female was entitled to vote, then it would be a subject of examination. If a female over the age of 21 was entitled to vote, then it would be within the judicial authority of the inspectors to examine and determine whether in the given case the female came within that provision. If a married woman was entitled to vote, or if a married woman was not entitled to vote, and a single woman was entitled to vote, I think the inspectors would have a right in a case before them to judge upon the evidence whether the person before them was married or single. If they decided erroneously, the[i]r judicial character would protect them. But under the law of this state, as it stands, under no circumstances is a woman entitled to vote. When Miss Anthony, Mrs. Leyden and the other ladies came there and presented themselves for registry, and presented themselves to offer their votes, when it appeared that they were women—that they were of the female sex—the power and authority of the inspectors was at an end. . . .

But upon the view which has been taken of this question of the right of females to vote, by the United States Court at

Washington, and by the adjudication which was made this morning, upon this subject there is no discretion and therefore I must hold that it affords no protection.

In that view of the case, is there anything to go to the jury?

Justice Hunt was trying to justify another directed verdict of guilty, just as he had done with Anthony. Curiously, as justification he cited U.S. Supreme Court precedent on woman suffrage, which, at this point, did not yet exist, as well as his own ruling in the *Anthony* case that morning. That ruling could not be cited as legally binding precedent, for it was not the ruling of an appeals court. Hunt sat as a trial court judge in the *Anthony* case.

Van Voorhis did not plan to let Hunt get away with it and engaged the justice. He started by answering the justice's last question:

VAN VOORHIS: The jury must pass upon the whole case, and particularly as to whether any ballots were received for representative in Congress, or candidates for representative in Congress, and whether the defendants acted wilfully and maliciously.

THE COURT: It is too plain to argue that.

VAN VOORHIS: There is nothing but circumstantial evidence.

THE COURT: Your own witness testified to it.

VAN VOORHIS: But "knowingly," your Honor, implies knowing that it is a vote for representative in Congress.

THE COURT: That comes within the decision of the question of law. I don't see that there is anything to go to the jury.

Hunt was clearly applying the rules for civil cases to this criminal case, just as he had with the *Anthony* case in the morning session.

Van Voorhis would not concede any of these points. Like Selden, he was boiling at Hunt's indifference to the federal rules of procedure in criminal cases. He forcefully argued the point: "I cannot take your Honor's view of the case, but of course must submit to it. We ask to go to the jury upon this whole case, and claim that in this case, *as in all criminal cases*, the right of trial by jury is made inviolate by the constitution—that the Court has no power to take it from the jury" (emphasis added).

Whether Van Voorhis made the point more forcefully or more clearly than his colleague Judge Selden earlier in the day, or if Justice Hunt now heard the constitutional issue and started to rethink his actions, Van Voorhis got the response from Hunt that had eluded Selden. Hunt grudgingly conceded: "I am going to submit it to the jury."

But Justice Hunt refused to admit defeat in his control of the outcome of the case. He still had his opportunity in framing his charge or instructions to the jury.

Gentlemen, the defendants are charged with knowingly, willfully and wrongfully receiving the votes of the ladies whose names are mentioned. . . . I decided in the case this morning, which many of you heard, probably, that under the law as it stands the ladies who offered their votes had no right to vote whatever. I repeat that decision, and I charge you that they had no right to offer their votes. They having no right to offer their votes, the inspectors of election ought not to receive them. . . . But, instead of doing as I did in the case this morning—directing a verdict—I submit the case to you with these instructions, and you can decide it here, or you may go out.

Hunt stepped around the constitutional problem of directing a verdict while at the same time "instructing" the jury that the defendants were guilty as charged. He then asked them, clearly thinking that after what he had told them, whether they actually needed to deliberate in private or could just give Hunt the verdict he was clearly asking for. Van Voorhis was not fooled. He rose to request that Justice Hunt "instruct the jury that if they find these inspectors acted honestly, in accordance with their best judgment, they should be acquitted." After all, Hunt had allowed that argument as Van Voorhis presented his case. But Hunt seemed to have changed his mind about that line of defense. He tersely responded by telling the jury: "I have expressly ruled to the contrary of that, gentlemen; that that makes no difference."

Van Voorhis was incensed and told Hunt (and the jury) "that in this country—under the laws of this country," but Hunt angrily interrupted him: "That is enough—you need not argue it, Mr. Van

Voorhis." Van Voorhis tried another tack by requesting an instruction about the fact that the inspectors could not have known what the ballots contained and thus could not have known that the women had voted in the federal election. And that, if the gentlemen of the jury found that to be true they had the "right to find for the defendants, if they choose."

Van Voorhis was insisting that whether to find the defendants guilty or not guilty was up to the jury. He reiterated his request to the justice: "I ask your Honor also to charge the jury that there is sufficient evidence to sustain a verdict of not guilty." But Hunt was determined, even if he had been forced to submit the case to the jury, and told Van Voorhis, "I cannot charge that." In frustration, Van Voorhis exclaimed: "Then why should it go to the jury?" This was the crux of the matter. Hunt was "allowing" the case to go to the jury and had not specifically "directed" a guilty verdict, but his "instructions" conceded no room for anything but the return of a verdict of guilty.

Hunt openly admitted that submitting the case to the jury was "as a matter of form." Van Voorhis was clearly nonplussed. He demanded of the justice: "If the jury should find a verdict of not guilty, could your Honor set it aside?" Hunt avoided a direct answer, telling counsel, "I will debate that with you when the occasion arises." Unbelievably, Hunt would not even admit the fundamental principle that a jury's not-guilty verdict ended the case. Judges cannot overturn a not-guilty verdict. In the heat of the moment, incensed that his expert judicial view of the case could be questioned and possibly rejected by laypersons sitting on a jury, Hunt overstepped and revealed his ignorance or extreme prejudice. Again, he told the jury that they could either deliberate in open court (and come to the obvious verdict) or retire to deliberate in private. The gentlemen of the jury chose privacy.

It was fairly late in the afternoon by the time the case went to the jury, so Hunt took a recess but did not call it a day. Perhaps he was optimistic that the jury would bring their guilty verdict in speedily. If so, he was doomed to disappointment. Finally, at 7 p.m. he had the court clerk summon the jury to ask them "if they had agreed upon their verdict." Probably to everyone's surprise, the foreman of the jury "replied in the negative." Justice Hunt asked the jurors, "Is there anything upon which I can give you any advice, gentlemen, or any information?"

Hunt was more than eager to help them along to a guilty verdict. One of the jurors responded, "We stand 11 for conviction, and 1 opposed." There was one holdout who, if he couldn't be brought around to change his mind, the jury would be hung—because they lacked unanimity—and Hunt would be forced to declare a mistrial. The prosecution could then try the defendants again before a new jury, but a mistrial would nevertheless hand the prosecution, and Hunt in particular, a galling defeat.

Hunt spoke to the jury: "If that gentleman desires to ask any questions in respect to the questions of law, or the facts in the case, I will give him any information he desires." But, the clerk noted that there was "no response from the jury." Hunt continued to press: "It is quite proper, if any gentleman has any doubt about anything . . . he should state it to the Court." Hunt was clearly attempting to intimidate the holdout juror. And though the lone juror spoke up to say "I don't wish to ask any questions," it became clear that Hunt's intimidation tactic had succeeded.

After the juror's response in open court, Hunt sent the jury out again. Though Hunt announced that "the Court will adjourn until to-morrow morning," after only ten minutes the jury "returned into court." In answer to the clerk's query as to whether they had now agreed upon a verdict, the jury foreman replied, "We have." Then in the ritual of all criminal trials, the clerk asked the jury: "How say you, do you find the prisoners at the bar guilty of the offense whereof they stand indicted, or not guilty?" A hush undoubtedly descended on the courtroom in anticipation of the foreman's response, though after the exchange that had taken place only a few minutes before, it was obvious what the verdict would be. Just as expected, the foreman announced, "Guilty."

The Last Day

On Thursday, June 19, both Judge Selden, for Susan B. Anthony, and John Van Voorhis, for the inspectors, filed motions for new trials for their clients. Hunt scheduled arguments in the Anthony case for that afternoon at 2 p.m. and in the inspectors' case the following day. Anthony had arrived in court supported by several of the women who had voted alongside her the previous fall. They listened as Judge Selden earnestly argued for the motion:

> *May it please the Court:*
> The trial of this case commenced with a question of very great magnitude—whether by the constitution of the United States the right of suffrage was secured to female equally with male citizens. It is likely to close with a question of much greater magnitude—whether the right of trial by jury is absolutely secured by the federal constitution to persons charged with crime before the federal courts.

While lawyers and legal scholars would undoubtedly agree with him about the importance of the constitutional issue of trial by jury raised by Hunt's actions in Anthony's trial, Judge Selden seemed to be dismissing the woman's suffrage cause as a secondary issue. This was not a position Anthony and her allies wanted to hear in their case. Nevertheless, Anthony later confided to her diary that she considered Selden's performance that day "masterly."

In fact, Selden simply reiterated many of the arguments he had previously made during the trial, emphasizing the least useful to the suffragists' cause, that Anthony had voted in good faith after consulting and receiving possibly erroneous advice from Selden himself; thus she lacked the guilty knowledge Selden believed necessary for conviction under the Enforcement Act. After belaboring this issue Selden finally got to the question of whether Hunt had violated her constitutional right to a trial by jury when he directed the jury to return a verdict of guilty. In recounting the events surrounding that ruling, Selden did make the point that the jury actually had not even had the opportunity to deliver the requested guilty verdict. Then he seemed to find his voice as he eloquently pleaded the constitutional argument:

> Now I respectfully submit, that in these proceedings the defendant has been substantially denied her constitutional right of trial by jury. The jurors composing the panel have been

merely silent spectators of the conviction of the defendant by the Court. They have had no more share in her trial and conviction than any other twelve members of the jury summoned to attend this Court, or any twelve spectators who have sat by during the trial. If such course is allowable in this case, it must be equally allowable in all criminal cases, whether the charge be for treason, murder or any minor grade of offence which can come under the jurisdiction of a United States court; and as I understand it, if correct, substantially abolishes the right of trial by jury . . .

I insist that in every criminal case, where the party has pleaded not guilty, whether upon the trial the guilt of such party appears to the Judge to be clear or not, the response to the question, guilty or not guilty, must come from the jury, must be their voluntary act, and cannot be imposed upon them by the Court.

Selden then tried to cite case law to support his constitutional claims. He admitted that Hunt's ruling the day before had caught him off guard and that he had "no opportunity . . . to consult precedents on this subject, but a friend [Van Voorhis, perhaps?] has referred me to an authority strongly supporting my position." The case Selden cited was *State v. Shule*, a North Carolina case from 1849. There were some differences between *Shule* and *Anthony*. In the former, the jurors had originally been given the case, but when they could not reach a verdict on one of the defendants, they were brought back into the courtroom to be questioned by the judge. This was reminiscent of what had taken place in Justice Hunt's courtroom the previous night in the inspectors' case.

Unlike *Anthony*, in which the jurors never got an opportunity to deliberate, in *Shule* the jurors consulted in the courtroom after the judge gave them additional instructions, but after only a few minutes the prosecuting attorney told the clerk to enter a guilty verdict for the jury against both defendants. Only then did the clerk ask the jury if that were their verdict. The judge, apparently, let the prosecutor get away with this stunt. In the *Anthony* case, of course, it was the judge himself who directed the verdict of guilty. On appeal to the Supreme Court of North Carolina, Judge Pearson wrote for the

Court that there was a clear error in the way the case had been tried and he ordered a new trial.

In chastising the judge and prosecutor for their conduct, Pearson wrote (and Selden quoted), "There was a departure from the established mode of proceeding, and the wisest policy is, to check innovation at once; particularly, as, in this case, it concerns the 'trial by jury,' which the 'bill of rights' declares 'ought to remain sacred and inviolable.'" The innovation Judge Pearson criticized was the usurpation of the jury's role in delivering a verdict by the prosecutor with the tacit assent of the judge. Pearson noted, "It is true, from the cases made out, there could be but little room to doubt, that both defendants were guilty, and the wonder is, why the jury should have hesitated about convicting both. Still that was a matter for the jury, and its being a plain case, although it accounts for, does not legalize, this novel mode in entering a verdict. If allowed, because this is a plain case, it may be extended to cases that are not plain, and become a positive mischief."

The North Carolina case was not a federal case nor a New York case, and so Selden could only use it as persuasive rather than binding authority. Nevertheless, the constitutional principle Judge Pearson articulated was very clear and very persuasive. Yet Selden did not stop at citing a nearly quarter-century-old case. He went on to discuss Anglo-American principles and authorities as far back as the Magna Carta to challenge Hunt's procedure in the *Anthony* case.

After Selden had finished his argument, the prosecutor had some words of rebuttal, though Anthony did not include these in the transcript she paid to have published and which is the best source of what took place in the court. Justice Hunt immediately and without comment ruled to deny Anthony's motion for a new trial.

Witnessing

One must not lose sight in the heated exchanges between defendants' counsel and Justice Hunt that Anthony repeatedly addressed the court. While defendants with counsel were often admonished to remain silent, Hunt allowed Anthony some latitude in this regard. Anthony's perspective was a little different. She did not see herself as a legal witness. Her testimony was of a different sort.

Anthony's education and background was distinctly Quaker. She retained her membership in the Rochester Hicksite Meeting to the day of her death. The founder of the Quaker movement, George Fox, described this central philosophy as "Be patterns, be examples, in all countries, places, islands, nations, wherever you come, that your carriage and life may preach among all sorts of people and to them; then you will come to walk cheerfully over the world, answering that of God in every one." Anthony's speeches to all and sundry throughout the United States on the issue of woman suffrage served as her "ministry." Even if she most often attended Unitarian services, her spiritual center incorporated the basic Quaker testimonies of "truth, equality, peace, simplicity and community."

Unlike the secular or legal use of the term "testimony," the Friends use the word "to describe a witness to the living truth within the human heart as it is acted out in everyday life. According to Hans Weening, it is not a form of words, but a mode of life based of the realisation that there is 'that of God in everyone,' that all human beings are equal, and that all life is interconnected. It is affirmative but may lead to action that runs counter to certain practices currently accepted in the society at large."

It is no wonder that Anthony received lifelong support from the Quaker community, particularly the liberal or "Progressives," in her commitment to the cause of woman suffrage. Another aspect of this adherence to the Quaker testimonies was the "call to witness," to "speak truth to power," if you will. And though Anthony had been denied the opportunity to "witness" at her trial, and her testimony at the trial of the inspectors was cut short, she finally found her moment at the time of her sentencing.

After summarily denying the motion for her new trial, Hunt ordered the defendant to stand and then, in the ritual of sentencing dating back hundreds of years, asked Anthony: "Has the prisoner anything to say why sentence shall not be pronounced?" This was her call to witness to the court her ministry of the Quaker Testimonies of integrity and equality.

Yes, your honor, I have many things to say, for in your ordered verdict of guilty, you have trampled under foot every vital principle of our government. My natural rights, my civil rights, my political rights, my judicial rights, are all alike ignored. Robbed of the fundamental privilege of citizenship, I am degraded from the status of a citizen to that of a subject; and not only myself individually, but all of my sex, are, by your honor's verdict, doomed to political subjection under this so-called, form of government.

Hunt, recognizing that Anthony was launching into one of her orations on woman suffrage, tried to silence her once again: "The Court cannot listen to a rehearsal of arguments the prisoner's counsel has already consumed three hours in presenting." The justice wanted nothing to do with an "uppity" woman preaching in open court. But Susan B. Anthony would not allow him to muzzle her.

May it please your honor, I am not arguing the question, but simply stating the reasons why sentence cannot, in justice, be pronounced against me. Your denial of my citizen's right to vote, is the denial of my right of consent as one of the governed, the denial of my right of representation as one of the taxed, the denial of my right to a trial by a jury of my peers as an offender against law, therefore, the denial of my sacred rights to life, liberty, property and—

Hunt interrupted to insist that "the Court cannot allow the prisoner to go on." He desperately tried to regain control of his courtroom. Anthony had, in what Hunt undoubtedly saw as an unfeminine and improper manner, usurped his authority. Anthony, in a barely polite but forceful response, complained that she had had no opportunity to speak (at least in court) before:

But your honor will not deny me this one and only poor privilege of protest against this high-handed outrage upon my citizen's rights. May it please the Court to remember that since the day of my arrest last November, this is the first time that either myself or any person of my disfranchised class has been allowed a word of defense before judge or jury—

An increasingly frustrated Hunt tried to order Anthony to cease her tirade, "The prisoner must sit down—the Court cannot allow it." Anthony persisted:

All of my prosecutors, from the 8th ward corner grocery politician, who entered the complaint, to the United States Marshal, Commissioner, District Attorney, District Judge, your honor on the bench, not one is my peer, but each and all are my political sovereigns; and had your honor submitted my case to the jury, as was clearly your duty, even then I should have had just cause of protest, for not one of those men was my peer; but, native or foreign born, white or black, rich or poor, educated or ignorant, awake or asleep, sober or drunk, each and every man of them was my political superior; hence, in no sense, my peer. Even, under such circumstances, a commoner of England, tried before a jury of Lords, would have far less cause to complain than should I, a woman, tried before a jury of men. Even my counsel, the Hon. Henry R. Selden, who has argued my cause so ably, so earnestly, so unanswerably before your honor, is my political sovereign. Precisely as no disfranchised person is entitled to sit upon a jury, and no woman is entitled to the franchise, so, none but a regularly admitted lawyer is allowed to practice in the courts, and no woman can gain admission to the bar—hence, jury, judge, counsel, must all be of the superior class.

Anthony had never been so eloquent in her cause. Too often in the speeches she gave on her tours of Ontario and then later Canandaigua counties, Anthony resorted to extensive quotations by others. Here the power of her true call to witness, her "spoken ministry" broke through. One can almost imagine how, as in the Quaker meeting, the Holy Spirit moved her to break the silence of the courtroom and defy Justice Hunt as again he interrupted her: "The Court must insist—the prisoner has been tried according to the established forms of law." But Anthony would not be denied her calling:

Yes, your honor, but by forms of law all made by men, interpreted by men, administered by men, in favor of men, and against women; and hence, your honor's ordered verdict of guilty, against a United States citizen for the exercise of *"that citizen's right to vote,"* simply because that citizen was a woman and not a man. But, yesterday, the same man made forms of law, declared it a crime punishable with $1,000 fine and six months' imprisonment, for you, or me, or any of us, to give a cup of cold water, a crust of bread, or a night's shelter to a panting fugitive as he was tracking his way to Canada. And every man or woman in whose veins coursed a drop of human sympathy violated that wicked law, reckless of consequences, and was justified in so doing. As then, the slaves who got their freedom must take it over, or under, or through the unjust forms of law, precisely so, now, must women, to get their right to a voice in this government, take it; and I have taken mine, and mean to take it at every possible opportunity.

Justice Hunt had enough. One can only imagine how the color must have risen in his face, a vein probably throbbing at his temple as "the prisoner" continued to defy him. "The Court orders the prisoner to sit down. It will not allow another word." But Anthony definitely got in another, actually several, words:

When I was brought before your honor for trial, I hoped for a broad and liberal interpretation of the Constitution and its recent amendments, that should declare all United States under its protecting aegis—that should declare equality of rights the national guarantee to all persons born or naturalized in the United States. But failing to get this justice—failing, even, to get a trial by a jury *not* of my peers—I ask not leniency at your hands—but rather the full rigors of the law.

Hunt began to chastise her once again—"The Court must insist"— but to his and probably everyone else in the courtroom's surprise, Anthony abruptly sat down. Hunt was momentarily flummoxed. After all, he was finally going to be able to pronounce sentence, but he must have suddenly realized that to do so she must stand up. So immediately after insisting that she sit, Hunt reversed himself and demanded that "the prisoner will stand up." And the transcript recorded that "here Miss Anthony arose again."

Hunt then announced that "the sentence of the Court is that you pay a fine of one hundred dollars and the costs of the prosecution." One hundred dollars was a reasonably small fine under the statute, though today it would have been the equivalent of nearly $1,770 dollars, a fairly large sum to the perennially impecunious Anthony. Nevertheless, Anthony could have undoubtedly raised even that sum from supporters, but standing on principle she again spoke defiantly to the court:

> May it please your honor, I shall never pay a dollar of your unjust penalty. All the stock in trade I possess is a $10,000 debt incurred by my publishing my paper—the *Revolution*—four years ago, the sole object of which was to educate all women to do precisely as I have done, rebel against your manmade, unjust, unconstitutional forms of law, that tax, fine, imprison and hang women, while they deny them the right of representation in the government; and I shall work on with might and main to pay every dollar of that honest debt, but not a penny shall go to this unjust claim. And I shall earnestly and persistently continue to urge all women to the practical recognition of the old revolutionary maxim, that "Resistance to tyranny is obedience to God."

As in the Quaker tradition, Anthony may have discerned her vocal ministry. The "message intended" for others came "from the Holy Spirit" and "not just" from herself. At any rate, she had answered the inner call to speak.

Hunt resisted both her message and her legal tactic. In refusing to pay the fine that Hunt had ordered, she not only resisted "tyranny" but also invited imprisonment for contempt of court. An imprisonment could then lead to a motion for a writ of habeas corpus. The "Great Writ" was the last resort for someone unjustly imprisoned and, unlike Hunt's denial of her motion for a new trial, denial of a motion for the writ was grounds for appeal to a higher court and ultimately to the Supreme Court. The judge simply announced: "Madam, the Court will not order you committed until the fine is paid." Though Hunt's refusal to send Anthony to jail despite her defiance in failing to pay her fine seems to have let the suffragist win the battle, in fact the wily jurist had won the war. Without imprisoning Anthony, he had denied her grounds to move for a writ of habeas corpus and circumvented her plan to appeal her case to the Supreme Court.

As for the other women voters indicted with Anthony, two days after Anthony's sentencing, the *New York Times* reported that prosecutor Richard Crowley had filed a *nolle prosequi* motion with the court, thus informing the court that he had no intention to pursue the charges against them. Anthony had been the test case, and Crowley probably believed that he had made his point with her conviction. To pursue cases against the other women would only sustain the public relations campaign of the suffragists to bring attention to their cause. In addition, such subsequent trials would be unlikely to be brought before Justice Hunt, which could increase the chances that a friendly jury might actually acquit one or more of the women. It must have made perfect sense to Crowley to quit while he was ahead. Thus ended the federal criminal trial of Susan B. Anthony.

CHAPTER 7

"Selfish Male Tyranny"
June 20, 1873–March 29, 1875

The outcome of Anthony's trial was widely reported. Henry Ward Beecher's *Christian Union* newspaper in New York editorialized that it "ended, as might have been expected, in her conviction." Beecher applauded the outcome, claiming that "the judgment of the Court upon the legal questions involved is no doubt in accordance with public opinion as well as judicial precedent." The editorial denounced the litigation strategy, arguing that "it is not in the interest of good government that Courts should have power, in the name of Justice, and against the well-settled interpretation of the Constitution and the conscious purpose and intent of the people to make such a revolution as the women-suffragists seek."

Beecher, of course, was a longtime acquaintance of Anthony's. More important, since 1869 he had affiliated himself with NWSA's rival, the AWSA, and served as its first president. Thus Beecher, like AWSA, had never endorsed the litigation strategy of claiming women had the right to suffrage and then seeking the Court's endorsement.

Beecher's admonition to the contrary notwithstanding, the response to Anthony's trial in newspaper editorials across the country largely focused on Justice Hunt's directed verdict of guilty. Typical of these was a piece published in the *Trenton State Sentinel and Capital* that came out two days after Anthony was sentenced. The paper asked its readers: "Is it not possible, yea, certain, that in this view of the case Judge Selden was right and Judge Hunt was wrong? Why have juries at all, if Judges can find verdicts—or direct them to be found, and then refuse to poll the jury, which amounts to just the same—without any reference whatever to the jury?" While Anthony certainly agreed with the constitutional principle the newspaper espoused and would certainly use Hunt's usurpation of the jury's role as part of her appeals to Congress and the public, she must also have been disappointed that their attention had been deflected from the woman suffrage question itself. Indeed, the Trenton, New Jersey, newspaper editorial concluded that "whether female suffrage is right or wrong, legal or illegal, it is not our intention now to discuss; but we do say now, and expect ever to say, that action so arbitrary and unjust as that of Judge Hunt in this case . . . should meet with condemnation from all lovers of fair-play."

Hunt on Trial

Even newspaper opponents of the suffragists condemned Hunt's high-handed maneuver around the jury in the *Anthony* case. The Democratic *Rochester Times* editorial on the Sunday after her conviction applauded the outcome and expressed the hope that "hereafter we shall hear no more of arguments as to the legal right, while the denunciation of selfish male tyranny and the oppression under which the shrill-voiced sex now groan." Yet even as it criticized the women who demanded the right to vote it condemned Justice Hunt for his "arbitrary conduct" in circumventing the jury in the case. The editorial asked, "whether we really have any jury system in the higher courts, or whether a prisoner arraigned before the more August tribunals has any right to a defense or any claim to be tried by a jury of his, or her, peers."

The editorial went on to liken what happened in Hunt's courtroom to "the old 'star-chamber' court of the English Tudors," which was infamous "because the cases were decided before they were heard and the hasty trials before prejudiced judges were meaningless forms preparatory to certain and prearranged convictions." In their dramatic account of the justice's machinations, "Judge Hunt threatened to keep those twelve good men and true on bread and water for some time and so he frightened the untutored rustics into a servile obedience to his arbitrary will." The paper even speculated on why Justice Hunt had acted has he had. It is not clear where they got this insight into his motivation, but they claimed that it was "supposed to be an ambition for the chief-justiceship of the United States." It is probable that the *Rochester Times* was simply adding the fact of the recent death of Chief Justice Salmon P. Chase to the fact that Hunt was serving on the Court. Though several of his fellow associate justices made no secret of their ambition to replace the chief justice, there was no hint that Hunt's ambitions led in that direction. Nevertheless, the editorial denounced him and any ambition he might have to advancement. Indeed, it called for his impeachment.

So much attention was paid to Justice Hunt's directed jury verdict that one cannot help but wonder if Hunt's real motivation may have been to deflate the impact of Anthony's test case on woman suffrage. As the writer in another article that appeared in the wake of the case summed it up: "The question of Miss Anthony's alleged misdemeanor is entirely absorbed and lost in contemplation of Judge Hunt's greater and overshadowing offence."

Anthony had no appellate route available to her since under the rules of federal appeals at that time, Justice Hunt's denial of Selden's motion for a new trial, based in part on the attorney's claim that Hunt's directed verdict of guilty was unconstitutional, and thus an error by the court, did not entitle Anthony to an appeal to the Supreme Court. Anthony and her allies tried to refocus attention on the suffrage question, though they used Hunt's directed verdict to incense the faithful. Two weeks after the events in Canandaigua, the woman suffragists held "an indignation meeting . . . at DeGarmo's Hall, Fifth-avenue and Fourteenth-street" in New York City. After speeches that must have aroused the ire of the audience, they adopted resolutions that both "sympathiz[ed] with Miss Anthony, and condemn[ed] the action of Judge Hunt." Similar resolutions were adopted by the Women Taxpayers Association a week later, though they agreed with the newspaper that had called for Justice Hunt's impeachment and, according to Ann Gordon, "promised to petition Congress to reverse his judgements against [Anthony] and the inspectors."

In late July 1873 federal authorities had sought to collect the fine (and court costs) Justice Hunt had imposed on her, but they were consistently thwarted by Anthony. The federal marshal visited Anthony, but as Anthony wrote on August 5 to her friend, the venerable former abolitionist Gerrit Smith, "when the Marshall in service of his master—asked me for the money, I refuse to pay it—& told him I had no property but my person—and I saw no way for Uncle

Sam to get his claim but to *imprison me for debt.*" By now, according to Ann Gordon, the sum she owed the court added up to $204.41. That would be $3,675.47 in 2010 dollars, not an insignificant sum for a woman with no profession other than suffrage activist. Ann Gordon also found that "Elisha Keeney reported to the [court] clerk on 24 July: 'I have made diligent search and can find no goods or chattels land or tenements' with which to answer the judgment against SBA." And, despite what Anthony told Gerrit Smith, imprisonment for debt was no longer an option according to a federal law passed in 1833.

The fall of 1873 was a stressful and anguished period for Susan B. Anthony. She recorded in her diary the slow and painful last illness of Guelma Anthony McLean, Anthony's older sister by only two years. Guelma, whom the family called Gula, owned the house in Rochester in which Susan, her mother, and their younger sister, Mary, all lived. Anthony curtailed her activities throughout those months to stay by her sister's bedside. On November 6 there was a "Women Tax-payers meeting," but she "did not attend." She bemoaned that "these days cover us with a fearful night-mare feeling," and Guelma's cries of "How long—Oh how long must this suffering continue & all of us perfectly powerless to relieve."

Three days later Anthony recorded that "Dear Sister Guelma passed away at 5.30 this A.M." Anthony herself, along with her two remaining sisters and her niece, "performed the last sad offices ourselves." Guelma had been not only a dear sister but also a stalwart ally to Susan in the suffrage cause. She would not have wanted her sister to abandon the fight to mourn her, and Anthony wasted little time in grieving before immersing herself in the fray once again. The Connecticut Woman Suffrage Association, led by Anthony's close colleague Isabella Beecher Hooker, held its annual meeting the second week of December in New Haven. Anthony attended.

In her scrapbook Anthony pasted an article about the meeting but not about her own presence. Rather it was a report of a letter from John Hooker to the "President of the Connecticut Woman suffrage association" read to the assemblage. John Hooker was a distinguished Connecticut lawyer and served as the reporter for the Connecticut Supreme Court 1858–1894. He had been married to Isabella Beecher Hooker for sixty years at the time of his death. His support for woman suffrage was not merely a concession to his wife but also a heartfelt principle he espoused his entire adult life. The lengthy letter to the woman suffragists endorsed Anthony and the cause. He told them that in his "opinion she had the right to vote and the conviction was wrong." Hooker's letter then went on to critique the prosecution in detail. The letter was similar to an article Hooker had written shortly after the trial. It was later included in the account of the "Proceedings" of Anthony's trial that she arranged to have published as a book by the *Rochester Democrat and Chronicle* in early 1874.

Neither the letter nor the version later included in Anthony's trial volume were amateur condemnations of Hunt's courtroom machinations. Hooker was a widely respected legal mind and had "declined a seat upon the Supreme bench [of Connecticut]." He wrote the following:

[Hunt's] conduct of the case was so utterly against the law and so unjust and oppressive that his name ought to go down to posterity with those of Jeffreys and other infamous judges who have been pilloried by history. I will do what I can to effect this. Immediately after the trial I wrote and published [a] review of his course, which I insert in these Reminiscences as worthy of a place here and as putting on record my abhorrence of the man. It is impossible to suppose for a moment that he could have any doubt of the well-established principles of law which he was setting at defiance: if he had such doubt, he was totally unfit for a place in any respectable court.

The constitutional issue of whether a trial judge could order a directed verdict in a criminal case remained undecided for nearly nine years. Neither Congress nor the Supreme Court responded to the editorial complaints about Justice Hunt's actions in the Susan B. Anthony case. It was only after Justice Hunt had, in 1878, suffered a paralyzing stroke that ended his active participation on the high court and was later forced to accept retirement that his extraordinary misuse of discretion was recognized officially by George Washington McCrary (a former secretary of war under Rutherford B. Hayes serving as U.S. judge for the eighth circuit court), who unequivocally established that a judge in a federal court could not direct a verdict of guilty. In *U.S. v. Taylor* (11 F. 470) (1882), McCrary opined that a directed verdict in a criminal case was a blatant and offensive violation of the Sixth Amendment's guarantee of trial by jury. The judge in a district court had agreed with the prosecution that "the facts being admitted or settled beyond dispute, the question of guilt or innocence depends wholly upon a question of law, which the court must determine, and that, therefore, the court may direct a verdict either way, in accordance with its opinion of the law." McCrary observed that the trial judge was, "no doubt, largely influenced by the ruling of Mr. Justice Hunt in the case of *U.S. v. Anthony*." But, McCrary continued, the overwhelming "authorities are, with entire unanimity, against the right of a court in a criminal case to direct a verdict of guilty." There was no distinction between questions of law and fact in a criminal case tried before a jury; thus "it is doubtless true that, in a certain sense and to a limited extent, this doctrine makes the jury the judges in criminal cases, of both law and fact; but this is the necessary result of the jury system." Judge McCrary was sensitive to the implication of his ruling on the reputation of the ailing and only recently retired Hunt. The correct inference from McCrary's opinion, however, was that Hunt had violated Susan B. Anthony's constitutional rights. McCrary concluded his opinion: "In view of this, and especially in view of the opinion above cited of Mr. Justice Hunt, for whose judgment I entertain the highest respect, I have considered the case with great care. I have also consulted Mr. Justice [Samuel] Miller [Hunt's former colleague on the high court], who authorizes me to say that he concurs in the conclusion which I have reached, which is that the district court erred in charging the jury to find the defendant guilty." McCrary and Miller had heard and decided the appeal that Hunt denied Anthony nine years earlier.

In January 1874 Anthony sent a petition to Congress. According to the *Journal of the House of Representatives* and the *Journal of the Senate*, old allies Congressman William Loughridge and Senator Aaron Sargent presented Anthony's petition, which recounted the events of her trial and Hunt's directed guilty verdict. She then requested that "inasmuch as the law has provided no means of reviewing the decisions of the Judge, or of correcting his errors, that the fine imposed upon your petitioner be remitted, as an expression of the sense of this high tribunal that her conviction was unjust." The House Judiciary Committee issued its report on Anthony's petition in May 1874. It roundly criticized the violation of Anthony's right to trial by jury and recommended that her fine be remitted. The *Albany Law Journal* criticized the report because "the committee seem to imagine that they have succeeded to the appellate jurisdiction of the House of Lords." The Senate report followed the next month. Unlike the House, the Senate Judiciary Committee "submitted an adverse report." Congress never granted her the relief she requested. Anthony herself told Isabella Beecher Hooker in a letter on July 14, "Of course I do not *expect* Congress to reverse Judge Hunts decision—nor order me a new trial." But the petition might have a secondary, and more worthwhile, purpose. "I should expect the petition to rouse the people—& to record the sentiment on the question," she told Hooker.

There was one last matter to resolve. According to the *Papers of Ulysses S. Grant*, "On February 26, 1874," while Anthony awaited word from Congress about action on her petition, "Anthony telegraphed Senator Butler informing him that the three convicted electors [the officials who had been convicted alongside her] were jailed. Butler told this to President Grant and Grant pardoned the inspectors on March 3, 1874.

A Case to Take to the High Court

No matter how committed John Hooker may have been to the cause of woman suffrage, he was a canny lawyer and observer of the courts. Some devotees of the litigation strategy were eager for the Supreme Court to rule on the question, and many believed that the high court would vindicate their position. Several cases were wending their way through the courts at the end of 1873, and one of them would be heard by the Supreme Court, though it was not Anthony's.

Another litigation suffragist attempted to test the constitutionality of state laws that limited the franchise to men in the election of 1872, but unlike Susan B. Anthony's thwarted attempt to test the law through an appeal of her criminal trial, Virginia Minor's civil suit against Reese Happersett, the registrar of elections for the western precinct of the Sixth Ward of St. Louis, Missouri, went all the way to the U.S. Supreme Court.

Virginia Louisa Minor, then forty-eight years old, was a member of NWSA, and a veteran of the women's movement. She was married to the lawyer Francis Minor, a distant cousin, for nearly thirty years. The couple's marriage was an equal partnership, which was unusual at the time. Since Francis and Virginia were cousins with the same last name, the bride did not need to give up her own name upon marriage. Francis also arranged joint ownership of the couple's property so they could circumvent Missouri's marital property rules that would have otherwise granted Francis sole ownership. Though Virginia had volunteered with the St. Louis Union Aid Society during the Civil War, by at least one account, she only turned to full-time political activism after the Minors' only child, their fourteen-year-old son, died in a shooting accident in 1866. Virginia's activism after the war focused on woman suffrage. In 1867 she organized and collected over three hundred signatures for a petition to the Missouri legislature to extend the franchise to women. When that effort was overwhelmingly defeated by an 89–5 vote, she helped found, and became the first president of, the Woman Suffrage Association of Missouri.

Francis Minor, a graduate of Princeton and the University of Virginia Law School, was the successful St. Louis attorney who wrote the 1869 "Resolutions" and introduced it at a national convention hosted by the association at the Mercantile Library in St. Louis. Susan B. Anthony attended the convention and heard the Minors present their strategy of appealing to the courts. Virginia addressed the convention, proclaiming, "I believe that the Constitution of the United States gives me every right and privilege to which every other citizen is entitled. . . . Failing before the Legislature, we must then turn to the Supreme Court . . . and ask it to decide what are our rights as citizens."

After introducing his resolutions, Francis wrote to Stanton and Anthony's journal, the *Revolution*, to submit them for publication. In his letter dated October 14, 1869, Francis explained to the journal's readers: "When I framed them, I looked beyond the action of this

Convention. These resolutions place the cause of equal rights far in advance of any position heretofore taken." Francis's constitutional arguments in the resolutions were probably the first public assertion that the Fourteenth Amendment granted women the right to vote as one of the privileges of citizenship protected against state law encroachment. But Francis's Fourteenth Amendment strategy signaled more than just a legal claim. "We no longer beat the air—no longer assume merely the attitude of petitioners. We claim a right, based upon citizenship," Francis declared.

Anthony was quite taken with this proposed change in posture, a shift from supplicant in the legislative antechamber to claimant in the courts. She believed that Francis was the "first person to assert a woman's right to vote under the Fourteenth Amendment," and that "no man has contributed to the woman suffrage movement so much valuable constitutional argument and proof as Mr. Minor." Anthony and Stanton rushed to publish Francis's "Resolutions" in a revised form with legal references—his legal brief, so to speak—in the October 28, 1869, issue of *Revolution*. They printed "ten thousand extra copies of the issue . . . including one sent to each member of congress." When Anthony and her allies were thwarted in their opposition to the restrictive language of the Fifteenth Amendment, they adopted Francis Minor's "Resolutions" and their judicial strategy based on the Fourteenth Amendment as the focus of their campaign after 1869. The "Resolutions" also served as the template for both Anthony's and Minors' cases after the 1872 election.

On October 15, 1872, Virginia Minor went to the election registration office at 2004 Market Street in St. Louis and attempted to have her name added to the list of registered voters so that she would be allowed to vote in the upcoming presidential election. Reese Grier Happersett, one of the registrars for elections for the western precinct of the Sixth Ward of St. Louis, refused to add Virginia Minor's name to the voting list. Virginia pointed out to the young elections clerk that she "was a resident of the thirteenth election district of the city and county of St. Louis, in the State of Missouri, and had been so residing in said county and election district, for the entire period of twelve months and more, immediately preceding . . . and for more than twenty years had been and is, a tax-paying, law-abiding citizen of the county and State aforesaid."

She insisted that she was conscientiously following the law as "she appeared before him, at his office . . . and then there offered to take and subscribe the oath to support the Constitution of the United States, and of the State of Missouri, as required by the registration law of said State . . . and respectfully applied to him to be registered as a lawful voter." Unintimidated by the older woman and her husband, who stood by her side, Happersett "was then thrown into an awkward dilemma, and scarcely knew what to do or say," according to the report of the incident the *St. Louis Times* published a little over two weeks afterward. The *Times* article, clearly sympathetic to the official's position, told its readers that Happersett "was gallant enough to have acquiesced, but the law of the State authorized him to register only males . . . [and he] firmly but politely declined."

The brief filed on behalf of the Minors in the appeal to the U.S. Supreme Court put Happersett's response somewhat less sympathetically: supposedly he refused her request and told her that "she was not entitled to be registered, or to vote, because she was not a 'male' citizen, but a woman." The language in the Minors' petition to the Court claimed that Happersett had "knowingly, willfully, maliciously and corruptly refused to place her name upon the list of registered voters, whereby she was deprived of her right to vote."

The *Times* was not entirely antagonistic toward Mrs. Minor; condescending would be a more accurate term. The editorial writer pointed out that "Mrs Minor is a lady of the highest respectability, and belongs to a class of reformers who would not stoop to any such action for the sake of creating a sensation." Locals knew exactly what the Minors had planned. The *Times* reminded its readers that "two years ago the leaders in the movement here, were just at the point of making a test case and carrying it up to the highest courts, but were unable to decide who should be made the victim in the test." The newspaper concluded, "It is very evident that a good deal more is intended than at first appears. . . . It is probable that the action of Mrs. Francis Minor is intended as the preliminary step toward a test case in the courts."

It was thus no surprise when little more than a week later, on November 9, 1872, Francis Minor filed a civil suit in the circuit court for St. Louis County, Missouri, on behalf of his wife and himself. As a married woman, Virginia Minor lacked standing to sue in her own name, a right not available to Missouri women until the Married Women's Act of 1889. The petition in the suit was formally filed by Francis and his co-counsel, John M. Krum and John B. Henderson, in December 1872.

John Marshall Krum, born in New York State, moved to St. Louis in 1840 after successfully practicing law and serving as the first mayor of Alton, Illinois. "In 1843 he was made Judge of the St. Louis Circuit Court and held that office until being elected mayor of St. Louis." He seems to be remembered primarily today for his work helping to establish the St. Louis public schools and "as a pioneer in planning the Sewer System." After retiring from politics, Krum "served as a director of Washington University. He was a professor at the St. Louis Law School." He was also the author of "a scholarly work, 'Missouri Justice.'" Like the Minors, Krum supported the Union and the Republican Party during the Civil War. He continued to practice law after the war. In the St. Louis Public Library profile of Krum published as a part of their historical exhibit on St. Louis mayors, no mention was made of Krum's role in the Minors' woman suffrage case.

John Brooks Henderson was probably the most prominent Missourian and lawyer of this era. Like the Minors and John Krum, he migrated to Missouri in the 1840s. Also, like Krum, Henderson had been an active Democrat before the war; he served two terms in the Missouri House of Representatives. Again, like Krum and the Minors, Henderson was an ardent Unionist who transferred his allegiance to the Republicans when the Civil War began. In 1862 Henderson was appointed a U.S. senator to replace Trusten Polk, who had been expelled from the Senate for supporting the Confederacy after the advent of the war. Henderson's place in Missouri and U.S. history was assured when Henderson coauthored and introduced in the Senate the Thirteenth Amendment prohibiting slavery, "because he was convinced that it would pass only if sponsored by a slave-state Senator." His senate career ended when he broke ranks with the majority of his fellow Republican senators to join six other Republicans in casting their vote for acquittal in the impeachment trial of President Andrew Johnson, an act for which he was "denounced, threatened and burned in effigy." He later ran unsuccessfully for governor and again for senator. At around the time the U.S. Supreme Court handed down its decision in *Minor v. Happersett*, Henderson was appointed by President Grant as special U.S. attorney to prosecute the Whiskey Ring, a major national bribery and corruption case involving over one hundred distillers, politicians, and internal revenue agents; he was later fired by Grant when he protested Grant's interference in the prosecutions.

This was a formidable legal team, one that might have reasonably thought they could prevail in the courts (after legislative petitions had failed), to uphold the right of women to vote. Norma Basch, an eminent women's legal historian, characterized their efforts as "as [a] meticulously planned and ingeniously argued case that probed the boundaries of the Fourteenth Amendment."

The civil suit brought by the Minors in the Missouri courts claimed that "by reason of the wrongful acts of the defendant [Happersett] . . . [Virginia Minor] has been damaged in the sum of ten thousand dollars, for which she prays judgment." The Minors were not avaricious. The damages they sought were a legal requirement to create a real case in controversy that could be tried in the circuit court and appealed to the higher courts. The arguments in the petition to support their case that Happersett had acted wrongfully were a somewhat expanded version of the resolutions Francis had drafted more than three years before. Francis, Krum, and Henderson directly challenged the validity of provisions in the Missouri constitution and election law claiming that they were "in conflict with, and repugnant to the Constitution of the United States, which is paramount to State authority" under the Supremacy Clause (Article VI, Section 2) of the Constitution.

Pleading in the alternative, the Minors' petition to the Missouri courts invoked a wide variety of additional constitutional provisions that they argued were violated by the Missouri law and constitution—namely, Article I, Section 9, Paragraph 3, which prohibited Congress from passing a Bill of Attainder (a legislative enactment finding a person guilty of a crime without a trial in court); Article I, Section 10, Paragraph 1, which prohibited the states from doing the same; Article IV, Section 4, which required the federal government to "guarantee to every state in this union a republican form of government"; the Fifth Amendment, which states that "no person shall be . . . deprived of life, liberty of property, without due process of law"; the Ninth Amendment, which states that "the enumeration in the Constitution of certain rights, shall not be construed to deny or disparage others retained by the people"; and the Fourteenth Amendment.

The Fourteenth Amendment was by far the most important and relevant constitutional section cited by the Minors and the backbone of their suit. It was the strategy that Francis Minor proposed in 1869. The first section of the Fourteenth Amendment stated that all persons "born or naturalized in the United States . . . are citizens of the United States, and of the State wherein they reside." While this provision responded to the deprivation of citizenship dictum in Chief Justice Taney's opinion in the *Dred Scott* case, the wording was general and seemingly applied to all Americans, including women. The section went further to prohibit any state from making or enforcing "any law, which shall abridge the privileges or immunities of citizens of the United States."

This wording was the crux of the Minors' case. Missouri could not pass laws that "abridged the privileges" of Virginia Minor as a citizen of the United States. And it seemed to them that one of the paramount privileges of citizenship was the right to vote. It logically followed that the Missouri constitution and election law limiting voting to men and disenfranchising women citizens of the state violated the Fourteenth Amendment.

Reese Happersett was represented by Smith P. Galt. Galt was a recent transplant from Lancaster, Pennsylvania, and had served during the Civil War as a captain in the 122nd Pennsylvania Volunteers, Company C. Shortly before leaving Pennsylvania for Missouri, he married Frances Olivia Franklin, daughter of his colonel in the 122nd, Thomas Emlin Franklin. Galt had a successful career as a corporate and railroad lawyer in Missouri, successful enough that his name was included in a volume of "Notable St. Louisians" published in 1900. He never achieved the illustrious ranks of Krum or Henderson, but, for that matter, neither did Francis Minor.

Galt responded to the Minors' civil suit against Happersett by filing a demurrer. A demurrer is a form of pleading in which the defendant does not challenge the facts as stated in the complaint by the plaintiffs but nevertheless argues that those facts fail to state a legitimate cause of action in law. Galt's pleading on behalf of Happersett was simple and contained only three short reasons for the demurrer: "1. Because said Virginia L. Minor plaintiff had no right to vote at the general election held in November, 1872 . . . 2. Because said Virginia L. Minor had no right to be registered for voting by said defendant . . . [and] 3. Because it was the duty of the defendant to refuse to place said Virginia L. Minor's name upon the list of registered voters," concluding that all of the factual information in the petition may be correct, but Missouri law precludes a successful suit against Happersett.

The petition and demurrer were formally filed on January 2, 1873. The Missouri trial judge would have to rule on whether the Minors could proceed to a trial or whether their suit should be summarily dismissed because Happersett's demurrer was correct in claiming that as a matter of law they had no legitimate case. Before the circuit court judge heard their case, Francis and his co-counsel filed a brief containing additional arguments based on the Bill of Right's guarantee of right of free speech, since "the right to vote or express one's wish at the polls, is embraced in the spirit, if not the letter, of the First Amendment. They also invoked the Thirteenth Amendment, arguing that without the vote women suffered under the yoke of "involuntary servitude." They concluded by claiming the right to vote under the Natural Law jurisprudential theory popular in the middle of the nineteenth century, because "suffrage is never conferred by government upon a citizen. He [bad choice of pronoun under the circumstances] holds it by higher title."

The first Missouri hearing took place in the recently erected Four Courts Building on Twelfth Street between Clark and Spruce in Circuit Court 5 of the old courthouse in St. Louis, now a historic site managed by the national park service. (Court 5 currently serves as the site library.) It was the same courtroom in which a federal circuit judge ruled that Dred Scott and his family were slaves. On February 3, 1873, the judge quickly ruled in favor of Happersett's demurrer and dismissed the case.

Francis and Virginia and their counsel were neither surprised nor disheartened by the circuit court judge's dismissal of their case. They had never expected to win in the lower state court. As the *St. Louis Times* had predicted the previous November: "It is expected that a decision adverse to the plaintiffs will be rendered, and in that case it will go before the State Supreme court at the arch term, and thence up to the Supreme court of the United States."

On May 7, 1873, the Minors' case was heard by the Missouri Supreme Court. Of the five judges who served on the Missouri Supreme Court in 1873, only four heard the Minors' appeal. The chief justice, David Wagner, was absent when the case was argued and so did not vote on their petition. Of the remaining four, at least one report claims that Judge E. B. Ewing died while the case was pending. The remaining judges, H. M. Vories, Wash Adams, and J. A. Sherwood, unanimously affirmed the circuit court ruling against the Minors.

As had the trial court, the Missouri Supreme Court relied on the Missouri constitution and election law, but faced their Fourteenth Amendment claim head on. Using an analysis that relied implicitly on the U.S. Supreme Court's majority opinion in the *Slaughter-House Cases*, the Missouri Supreme Court stated that the Fourteenth Amendment had been passed *only* to protect the former slaves from "unfriendly legislation." With the history of the Reconstruction amendment still fresh in these judges' memories, the Fourteenth Amendment was passed and ratified because "unless . . . [former slaves] had the right to vote and thus protect themselves against oppression, their freedom from slavery would be a mere mockery." Virginia Minor, not being a former male slave, was obviously not the object of the Framers of the Fourteenth Amendment, and so "there could have been no intention [in the amendment] to abridge the power of the States to limit the right of suffrage to the male inhabitants."

Briefing the Case for Women's Right to Vote

Now the Minors brought their appeal to the U.S. Supreme Court. The Court that heard the Minors' appeal was little changed from the politicized post–Civil War Court of Chief Justice Salmon P. Chase. Indeed, the only change in its personnel was the position of chief justice itself. Eight months after Chase's death, and after several missteps in Grant's attempt to replace him, Morrison Remick

Waite was confirmed as the sixth (or seventh depending on how you count John Rutledge who had been a recess appointment by Washington but then was rejected by the Senate before actively taking up the position) chief justice of the U.S. Supreme Court. He was Grant's fourth pick for the chief justiceship and his third nominee (Grant had previously asked Senator Roscoe Conkling to take the chief's seat and was turned down; he then nominated but withdrew the nominations of George Williams, a former senator from Oregon and Grant's attorney general, and Caleb Cushing, a former attorney general under President Peirce, a justice of the Massachusetts Supreme Court and a diplomat serving as Grant's minister to Spain). Grant's options were limited also by the fact that two of the associate justices currently serving on the Court, Stephen J. Field and Joseph Bradley, had actively campaigned for the chief justiceship. Waite thus came to the Court a weakened choice for chief.

In other words, Waite, who would write the opinion for the Court in *Minor v. Happersett*, was not the strong leader a Reconstruction and post-Reconstruction era Court needed to protect the rights of minorities. Waite, a native of Connecticut, was a graduate of Yale and a member of Phi Beta Kappa. He was an intelligent man, particularly interested in constitutional jurisprudence; a hardworking lawyer; and a leader of the Toledo, Ohio, bar. He had served a term as a state senator and presided over the Ohio constitutional convention. His Republican credentials were unassailable.

Two other justices and fellow Grant appointees sitting with Waite on the Court that term are worth noting. The first was Ward Hunt. The other was Joseph Bradley, the justice who wrote a strikingly antifeminist concurrence in the case of *Myra Bradwell v. State of Illinois*. He opined that

> the civil law, as well as nature herself, has always recognized a wide difference in the respective spheres and destinies of man and woman. Man is, or should be, woman's protector and defender. The natural and proper timidity and delicacy which belongs to the female sex evidently unfits it for many of the occupations of civil life. The constitution of the family organization, which is founded in the divine ordinance, as well as in the nature of things, indicates the domestic sphere as that

which properly belongs to the domain and functions of womanhood. The harmony, not to say identity, of interest and views which belong, or should belong, to the family institution is repugnant to the idea of a woman adopting a distinct and independent career from that of her husband. . . . The paramount destiny and mission of woman are to fulfil the noble and benign offices of wife and mother. This is the law of the Creator.

It should be noted that the Illinois legislature apparently disagreed with Justice Bradley's theology, for less than a decade later it passed a law forbidding the exclusion of any person "from any occupation, profession, or employment (except military), on account of sex."

The brief Francis Minor, John Krum, and John Henderson filed was nearly thirty pages long, considerably longer than Francis's 1869 "Resolutions." It began with a summary of how the case came to the Supreme Court, including a copy of the Minors' original petition to the St. Louis circuit court and Happersett's demurrer and the legal basis of why the U.S. Supreme Court had jurisdiction to hear the Minors' appeal: "The question is thus broadly presented of a conflict between the Constitution of the State of Missouri and that of the United States, as contemplated by the twenty-fifth section of the judiciary act of 1789, and the supplemental act of February 5, 1867."

The brief then cited three errors the Missouri Supreme Court made when it upheld the circuit court in sustaining Happersett's demurrer. The first error was simply the fact that the Missouri high court had affirmed the lower court's ruling. The second error was that in upholding the circuit court in ruling for Happersett the state supreme court declared "that the plaintiff in error [Virginia Minor] was not entitled to vote at the election mentioned in the record." The third and final error was that the Missouri court had "in effect, declar[ed] that the Constitution and laws of Missouri . . . do not conflict with the Constitution of the United States," which Virginia Minor and her lawyers claimed they did.

As simple as these errors appeared on their face, the legal arguments presented in the remaining twenty-eight pages of the brief Francis and his co-counsel filed on behalf of Virginia were complex and sophisticated. On first glance, some of their claims might seem outlandish or even silly—likening the denial of suffrage to women to "indentured servitude" or a "bill of attainder"—but closer analysis of their arguments and the authorities they invoked were clever and compelling. It is also apparent from some of the language of the brief that Francis Minor (and perhaps his colleagues as well) felt passionately about the issue of woman suffrage.

The opening of the brief is surprising given that the appellants were trying to argue a question of law before the High Court. "We think," the lawyers began their argument, "the chief difficulty in this case, is one of fact rather than of law." They made a risky admission: "The practice is against the plaintiff," since the states "have uniformly claimed and exercised the right to act, as to the matter of suffrage, *just as they pleased*—to limit or extend it, as they saw proper" (emphasis added). They also admitted that the state legislatures' actions in thus limiting the vote to men reflected the cultural norm because "this is the popular idea on the subject." Indeed, "men accept it as a matter of fact, and take for granted that it must be right." Were they conceding that they had no case in law? Not at all. After all, recent history had shown that accepted and even popular legal and cultural norms—in slavery—were not necessarily right. "So in the days of African slavery," they pointed out, "thousands believed it to be right—even a Divine institution." They knew that the justices were with one exception Republicans. "We all know," the brief asserted, that now "this belief has passed away." So, too, they vociferously argued that "in like manner, this doctrine of the right of the States to exercise unlimited and absolute control over the elective franchise of citizens of the United States, must and will give way to a truer and better understanding of the subject."

But changes in public opinion, even if true, are not enough to hold sway with the Court. The appellants must have a valid constitutional claim for the U.S. Supreme Court to overturn a ruling by a state supreme court. Thus the Minors' brief arrived at the crux of their argument: "We claim, and presume, that the elective franchise is a privilege of citizenship within the meaning of the Constitution of the United States." Over and over the suffragists had recited this mantra; Anthony had claimed it as fact; now it was to be tested before the highest tribunal in the land.

But less than two years before Francis filed his brief, the Supreme Court on April 14, 1873, had delivered a fatal blow to such a generous reading of the Privileges or Immunities Clause of the Fourteenth Amendment in the *Slaughter-House Cases* (1873). In cases that had nothing to do with either women or African Americans, Justice Miller, writing for the majority (the case was decided by a 5–4 vote) upheld a regulation of the slaughterhouse industry in Louisiana against the butchers' claim that the law, which had created a monopoly in the industry from which they were excluded, had impinged on their rights under the Privileges or Immunities Clause of the Fourteenth Amendment. Miller narrowly construed what constituted the protected "privileges" under the amendment. As Miller wrote in his opinion, "Of the privileges and immunities of the citizen of the United States, and of the privileges and immunities of the citizen of the State, and what they respectively are, we will presently consider; but we wish to state here that it is only the former which are placed by this clause under the protection of the Federal Constitution, and that the latter, whatever they may be, are not intended to have any additional protection by this paragraph of the amendment."

The justice only cited a very few privileges of U.S. citizenship, but he went into a detailed survey of pre–Civil War case law to illustrate that antebellum judges believed the privileges derived from state citizenship included most "fundamental" rights. Justice Miller concluded that any other reading of the amendment to extend federal protection of a citizen's rights against the states "radically changes the whole theory of the relations of the State and Federal governments to each other and of both these governments to the people. . . . We are convinced that no such results were intended by the Congress which proposed these amendments, nor by the legislatures of the States which ratified them." In point of fact, Miller cited no evidence from the record of the debates in Congress or from the state legislative debates over ratification to support this assertion.

Nevertheless, when taken in conjunction with *Bradwell* discussed earlier, and which the Court decided only a day after it handed down its opinion in the *Slaughter-House Cases*, it is impossible not to view the Supreme Court precedent at the time that the Court considered the *Minor* case, as anything but hostile toward an application of the Fourteenth Amendment's protection of the "privileges or immunities" of U.S. citizens to cover any substantive or fundamental rights. The Court itself pointed out the following:

> The opinion just delivered in the Slaughter-House Cases renders elaborate argument in the [*Bradwell*] case unnecessary; for, unless we are wholly and radically mistaken in the principles on which those cases are decided, the right to control and regulate the granting of license to practice law in the courts of a State is one of those powers which are not transferred for its protection to the Federal government, and its exercise is in no manner governed or controlled by citizenship of the United States. . . . It is unnecessary to repeat the argument on which the judgment in those cases is founded. It is sufficient to say they are conclusive of the present case.

Yet Minor, Krum, and Henderson tried to "claim, and presume it will not be disputed," that voting, unlike one's occupation at issue in both the *Slaughter-House Cases* and *Bradwell*, was a fundamental privilege of U.S. citizenship, not merely a privilege derived from and subject to the will of the states. While the odds were that the Court would not side with them, the argument of the Minors' attorneys was not completely far-fetched; voting has a more convincing nexus to citizenship than employment, after all.

The brief attempted to demonstrate how the concept of citizenship came to be understood in American law. It was, Minor argued, in direct contradiction to the pre-Revolutionary situation in which the colonists had been "subjects" of the Crown. "But when these 'bands,' as they are termed in the Declaration of Independence, were dissolved, the political relation became changed, and we no longer hear in the United States the [term] 'subject' . . . The term citizen was substituted for that of 'subject.'" This was no mere change of nomenclature, according to the brief, "the men who framed the Constitution of the United States had all been 'subjects' of the English king, and they well knew the radical change wrought by the revolution." Such a "radical change" meant that the idea of "independence" had supplanted the "feudal idea of dependence." It is in this context that the brief's authors insisted the Court read the word of the Constitution, in which "WE MUST LOOK FOR THE LIMITATIONS, IF ANY, THAT MAY BE PLACED UPON THE POLITICAL RIGHTS OF THE PEOPLE OR CITIZENS OF THE UNITED STATES. . . . A LIMITATION NOT FOUND THERE, OR AUTHORIZED BY THAT INSTRUMENT, CANNOT BE LEGALLY EXERCISED BY ANY LESSER OR INFERIOR JURISDICTION." This was dangerous ground because the only mention of voting in the Constitution assigned that task to the states. Minor's counsel were undeterred, however, pointing out that discretion on suffrage was intended by the Framers only "to be regulated by them; not to limit or restrict the right of suffrage, but to carry the same fully into effect." How did they know this? Again, they asserted that "it is impossible to believe that anything more than this was intended. In the first place, it would be inconsistent and at variance with the idea of the supremacy of the federal government; and, next, if the absolute, ultimate and unconditional control of the matter had been intended to be given to the States *it would have been so expressed.* It would not have been left to doubt or implication." In other words, the absence of an express authorization could only lead to the conclusion that such an interpretation was never intended. Furthermore, "in so important a matter as suffrage, the chief of all political rights or privileges, by which indeed, life, liberty and all others are guarded and maintained, and without which they would be held completely at the mercy of others; we repeat, it is impossible to conceive that this was intended to be left wholly and entirely at the discretion of the States." The way the word "impossible" was employed in this context was clearly an attempt to persuade by hyperbole; they would go on to utilize that word several more times in the course of the brief to emphasize the rightness of their position.

The brief next argued that Missouri's election law limiting suffrage to men, "inflict[ed] upon the plaintiff and the class to which she belongs, the bar of *perpetual disenfranchisement,* where no crime or offence is alleged or pretended, and without 'due process of law.'" This amounted to "a 'bill of attainder' of the most odious and oppressive character." A bill of attainder, prohibited by both Article I, Section 9 (vis-à-vis Congress) and Section 10 (applied to the states) is a legislative act that singles out an individual or group for punishment without a trial. The vote was an essential right and its deprivation clearly a punishment, and the brief quoted the father of the Constitution, James Madison, to the effect that such deprivation "violates the vital principle of free government, that those who are to be bound by laws, ought to have a voice in making them."

Thus the disenfranchisement of Virginia Minor, and all the other women residing in Missouri, was a punishment laid against members of one sex because "any deprivation or suspension of any of these rights . . . is punishment, and can be in no otherwise defined." In other words, "to single out a class of citizens and say to them, 'Notwithstanding you posses[s] all these qualifications, you shall never note, or take part in your government,' what is it but a bill of attainder?"

To support their contention that the privileges of citizenship included the elective franchise, Minor, Krum, and Henderson quoted Justice Bushrod Washington from the same 1823 case Anthony's counsel cited and Justice Miller invoked in the *Slaughter-House Cases*, though they found a passage Justice Miller seems to have ignored. In *Corfield v. Coryell*, Justice Washington opined, "We feel no hesitation in confining these expressions to those privileges and immunities which are in their nature *fundamental*; which belong of right to the citizens of all free governments. . . . What those fundamental principles are, it would perhaps be more tedious than difficult to enumerate." Washington went on to enumerate those rights, and Minors' counsel concluding the justice's listing: "to which may be added, THE ELECTIVE FRANCHISE."

While it is true that Justice Washington characterized the elective franchise as a fundamental right, Minor and his colleagues might not have been best served in quoting the passage, since the justice immediately qualified this assertion with the language "as regulated and established by the laws or Constitution of the State in which it is to be exercised." Thus Justice Washington, quoted in full, actually undermined the brief's ultimate point, that suffrage was a fundamental right of national citizenship, not a privilege awarded at the discretion of the states.

Finally, the Minors' brief decided to confront the precedent of the *Slaughter-House Cases* head on since they could anticipate that it would be cited against them. The Minors' counsel quoted Justice Miller: "the negro having, by the Fourteenth amendment, been declared a citizen of the United States, *is thus made a voter in every State of the Union*" (emphasis added in the brief). They then immediately reasoned by analogy that "if this be true of the negro citizen of the United States, it is equally true of the woman citizen." Francis Minor knew that this very issue had divided the woman suffrage movement, and that the Framers of the Fourteenth and Fifteenth Amendments had excluded women. Would the high court ignore these facts?

Francis Minor included in his brief to the Supreme Court an eloquent plea:

> We ask the Court to consider what it is to be disf[r]anchised; not this plaintiff only, but an entire class of people, utterly deprived of all voice in the government under which they live! We say it is to her, and to them, a DESPOTISM, and not a Republic. What matters it that the tyranny be of many instead of one? Society shudders at the thought of putting a fraudulent ballot into the ballot-box! What is the difference between putting a fraudulent ballot in, and keeping a lawful ballot out? Her disfranchised condition is a badge of servitude . . . a married woman cannot, by the law of Missouri, own a dollar's worth of personal property, except by the *consent of another!* It makes no difference that that other is her husband. This, it is true, is a State law, a matter exclusively of State legislation; but we mention it to show how utterly helpless and powerless her condition is without the ballot.

In the conclusion to the brief, Minor and co-counsel appealed to the conscience of the Court: "It is impossible that that can be a republican government in which one-half the citizens thereof are forever disfranchised. A citizen disfranchised is a citizen attainted; and this, too, in face of the fact, that you look in vain in the great charter of government, the Constitution of the United States, for any warrant or authority for such discrimination. To that instrument she appeals for protection." And with those words Virginia Minor's counsel placed her case before the Court. The "defendant in error," Reese Happersett, was not represented by counsel and did not file a brief with the Supreme Court.

In the Well of the High Court

On February 9, 1875, after the Court had an opportunity to review their brief, Francis Minor appeared to make his oral argument. Francis reiterated many of the arguments from his brief, according to the *New York Times* account of the proceedings. But the questioning he faced from Justice Field did not go so well. Associate Justice Stephen J. Field, was the intellectual heavyweight on the Court in this era. A transplant to California from Connecticut, a Democrat whose loyalty to the Union had gained him the trust of Lincoln and his advisers, Field was a conservative jurist from an exceptionally distinguished family. One of his younger brothers was David Dudley Field II, a famous attorney in his own right and the author of the Field Code, which reformed the practice of civil procedure in New York State and influenced many others. Another brother was the millionaire entrepreneur Cyrus Field, the man responsible for the first trans-Atlantic cable. His sister's son, David Josiah Brewer, served as an associate justice on the Supreme Court with his uncle between 1889 and 1897. At the time of the *Minor* oral arguments Justice Field, who had dissented in *Bradwell*, had served on the Court for twelve years.

If Francis thought Field would make things easy for him, he was disappointed. According to the *Times* account of the "colloquy" between Field and Minor, the justice asked Minor: "So you hold that citizenship confers the right to vote?" To which Minor politely responded: "Yes, Sir." Field then pressed Minor to ascertain the limits of counsel's argument: "Have children then the right to vote?" Here he seems to have caught Francis left-footed. There are so many ways, in hindsight, Francis might have responded to Field, but all he could say was "Yes, Sir." The *Times* duly added with some hint of criticism: "[Without any further explanation.]" Francis was a novice litigant before the high court and did not serve his case and client well. The newspaper's report of the proceedings concluded that "the court generally seemed inclined to rally the counsel, but as he either did not relish the piquant interruption and therefore purposely refrained from replying, or was unable to respond to the satisfaction of their Honors, they soon ceased to ply him with questions." Again, Reese Happersett was not represented at the oral arguments.

The Court reporter's headnote for the *Minor* case succinctly framed Francis's "elaborate argument" as "partially based on what he deemed true political views, and partially resting on legal and constitutional grounds." The Court implied that the former was beyond the scope of the Court's purview, but "these last seemed to be thus resolvable." It then logically summarized Minor's "elaborate argument" in five simple points:

1st. As a citizen of the United States, the plaintiff was entitled to any and all the "privileges and immunities" that belong to such position however defined; and as are held, exercised, and enjoyed by other citizens of the United States.

2d. The elective franchise is a privilege of citizenship, in the highest sense of the word. It is the privilege preservative of all rights and privileges; and especially of the right of the citizen to participate in his or her government.

3d. The denial or abridgment of this privilege, if it exist at all, must be sought only in the fundamental charter of government, the Constitution of the United States. If not found there, no inferior power or jurisdiction can legally claim the right to exercise it.

4th. But the Constitution of the United States, so far from recognizing or permitting any denial or abridgment of the privileges of its citizens, expressly declares that "no State shall make or enforce any law which shall abridge the privileges or immunities of citizens of the United States."

5th. [It] follows that the provisions of the Missouri constitution and registry law before recited, are in conflict with and must yield to the paramount authority of the Constitution of the United States.

Chief Justice Waite delivered the opinion for the unanimous court. He deliberately limited the opinion to the central question of "whether, since the adoption of the fourteenth amendment, a woman, who is a citizen of United States and of the State of Missouri, is a voter in that State," though the justices "might, perhaps, decide the case upon other grounds." After all, Waite observed, "the case was undoubtedly brought to this court for the sole purpose of having that question decided by us." Again, he summarized the question as framed by Francis and his co-counsel: "It is contended that the provisions of the constitution and laws of the State of Missouri which confine the right of suffrage and registration therefore to men, are in violation of the Constitution of the United States, and therefore void." He then got to the crux of the Minors' case against Happersett, "The argument is, that as a woman, born or naturalized in the United States and subject to the jurisdiction thereof, is a citizen of the United States and of the State in which she resides, she has the right of suffrage as one of the privileges and immunities of her citizenship, which the State cannot by its laws or constitution abridge."

But Waite did not immediately address this central issue. Instead, he went into a rather lengthy exegesis about what constitutes citizenship, beginning with the unequivocal conclusion, and stating for what was the first time in the Court's history, that "there is no doubt that women may be citizens." It is clear from the analysis that follows that "may be" simply referred to the fact that, like men, women might be foreign transplants who had not yet become naturalized citizens. After all, Waite pointed out, "They [women] are persons." Quoting the Fourteenth Amendment language that by now was familiar, he continued: "'all persons born or naturalized in the United States and subject to the jurisdiction thereof' are expressly declared to be 'citizens of the United States and of the State wherein they reside.'" But the Fourteenth Amendment was not essential to the assertion that women born or naturalized are citizens. "Before its adoption," Waite discoursed, "the Constitution of the United States did not in terms prescribe who should be citizens of the United States or of the several states, yet there were necessarily such citizens without such provision."

Waite then indulged in a tangential discourse on the meaning of the term "citizen." Obviously, a nation by definition must have "citizens," since "there cannot be a nation without a people." And these people in a nation form some kind of "political community," which "for convenience it has been found necessary to give a name to this membership. The object is to designate by a title the person and the relation *he* bears to the nation" (emphasis added). What to call these members of the nation's "political community"? Waite suggested several answers drawn from history as "the words 'subject,' 'inhabitant,' and 'citizen' have been used, and the choice between them is sometimes made to depend upon the form of the government." But Waite's digression had a point. Since the term "Citizen is now more commonly employed, however, and as it has been considered better suited to the description of one living under a republican government, it was adopted by nearly all of the States upon their separation from Great Britain, and was afterwards adopted in the Articles of Confederation and the Constitution of the United States."

With that historical and constitutional pedigree established, it was clear to Waite that a citizen "is understood as conveying the idea of membership of a nation, *and nothing more*" (emphasis added). Thus, on the one hand, Waite deftly conferred on women membership in the nation as citizens, while with the other hand, and consistent with the Court's prior stance in the *Slaughter-House Cases* and the even more recent and relevant *Bradwell*, deprived such citizenship of any real value. Nevertheless, Waite concluded that "whoever then was one of the people of either of these States when the Constitution of the United States was adopted, became ipso facto a citizen." The chief justice cited statute and case law to support this interpretation of citizenship and the conclusion that women just like men were citizens. Unlike modern justices who have the assistance of bright young recent law school graduates, Waite did his own research and writing.

"In this respect," Waite optimistically averred, "men have never had an advantage over women," since "the same laws precisely apply to both." And subsequent amendments such as the Fourteenth "did not affect the citizenship of women any more than it did of men." Applied to the present case this meant that "the rights of Mrs. Minor do not depend upon the amendment. She has always been a citizen from her birth, and entitled to all the privileges and immunities of citizenship." Missouri, under the amendment, was prohibited "from abridging any of her privileges and immunities as a citizen of the United States; but it did not confer citizenship on her. That she had before its adoption." Thus the Supreme Court officially recognized women as U.S. citizens. With the question of whether women were citizens decided in the affirmative (if, in fact, that was ever really in doubt), would the privileges of her citizenship entitle Virginia Minor and the rest of American women to vote?

The Court now had to answer that question, and the answer would clearly be contingent on the answer to another question. Chief Justice Waite cut right to the heart of the matter: "The direct question is, therefore, presented whether all citizens are necessarily voters." Because if the answer were yes and the right of suffrage were "one of the necessary privileges of a citizen of the United States, then the constitution and laws of Missouri confining it to men [would be] in violation of the Constitution of the United States, as amended, and consequently void."

Where would the Court find the answer to that question? The conundrum it faced was that "the Constitution does not define the privileges and immunities of citizens," but the task was simplified because "we need not determine what" *all* the privileges and immunities of citizens might be, "but only whether suffrage is necessarily one of them." The Court first looked to the text of the Constitution. How did that fundamental law treat the question of suffrage? "The United States has no voters in the States of its own creation," Waite observed. When one looked at the constitutional provisions for the election of federal officials "all [are] elected directly or indirectly by State voters." The circumstances for voting were also controlled by state law because "the times, places, and manner of holding elections for Senators and Representatives" were to be "prescribed in each State by the legislature thereof."

Waite next proceeded to make a close examination of the voting practices of all the original states, and it was clear that there was wide variation in the granting of suffrage. While such diligence was not unusual for a practicing counsel, Waite's journey through the state statute books was a kind of pedantry that would mark the rest of his tenure. Indeed, he would take on more than his share of opinion writing and literally die at his desk. From his research, Waite concluded that "in this condition of the law in respect to suffrage in the several States it cannot for a moment be doubted that if it had been intended to make all citizens of the United States voters, the Framers of the Constitution would not have left it to implication . . . if intended, would have been expressly declared." The original Con-

206   { *Chapter Seven* }

stitution clearly conveyed the right to vote on no one; it left it to the states to determine who could vote.

To Waite's mind, the Fourteenth Amendment did not change any of this. "The [Fourteenth] amendment did not add to the privileges and immunities of a citizen. It simply furnished an additional guaranty for the protection of such as he already had." Thus, "no new voters were necessarily made by it." Another fact reinforces this conclusion. "After the adoption of the fourteenth amendment, it was deemed necessary to adopt a fifteenth," which specifically guaranteed "the right of citizens of the United States to vote . . . [regardless] of race, color, or previous condition of servitude." Thus, just as the suffragists had feared, the Fifteenth Amendment's failure to list sex in the list of characteristics that could not be used to deprive a citizen the franchise worked against them in their claim to a constitutional right of suffrage. Predictably, Waite pointed out that "if suffrage was one of these privileges or immunities, why amend the Constitution to prevent its being denied on account of race &c.?" Simple and well-established rules of statutory interpretation dictated that "nothing is more evident than that the greater must include the less, and if all were already protected why go through with the form of amending the Constitution to protect a part?"

Having disposed of the Minors' major constitutional claim under the Fourteenth Amendment, Waite now turned his attention to the less compelling arguments raised in their brief. In short order he dealt with them. On the constitutional guarantee of a republican form of government, Waite pointed out that no particular style of government was defined in the Constitution. He then repeated his earlier examples of various state laws on voting qualifications. Their claim that the Missouri law restricting the vote to male citizens was the equivalent of a constitutionally prohibited bill of attainder failed because no explicit legislative provision had been passed *against* women. And the constitutional language, "which declares that no person shall be deprived of life, liberty, or property without due process of law," could not apply to woman suffrage, since "he who has it can only be deprived of it by due process of law, but in order to claim protection he must first show that he has the right." Another quick historical look at the various states' record on voting, now adding in all of the states added to the Union since the original thirteen, concluded the opinion's examination of precedent on the issue of American suffrage.

Immediately before announcing the ruling, Waite added some very interesting dicta, comments not necessary to the ruling in the case. First, he pointed out that the Court gave "this case the careful consideration its importance demands." Second, in stark contrast to the conservative social commentary his colleague, Justice Bradley, promoted in his concurrence in the *Bradwell* case, the chief justice carefully pointed out that the Court's "province is to decide what the law is, not to declare what is should be." Waite allowed for a legislative change of heart on woman suffrage, conceding that "the arguments addressed to us bearing upon such a view of the subject may perhaps be sufficient to induce those having the power, to make the alteration."

The chief justice seemed almost regretful that those arguments "ought not to be permitted to influence our judgment in determining the present rights of the parties now litigating before us." In the end, "no argument as to woman's *need* of suffrage can be considered. We can only act upon her rights as they exist. It is not for us to look at the hardship of withholding" (emphasis added). He claimed that the Court's hands were tied. Arguing from the position of judicial restraint, he concluded: "Our duty is at an end if we find it is within the power of a State to withhold."

All the precedent Chief Justice Waite had recited could lead the Court to only one conclusion: "the Constitution of the United States does not confer the right of suffrage upon any one, and that the constitutions and laws of the several States which commit that important trust to men alone are not necessarily void." Thus the Court held that it affirmed the judgment of the Missouri Supreme Court. Neither Virginia Minor nor any woman would have the right to vote if the state in which they resided did not permit it. On March 29, 1875, the U.S. Supreme Court put paid to the litigation strategy envisioned by Francis Minor and adopted by the Anthony and Stanton suffragists back in 1869. There would be no judicial recognition of a woman's right to vote.

To the Nineteenth Amendment

By 1875 the struggle for woman suffrage had become the center-piece of the women's movement, and Susan B. Anthony stood in the center of the battle. After her trial, she turned her attention to a cause she had espoused in the 1840s, equal opportunities for women in education and teaching, but she never ceased her lobbying for the woman's franchise. She toured, raised funds, spoke, and wrote about women's rights. Wearied but unbowed, she continued to agitate, but in the final years of the century her body was not as strong as her will. She died in 1906, revered by all and loved by some in the movement. At her funeral in Rochester, Anna Howard Shaw spoke for everyone who had labored alongside Anthony: "She merged a keen sense of justice with the deepest love; her masterful intellect never for one moment checked the tenderness of her emotions; her splendid self-assertion found its highest realization in perfect self-surrender; she demonstrated the divine principle that the truest self-development must go hand in hand with the greatest and most ar-duous service for others . . . she was nothing, her cause was everything; she knew no existence apart from it; in it she lived and moved and had her being. It was the first and last thought of each day; it was the last word upon her faultering lips; to it her flitting soul responded when the silenced voice could no longer obey the will, and she could only answer our heart-broken questions with the clasp of her trembling hand." Eulogies are occasions for exaggera-tion, but Shaw did not exaggerate.

Anthony had not labored alone. An entire generation of feminists had worked together in the movement, and now all were gone. Eliz-abeth Cady Stanton, Anthony's friend, confidant, and fellow cam-paigner, died in 1902. Family life had not prevented her from tour-ing Europe, tutoring Congress on the need for women's rights, and promoting causes like a woman's right to birth control. She was survived by six of her seven children. When she learned of Stanton's passing, Anthony told a reporter, "Mrs. Stanton was a most courageous woman, a leader of thought and action. I have always called her the statesman of our movement." To their younger protégé, Ida Husted Harper, Anthony was more forthcoming. A letter dated October 28, 1902, revealed Anthony's sense of loss: "Well, it is an awful hush—it seems impossible—that the voice is hushed—that I have longed to hear for 50 years—longed to get her opinion of things—before I knew exactly where I stood—It is all at sea—but the Laws of Nature are still going on—with no shadow or turning—What a world it is—it goes right on & on—no matter who lives or who dies!!"

With Anthony and Stanton gone, advocacy of woman suffrage lay in the hands of a new generation of feminists. Some were more conservative in their view of women's roles than Anthony and Stanton had been. Others, taking advantage of the opportunities for women's formal education and professional standing that Anthony and Stanton had promoted, were college graduates and Progressives. Progressive victories in state elections in 1910 and 1912 led to woman suffrage throughout the West and much of the East Coast by 1919. Reluctantly President Woodrow Wilson asked Congress to pass the amendment, and after failing to get the necessary two-third vote in 1918, Congress acceded in 1919. The amendment was sent to the states and ratified the following year. It read: "The right of citizens of the United States to vote shall not be denied or abridged by the United States or by any State on account of sex. Congress shall have power to enforce this article by appropriate legislation."

CHRONOLOGY

1815	Elizabeth Cady Stanton born in Johnstown, New York
1820	Susan B. Anthony born in Adams, Massachusetts
1826	Anthony family moves to Upstate New York
1848	Seneca Falls Convention, drafting and passage of the Declaration of Sentiments
1849	Anthony family moves to Rochester, New York, a hotbed of reform activity
1851	Anthony and Stanton meet in Seneca Falls
1853–1855	Anthony and Stanton shift from temperance reform to focus on woman suffrage
1860–1865	Civil War; Anthony campaigns in Upstate New York for abolition of slavery and for women's rights; ratification of Thirteenth Amendment
1866–1869	American Equal Rights Association founded and then split over woman suffrage question
1868	Anthony and Stanton begin the *Revolution*, a journal devoted to women's rights; ratification of Fourteenth Amendment
1869	Anthony and Stanton found the National Woman Suffrage Association
1869	Founding of rival American Woman Suffrage Association
1869–1872	Efforts to unify NWSA and AWSA fail; ratification of Fifteenth Amendment
1870	Federal Voting Enforcement Act passed
1871–1872	Victoria Woodhull testifies before Congress and runs for president
1872	Major parties' platforms for 1872 election omit universal suffrage plank, but Republicans more friendly to women's rights
November 1, 1872	Anthony and others register to vote in the federal election in Rochester, New York
November 5, 1872	Anthony and others vote in the federal election

November 14, 1872	Anthony and other voters called before federal commissioner for offense of illegal voting
November 29, 1872	Preliminary hearing on the charges against Anthony
December 23–26, 1872	Hearings on the charges resume; Anthony case removed to federal court
January 20–24, 1873	Anthony case motions heard in federal court in Albany; grand jury indictment filed; trial postponed
April 14–15, 1873	U.S. Supreme Court hands down decisions in the *Slaughter-House Cases* and *Myra Bradwell v. Illinois*
May 22, 1873	Anthony trial begins, then is carried over to next session of federal circuit court with Justice Ward Hunt to preside
June 17–18, 1873	Anthony trial and trial of voting registrars in federal court, Justice Ward Hunt presiding; Hunt's directed verdict
February 9–March 29, 1875	*Minor v. Happersett* argued and decided in U.S. Supreme Court
October 26, 1902	Elizabeth Cady Stanton dies
March 13, 1906	Susan B. Anthony dies
May–June, 1919	Nineteenth Amendment passes both houses of Congress
August 18, 1920	Nineteenth Amendment ratified

BIBLIOGRAPHICAL ESSAY

Note from the Series Editors: The following bibliographical essay contains the major primary and secondary sources the author consulted for this volume. We have asked all authors in the series to omit formal citations in order to make our volumes more readable, inexpensive, and appealing for students and general readers. In adopting this format, Landmark Law Cases and American Society follows the precedent of a number of highly regarded and widely consulted series. However, a version with complete footnote documentation has been deposited with the Law Library at Rutgers University School of Law–Camden.

The primary sources for any account are the Susan B. Anthony Papers at the Library of Congress and the Anthony Papers at the University of Rochester Library. In particular, Susan Brownell Anthony Papers, University of Rochester Archives, Rare Books, 1846–1904, Location: A.A62, Box 1: Correspondence, two items: November 12, 1872: SBA to "My Dear Young Friend"; January 24, 1873: SBA to Francis S. Rew; also Volume 1: Scrapbook of newspaper clippings from the 1870s related to the woman suffrage movement; many dealing with the 1873 trial of Susan B. Anthony for voting in the election of 1872. The clippings are glued into a copy of State of New York Court of Appeals Reports.

Ann D. Gordon, ed., *The Selected Papers of Elizabeth Cady Stanton and Susan B. Anthony*, vol. 1, *In the School of Anti-Slavery, 1840 to 1866* (New Brunswick, NJ: Rutgers University Press, 1997); vol. 2, *Against the Aristocracy of Sex, 1866–1873* (New Brunswick, NJ: Rutgers University Press, 2000); and vol. 3, *National Protection for National Citizens, 1873–1880* (New Brunswick, NJ: Rutgers University Press, 2003), the Anthony-Stanton material is the single best source for anyone studying the nineteenth-century woman suffrage movement. Gordon and her editorial team have produced a monumental work. I recommend that if anyone is interested in the suffrage movement and its leaders, they should read the collected material and the exhaustive footnotes following each document. (Quotations from Gordon herself in my text are from 1:572n1; 2:242n1; 2:284 head note; 317n2; 374n5; 385n3; 404n1; 532n1; 552n3; 542 head note; 590n1; 619n6; 621n1; 3:30n5.)

Two other primary sources are extremely important. The first is the *History of Woman Suffrage*, 3 vols. (New York: Fowler & Wells, 1881), written and edited by Elizabeth Cady Stanton, Susan B. Anthony, and Matilda Joslyn Gage. Ida Husted Harper continued the project with three more volumes (New York: Fowler & Wells, 1922). The *History* is actually a collection of documents with a loose narrative connecting them. There are two problems with it. First, it is sometimes hard to follow, for it does not strictly follow a chronological line, and, second, like many memoirists the authors sanitize and rewrite some of the story. But the three women were eyewitnesses to these events and carefully preserved items that would have otherwise been lost to later historians.

Another very personal eyewitness account by Elizabeth Cady Stanton is her memoir *Eighty Years and More: Reminiscences, 1815–1897* (dedicated to Susan B. Anthony) (New York: European Publishing, 1898). Again, this is a somewhat quirky volume with some questions about the accuracy of her memories but full of detail and insight. The editions I used for both the *History* and *Eighty Years* were the e-text prepared by the Project Gutenberg Online at http://www.gutenberg.org. Printed collections of primary sources also include Ellen Carol DuBois, ed., *The Elizabeth Cady Stanton–Susan B. Anthony Reader* (Boston: Northeastern University Press, 1992) (quotations from the editor in my text from pp. 88, 89, 91, 101).

New York Times archives is an invaluable source of biography (the obituaries) and politics accessed through http://www.nyt.com. For much of the trial coverage and local news reportage, I used the *Rochester Democrat and Chronicle* on microfilm, Rush Rhees Library, University of Rochester, reel dates November 1, 1872, to July 31, 1873 (accessed through Interlibrary Loan at the University of Georgia, Athens); *Rochester Union and Advertiser* microfilm accessed through interlibrary loan from Rush Rhees Library, University of Rochester, reel dates November 1, 1872, to July 31, 1873.

The best and most reliable available edition of the trial transcript is *An Account of the Proceedings on the Trial of Susan B. Anthony*, a facsimile edition of the original published by the *Rochester Democrat and Chronicle* (Rochester, NY, 1874), and reprinted by the Lawbook Exchange, Ltd. (Union, NJ, 2002). The newspaper, along with others in Rochester and as far away as Worcester, Massachusetts, covered the events. See also Gordon, *The Trial of Susan B. Anthony* (Washington, DC: Federal Judicial Center, 2005), a very useful primer about the trial written as a pamphlet for the Federal Judicial Center and available online; Godfrey D. Lehman, "Susan B. Anthony Cast Her Ballot for Ulysses S. Grant," *American Heritage* 37, no. 1 (December 1985): 25–31; idem, "The Trial of Susan B. Anthony," http://www.law.umkc.edu/faculty/projects/ftrials/anthony/sbahome.htm; idem, *The Trial of Susan B. Anthony*, with an introduction by Lynn Sherr, Classics in Women's Studies series (New York: Federal Judicial Center, 2003).

A search of online catalogs for volumes about Susan B. Anthony yielded over three hundred results. There were numerous biographies, beginning with Ida Husted Harper's three-volume magnum opus, *The Life and Work of Susan B. Anthony: Including Public Addresses* . . . (Indianapolis: Hollenbeck, 1898–1908), and an almost endless list of many small volumes, most of which have been written for young adults. Anthony was and continues to be treated as an icon who inspires girls and boys. Kathleen Barry, *Susan B. Anthony: A Biography of a Singular Feminist* (New York: New York University Press, 1988) (quotations are from pp. 235, 243, 244, 245, 246), does not go into great detail on the trial, but Barry's biography is the best modern treatment of Anthony's life. Judith E. Harper, *Susan B. Anthony: A Biographical Companion* (Santa Barbara, CA: ABC-CLIO, 1998) is an excellent reference work for anyone studying Anthony, though men involved in the suffrage movement are omitted.

Edward T. James, Janet Wilson James, and Paul S. Boyer, eds., *Notable American Women, 1607–1950: A Biographical Dictionary* (Cambridge, MA: Harvard University Press, 1971) is a trustworthy reference tool and one on which most other sources, including Judith Harper's, seemed to have relied. Biographies of other figures who loomed large in the story include Debby Applegate, *The Most Famous Man in America: The Biography of Henry Ward Beecher* (New York: Doubleday, 2006), a fascinating biography of a significant figure in the abolition and woman suffrage movements in the nineteenth century, and T. J. Stiles, *The First Tycoon: The Epic Life of Cornelius Vanderbilt* (New York: Vintage, 2009), the man who sponsored Victoria Claflin Woodhull's financial enterprise, which enabled her brief rise to prominence in the suffrage movement. Williamjames Hull Hoffer, *The Caning of Charles Sumner: Honor, Idealism, and the Origins of the Civil War* (Baltimore: Johns Hopkins University Press, 2010), is an excellent source on the Massachusetts senator. On others in the Senate, see John F. Kennedy, *Profiles in Courage: Decisive Moments in the Lives of Celebrated Americans* (New York: Harper, 1956). Joelle Million, *Woman's Voice, Woman's Place: Lucy Stone and the Birth of the Woman's Rights Movement* (Westport, CT: Praeger, 2003) examines Stone's role in the early events. Frances Murray, "Henry Rogers Selden," *Green Bag* 11 (Summer 2008): 2D, 443, traces the life of the counselor. This article originally appeared in Albert M. Rosenblatt, ed., *The Judges of the New York Court of Appeals: A Biographical History* (New York: Fordham University Press, 2007). Lelia J. Robinson, "Women Lawyers in the United States," *Green Bag: A Useless but Entertaining Magazine for Lawyers* 2 (Boston, MA: Thomas & Wentworth, 1890), 14, and Albert M. Rosenblatt, ed., *The Judges of the New York Court of Appeals: A Biographical History* (New York: Fordham University Press, 2007) were also helpful.

On Stanton, see Lori D. Ginzburg, *Elizabeth Cady Stanton: An American Life* (New York: Hill & Wang, 2010); Geoffrey C. Ward and Ken Burns, *Not for Ourselves Alone: The Story of Elizabeth Cady Stanton and Susan B. Anthony* (New York: Knopf, 1999); and Judith Wellman, *The Road to Seneca Falls: Elizabeth Cady Stanton and the First Woman's Rights Convention* (Urbana: University of Illinois Press, 2004).

The movement for women's rights has an extensive literature of its own. A partial listing includes Margaret Hope Bacon, *Mothers of Feminism: The Story of Quaker Women in America*, 2nd ed. (Philadelphia: Friends General Conference, 1986) (quote from page 117), several chapters of which provide a succinct and excellent overview of the role of Quaker women in the early suffrage movement as well as an explanation of their Quaker philosophy, allegiances, and views. Eleanor Flexner and Ellen Fitzpatrick's *Century of Struggle: The Woman's Rights Movement in the United States*, enlarged ed. (Cambridge, MA: Friends General Conference, 1975) (quotation from page 147), is the updated version of Flexner's brilliant and path-breaking study of the early woman's rights movement. It is an inspiration for a generation of women historians and absolutely essential background to the "first wave" of American feminism. See also Sylvia D. Hoffert, *When Hens Crow: The Women's Rights Movement in Antebellum America* (Bloomington: Indiana University Press, 1995); Jean V. Matthews, *Women's Struggle for Equality: The First Phase, 1828–1876* (Chicago: Ivan R. Dee, 1997); Frances M. Clarke, "Forgetting the Women: Debates over Female Patriotism in the Aftermath of the Civil War," *Journal of Women's History* 23 (2011): 64–86; and Nancy A. Hewitt and Suzanne Lebsock, *Visible Women: New Essays on American Activism* (Urbana: University of Illinois Press, 1993). Robert E. Riegel, *American Feminists* (Lawrence: University Press of Kansas, 1963), is a lively, sometimes speculative pioneering study of the early feminist movement. Christine Stansell, *The Feminist Promise: 1792 to the Present* (New York: Modern Library, 2010) mentions other cases but not the trial of Anthony.

On women and suffrage, see Jean H. Baker, *Sisters: The Lives of America's Suffragists* (New York: Hill & Wang, 2005), a modern biographical study of some of the five most important suffragists, focusing on their personal lives. Baker makes a plausible case, though perhaps a little overemphasized, that Anthony was a lesbian in some of her relationships with women, particularly Anna Dickinson. Baker also edited *Votes for Women: The Struggle for Suffrage Revisited* (New York: Oxford University Press, 2002). Norma Basch, "Reconstructing Female Citizenship: *Minor v Happersett*," in *The Constitution, Law, and American Life: Critical Aspects of the Nineteenth-Century Experience*, ed. Donald G. Nieman (Athens: University of Georgia Press, 1992), 52–65 (quotation from p. 52), though short, Basch's piece provides an interesting analysis of the case. Mari Jo Buhle and Paul Buhle, eds., *The Concise History of Woman Suffrage: Selections from History of Woman Suffrage* (Urbana: University of Illinois Press, 2005). See also Olivia Coolidge, *Women's Rights: The Suffrage Movement in America, 1848–1920* (New York: E. P. Dutton & Co., 1966).

Ellen Carol DuBois, *Feminism and Suffrage: The Emergence of an Independent Women's Movement in America, 1848–1869* (Ithaca, NY: Cornell University Press, 1978; reprint with new preface, 1999), is a classic reexamination of the woman suffrage movement and essential reading. DuBois, *Woman Suffrage and Women's Rights* (New York: New York University Press, 1998) is a collection of DuBois's later essays. Aileen S. Kraditor, *The Ideas of the Woman Suffrage Movement, 1890–1920* (New York: Columbia University Press, 1981) is a standard. On black women and the vote, see Rosalyn Terborg-Penn, *African American Women in the Struggle for the Vote, 1850–1920* (Bloomington: Indiana University Press, 1998).

Marjorie Spruill Wheeler, ed., *One Woman, One Vote: Rediscovering the Woman Suffrage Movement* (Troutdale, OR: New Sage Press, 1995), is a collection of primary documents and essays by several prominent women historians, including Linda Kerber, Ellen Carol DuBois, and Nancy Cott, on the occasion of the seventy-fifth anniversary of the Nineteenth Amendment. It is also the companion volume for a similarly titled video documentary.

The phrase "a new departure" commonly applied to the litigation strategy of 1869–1875 in the secondary scholarship requires some qualification. Though the *History of Women's Suffrage* used the phrase as the title of the chapter, it nowhere appears in the body of the chapter. As far as my researches have discovered, Ellen DuBois pulled this out and used it to describe the constitutional strategy in the published version of her dissertation, *Feminism and Suffrage: The Emergence of an Independent Women's Movement in America, 1848–1869* (Ithaca, NY: Cornell University Press, 1978; reissue with new Preface, 1999). DuBois later asserted that "this approach . . . was known among the suffragists as the New Departure." But, frustratingly, DuBois provides no quotations or citations as evidence for her claim that the expression was in common usage in her essay "Taking the Law into Our Own Hands: *Bradwell, Minor* and Suffrage Militance in the 1870s," reprinted in *One Woman, One Vote*. Nevertheless, it has been picked up by almost every historian of woman suffrage since that time.

I can find no evidence that "New Departure" was an expression commonly used by woman suffragists themselves, including Susan B. Anthony. An exhaustive search of published and online primary material shows only one other appearance of "New Departure" in the woman suffrage context: Ida Husted Harper, "Republican Splinter—Miss Anthony Votes," chapter 24 in *The Life and Work of Susan B. Anthony: Including Public Addresses* (Indianapolis: Bowen-Merrill, 1898),1: 409–413. Harper quotes the NWSA call to the Washington, DC, meeting in January 1872. The term does not appear in subsequent documents, and the fact that it was set off by quotation marks suggests that the one-time use was an adaptation. Post–Civil War Democrats in 1870 coined the term to indicate that they had ceased their opposition to Reconstruction, were just as loyal as the Republicans, and wanted to resuscitate their party's fortunes. See http://en.wikipedia.org/wiki/New_Departure_(Democrats).

On Quaker traditions within the reform movement, in addition to Bacon, see Michael L. Birkel, *Silence and Witness: The Quaker Tradition* (Maryknoll, NY: Orbis Books, 2004) and Elizabeth Potts Brown and Susan Mosher Stuard, eds., *Witness for Change: Quaker Women over Three Centuries* (New Brunswick, NJ: Rutgers University Press, 1989), a collection of essays about women's changing roles within Quakerism. Nancy Hewitt wrote the essay on nineteenth-century fragmentation of the society and how women were involved. Pink Dandelion's *An Introduction to Quakerism* (Cambridge: Cambridge University Press, 2007) is an exceptionally cogent history and theological introduction, probably the best for non-Quakers. It emphasizes the British history but also covers the Quakers in America, and it is particularly useful for explaining the various schisms and splits—with helpful charts, tables, and diagrams.

A trustworthy source for the larger political context of these events is in Eric Foner, *Reconstruction: America's Unfinished Revolution, 1863–1877* (New York: Harper, 1989). More specific material appears in Robert M. Goldman, *Reconstruction and Black Suffrage: Losing the Vote in Reese and Cruikshank* (Lawrence: University Press of Kansas, 2001) (quotation from p. 99), and Melanie Susan Gustafson, *Women and the Republican Party, 1854–1924* (Urbana: University of Illinois Press, 2001). Special attention to politics and women's voting appears in Alexander Keyssar, *The Right to Vote: The Contested History of Democracy in the United States* (New York: Basic, 2000).

On Rochester's place in the story, see Nancy A. Hewitt, *Women's Activism and Social Change: Rochester, New York, 1822–1872* (Ithaca, NY: Cornell University Press, 1984); Blake McKelvey, *Rochester: The Flower City, 1855–1890* (Cambridge, MA: Harvard University Press, 1949); and Blake McKelvey, *Rochester on the Genesee: The Growth of a City*, 2d. ed. (Syracuse, NY: Syracuse University Press, 1993). The latter has good background on SBA's home city and the site of her voting. Also see William Farley Peck, *History of Rochester and Monroe County, New York: From the Earliest Historic Times to the Beginning of 1907*, vol. 1 (St. Paul: Pioneer Publishing Co., 1908). Page 365 records William C. Storrs as a member of the Rochester bar in 1844.

On Minor v. Happersett, 88 U.S. 162 (1875) is the official report. See also Philip B. Kurland and Gerhard Casper, eds., "Minor v. Happersett" (1875), in *Landmark Briefs and Arguments of the Supreme Court of the United States: Constitutional Law* (Arlington, VA: University Publications of America, 1975), 7:212–213; Angela G. Ray and Cindy Koenig Richards, "Inventing Citizens, Imagining Gender Justice: The Suffrage Rhetoric of Virginia and Francis Minor," *Quarterly Journal of Speech* 93, no. 4 (November 2007): 375–402; "Virginia Minor Trial," Jefferson National Expansion Memorial,

National Park Service, http://www.nps.gov/jeff/forteachers/upload/Minor3.pdf; Helen R. Pinkney, "Virginia Louisa Minor," *Notable American Women*, 2550–2551; Carol Ferring Shepley, *Movers and Shakers, Scalawags and Suffragettes: Tales from Bellefontaine Cemetery* (Columbia: University of Missouri Press and Missouri History Museum, St. Louis, 2008); Laura Staley, "Suffrage Movement in St. Louis during the 1870s," *Gateway Heritage* 3, no. 4 (Spring 1983): 34–41; and LeeAnn Whites, "The Tale of Two Minors: Women's Rights on the Border," in *Women in Missouri History: In Search of Power and Influence*, ed. LeeAnn Whites, Mary Neth, Gary R. Kremer (Columbia: University of Missouri Press, 2002), 101–118. The *St. Louis Times* coverage was also helpful.

The constitutional issues involved are traced in Peter Charles Hoffer, Williamjames Hull Hoffer, and N.E.H. Hull, *The Supreme Court: An Essential History* (Lawrence: University Press of Kansas, 2007), 131–158; Linda J. Kerber, *No Constitutional Right to Be Ladies: Women and the Obligations of Citizenship* (New York: Macmillan, 1998), a prize-winning account; William E. Nelson, *The Fourteenth Amendment: From Political Principle to Judicial Doctrine* (Cambridge: Harvard University Press, 1988) (quotation in my text from p. 24); Donald Grier Stephenson Jr., *The Waite Court: Justices, Rulings, and Legacy* (Santa Barbara, CA: ABC-CLIO Supreme Court Handbooks, 2003).

INDEX

AASS. *See* American Anti-Slavery
Society
abolitionist movement
alliance with suffrage movement,
xxiii, 6–8 (*see also* universal
suffrage movement)
Anthony and, xxiii
origins of suffrage movement in,
xviii
post-war abandonment of
suffrage movement, 2–3, 5
Adams, Wash, 193
African American voting rights
debate on, 2–5
as impetus for suffrage
movement, 1, 4
as priority for some activists, 1,
2–3, 7–8, 9, 20–21
Albany Law Journal, 185
American Anti-Slavery Society
(AASS)
post-war role of, 2, 6
suffragists' and, 7–8
American Equal Rights Association
(AERA)
conflicts over black *vs.* women's
rights at, 10–21
constitution of, 8–9
demise of, 21
founding of, 7–10
officers of, 9, 13, 17–18, 19–20
suffragists' dissatisfaction with,
22
union with UWSA, 33
American Woman Suffrage
Association (AWSA)
Anthony at inaugural meeting of,
26–27
Anthony on, 25–26

convention of November, 1870,
35–38
criticisms by Stanton, 34–35
efforts to reconcile with NWSA,
27–30, 34–38
establishment of, 23–24
hierarchical structure of, 30
and litigation strategy, 179
rivalry with NWSA, 24, 27, 29
Stanton on, 24–25
universal suffrage as platform of,
24
Anneke, Mathilde Franziska, 89
Anthony, Guelma, 60, 104–5, 109,
182
Anthony, Lottie, 60, 108
Anthony, Mary, 60
Anthony, Susan B.
activism in education and
teaching, 209
and AERA, founding of, 6, 7
and AERA, struggle over agenda
of, 12–13, 18–21
as AERA officer, 13, 17–18,
19–20
arguments for universal suffrage,
91–96
on AWSA, 25–26, 35
at AWSA inaugural meeting,
26–27
and AWSA-NWSA
reconciliation efforts, 28–29,
30, 33, 36–38
background, xvii–xviii, 91–92,
173
call for suffragist unity, 31–32
death of, 209
and election of 1872, 53–56
family of, xvii–xviii

{ *Index* }

Crowley, Richard, *continued*
  at election inspectors' trial,
    159–65
  at grand jury hearing, 100
  at trial of Anthony, 123–30, 132,
    134–35, 146–49
  at trial postponement hearing,
    110–11
  views on women, 147
Cushing, Caleb, 194

Daniel, Peter, 144
Daughters of Temperance, xix
"Declaration of Sentiments" (1848),
    xix
DeGarmo, Rhoda, 60, 64
Democratic Party, NWSA lobbying
    of, 55
demurrer, in *Minor v. Happersett*,
    191–92
Denio, Hiram, 59, 115
divorce, Stanton's controversial
    views on, 34, 37–38, 46
Douglass, Frederick
  and AERA, 7, 13, 14–15
  and AWSA-NWSA
    reconciliation efforts, 35
  escape of, 59
  on prioritization of African
    American rights, 20–21
Downing, George T., 10
Dred Scott v. Sanford (1857), 144
DuBois, Ellen, 1, 40, 41

election inspectors
  hearing for, 85
  pardoning of, 185
election inspectors' trial, 159–69
  defense team for, 135
  jury deliberations, 168–69
  Justice Hunt's irregularities
    during, 162, 165–69

motion for new trial, 169
  relocation of, 109–10
election of 1872
  NWSA lobbying of political
    parties, 53–57
  women turned away from polls,
    64
  See also voting by Anthony
Ely, A. P., 85
emancipation of slaves, as impetus
    to suffrage movement, xxiii, 1
Enforcement Act of 1870
  arrests under, 70
  history of, 67–68
  Hunt on, 151–52
  provisions of, 68
Ewing, E. B., 193

Field, Cyrus, 202
Field, David Dudley II, 202
Field, Stephen J., 108, 194, 202
Fifteenth Amendment
  AWSA support for, 24
  exclusion of women from, 1,
    148–49, 152, 154, 201, 207
  Hunt's ruling on, 150–51
  implied voting rights of women
    in, 39, 47, 142, 143
  interpretation of, as legal issue, 84
  suffragists' opposition to, 13,
    15–18, 187
Fillmore, Millard, 73, 97
fine, Anthony's refusal to pay,
    177–78, 181–82
Fitzpatrick, Ellen, 39
Flexner, Eleanor, 39
Foster, Abby Kelley
  and AERA, 7, 11–12
  and origin of suffrage movement,
    xx
  prioritization of African
    American voting rights, 7

judicial strategy
  critics of, 179
  failure of, 208
  New York Times on, 99
  past failures of, 60
  See also Minor v. Happersett;
    Missouri Resolutions strategy;
    New Departure strategy
Judiciary Act of 1789, 132–33
Julian, George. W., 16
jury trial, Anthony's right to
  as distraction from suffrage issue,
    179–80
  Hunt's denial of, 156–59
  Selden on, 169–72

Keeney, Elisha J., 69–70, 86, 90, 98,
    182
Kent, James, 144
Krum, John Marshall, 189, 190,
    195, 198, 200
Ku Klux Klan Act (Civil Rights Act
  of 1871), 93

legal standing of women, xviii, xxi,
    122, 139–40, 189
Lewis, Sylvester
  and Anthony's voter registration,
    63–64, 67
  at election inspectors' trial, 159–60
  at preliminary hearing, first, 75,
    79–80
Leyden, Margaret, 60, 160–61
Life Insurance Co. v. Terry (1873),
    118–20
litigation strategy. *See* judicial
    strategy
Livermore, Mary, 22
Lockwood, Belva, 90
London World Anti-Slavery
    Conference (1840), xviii

Loughridge, William, 43–44, 83,
    184
Luther v. Borden (1849), 143

Madison, James, 200
"Manhood Suffrage" (Stanton), 18,
    20
Mansfield, Mrs. L. D., 60
marriage, Anthony on, 95–96
Married Women's Act of 1889,
    189
Marsh, Edwin T., 60–61, 63, 75–76.
    See also election inspectors
Marsh, Luther R., 56–57
McCrary, George Washington,
    183
McDowell, Anne E., 54–55
McLean, Guelma Anthony. *See*
    Anthony, Guelma
Miller, Francis, 105–6, 108
Miller, Samuel F., 153, 158, 184,
    97
Millerd, Brace, 101
Minor, Francis
  background, 186
  and *Minor v. Happersett*, 188–89,
    190–92, 195–96, 198, 200–203
  and Missouri Resolutions, 23, 39,
    41, 42, 186–87, 208
Minor, Virginia, 23, 92, 108, 144,
    186. See also *Minor v.
    Happersett*
Minor v. Happersett (1874)
  circumstances of case, 187–88
  14th Amendment as issue in,
    191, 193, 197–98, 203–4,
    204–5, 207
  impact on suffrage movement,
    xiv
  legal team behind, 188–90
  in Missouri courts, 190–93

New Jersey, history of women
voting in, xiv
newspapers
and Anthony's public relations
campaign before trial, 98–99,
103
coverage of *Bradwell* case, 106
and election of 1872, 64
on trial of Anthony, 179–81
New York State
law on voting by women in, 142,
148
property rights of married
women in, xviii, xxi
Republican Party in, founding
of, 116
suffragist activism in, xxii, 3
New York Times (newspaper)
on AERA, 15, 17, 19
Anthony's 50th birthday party
coverage, 27
on Crowley, 100
on election inspectors' trial,
85
Hall obituary, 96
on Hunt, 115
letters to the editor, 113
on *Minor v. Happersett*, 202
on NWSA, 51, 56, 90
NWSA notices in, 48
on trial of Anthony, 74, 99, 103,
111
on voting by Anthony, 65
on Woodhull, 40, 44
New York Tribune (newspaper),
34–35
Nineteenth Amendment
early versions of, 16–17
passage of, 210
as Susan B. Anthony
Amendment, xiv

NWSA. *See* National Women's
Suffrage Association

Osborn, Loring W., 101
Owen, Robert Dale, 3

Parmelee, William, 101
Peck, William Farley, 73
Pennsylvania Anti-Slavery Society,
6
Pennsylvania Citizens Suffrage
Association, 103–4
People's Party, Woodhull's effort to
create, 51–52
Philadelphia Evening Telegraph
(newspaper), 54–55
Philadelphia Inquirer (newspaper),
104
Phillips, Wendell
and AASS, 2
and AERA, 6–7, 13
prioritization of African
American voting rights, 7–8, 9
suffragist impatience with, 9, 15
support for suffragists, xxiii
Pillsbury, Parker, 6
police, harassment of suffragist
meetings, 104
political question doctrine, and
woman suffrage, 143
Polk, Trusten, 189
Post, Ann, xx
Pound, John E.
at election inspectors' hearing, 85
at preliminary hearing, first, 74,
75–81
at preliminary hearing, second,
83–86
at trial of Anthony, 134–35
at trial postponement hearing,
109

preliminary hearings
  defendants, described, 86–87
  finding of probable cause, and
    bail, 86, 87
  first, 75–81
  intent as issue in, 76–79, 80–81,
    83–85
  second, 82–86
Progressivism, and woman suffrage,
  210
property rights of women, in New
  York State, xviii, xxi, 122
Pulver, Mary, 60

Quakers
  Anthony as, 91–92, 105, 163,
    173, 175, 177
  philosophy of, 91–92, 173
  support of Anthony, 173

Reconstruction, limited success of,
  11–12
registering to vote
  by Anthony and companions,
    60–63, 76
  as issue at Anthony's trial,
    125–29, 136
  as issue at election inspectors'
    trial, 161–62, 163
  Minor v. Happersett and, 187–88
  as strategy, 42
  women denied registration, in
    election of 1872, 66
Remond, Charles Lenox, 7, 10, 11
Republican Party
  in New York State, founding of,
    116
  NWSA and, 53–57
  suffragists' break with, 108
Revolution (periodical)
  Anthony call for unity in, 31–32
  AWSA criticisms of, 35, 37–38

on AWSA-NWSA reconciliation
  efforts, 32, 35
failure of, 96
on 15th Amendment, 17, 18, 20
financial problems, 19, 63, 177
and Missouri Resolutions, 23,
  186–87
on 16th Amendment, 22
Stanton article on AWSA, 24–25
Riddle, Albert Gallatin, 41, 93
Rochester Democrat and Chronicle
  (newspaper)
  on Anthony registration, 63
  on Anthony voting, 64, 66–67,
    70
  defendants, description of, 86–87
  on habeas corpus petition, 97, 98
  letters to the editor, 65–66,
    70–72
  on moving of trial, 110
  on preliminary hearings, 74–75,
    85
  publication of Anthony's trial
    account by, 183
Rochester Evening Express
  (newspaper), 83
Rochester Times (newspaper), 180–81
Rochester Union and Advertiser
  (newspaper), 98
Rose, Ernestine, 13, 22
Rules of Decision Act, 158
Rutledge, John, 194

*Sarah Brandon v. The People of the
  State of New York*, 132–33
Sargent, Aaron, 184
Savage, John, 115
Selden, Henry R.
  Anthony's consultation of, 58,
    59, 77–78, 99, 131–32
  Anthony's faith in, 61

Anthony's public relations
   campaign and, 98–99
background of, 58–59
bail for Anthony, 102
career of, 130
competency as lawyer, 138
at habeas corpus hearings, 89–90,
   97–98
health of, 130
at initial Anthony hearing, 74
motion for new trial, 169–72
at preliminary hearing, first, 75,
   76, 80–81
at preliminary hearing, second,
   82–86
at trial of Anthony, 124–28,
   130–33, 134, 136: closing
   arguments, 136–45; verdict,
   protest against, 156–57
at trial postponement hearing,
   110–11
trial preparation, 105, 108
on woman suffrage, arguments
   for, 137–45
Selden, Samuel Lee, 58, 59
Seneca Falls, as center of reform,
   xvii
Seneca Falls convention (1848), xiii,
   xviii–xix
sentencing hearing of Anthony,
   172–76
Seward, William Henry, 97
Shaw, Anna Howard, 209
Sherwood, J. A., 193
Silver v. Ladd (1868), 92
Sixteenth Amendment
   abandonment of as strategy, 41
   Anthony's advocacy for, 26, 27,
      31
   Stanton's advocacy for, 16–17,
      22–23
   Sumner on, 93

Slaughter-House Cases
   and Anthony's case, 105, 108, 153
   and Fourteenth Amendment,
      interpretation of, 197–98,
      200–201, 205
   and *Minor v. Happersett*, 193,
      200–201
Smith, Gerrit, 181
Springfield [Massachusetts]
   Republican (newspaper), 32
St. Louis Times (newspaper), 188,
   192–93
Stanton, Elizabeth Cady
   as advocate for universal
      suffrage, 3
   and AERA, founding of, 7, 9
   and AERA, struggle over agenda
      of, 11, 19
   as AERA officer, 13, 17–18,
      19–20
   and AWSA, 23–25, 26
   and AWSA-NWSA
      reconciliation efforts, 27–28,
      32–33
   background, xvii
   career of, 209–10
   character and personality, xiii
   death of, 209–10
   on divorce, controversial views
      of, 34, 37–38, 46
   and election of 1872, 54–55, 56
   family of, xxi–xxii
   on 15th Amendment, 16–18,
      18–19
   first meeting of Anthony, xvii, xix
   and 14th Amendment, 12–13
   History of Woman Suffrage, 4, 5,
      12, 13, 41, 49
   on Hunt (Ward), 114, 150
   "Manhood Suffrage," 18, 20
   and Missouri Resolutions,
      186–87

voting by Anthony, 63–64
  challenging of, 63–64
  in city election, after indictment,
    103
  and Enforcement Act of 1870,
    67–68
  Lewis (complainant) on, 70–72
  planning for, 58, 59, 77–78
  reactions to, 65–67
  as strategy, 60
voting by women, history of, xiv, 60
voting rights for African Americans
  debate on, 2–5
  as impetus for suffrage
    movement, 1, 4
  as priority for male activists, 1,
    2–3, 7–8, 9, 20–21
  vulnerability of women, as basis for
    woman suffrage
    Minor on, 201
    Selden on, 139–42

Wagner, David, 193
Wagoner, S. J., 61
Waite, Morrison Remick, 151–52,
    193–94, 203–8
Warbasse, Elizabeth B., 113
Warner, Daniel, 61, 161
Washington, Bushrod, 92–93, 144,
    200
Washington Republican (newspaper),
    41
Wasson, James D., 101
Weening, Hans, 173
Whiskey Ring, 190
Williams, George, 194
Wilson, Henry, 57
Wilson, Woodrow, 210
Woman's Bureau
  birthday party for Anthony, 27
  and NWSA, establishment of,
    21–22

Woman's Journal (periodical)
  on AWSA-NWSA reconciliation
    efforts, 29–30, 32
  criticisms of Stanton, 34, 37
woman suffrage
  concerns raised by, 142
  Selden on arguments for,
    137–45
  vulnerability of women as basis
    for, 139–42, 201
  See also suffrage movement;
    universal suffrage
Woman Suffrage Association of
    Missouri, 186
women
  Crowley's views on, 147
  Hunt's views on, 116–22, 155
  legal standing of, xviii, xxi, 122,
    139–40, 189
Women's New York State
    Temperance Society, xxi
Women Taxpayers' Association of
    Monroe County, 109, 181
Woodhull, Victoria Claflin
  Anthony and, 44–45, 45–46,
    50–51, 88
  background, 39
  Comstock Act prosecution, 88
  Congressional petition, 39–40
  Congressional petition,
    congressional reports on,
    43–44, 83, 84
  Congressional petition, lobbying
    for, 44
  congressional testimony,
    39–41
  and NWSA, effort to co-opt,
    50–53
  at NWSA convention of May,
    1871, 46, 48
  presidential bid, 47, 48, 50–53,
    55